SUCH STUFF AS DREAMS ARE MADE ON

Nelles Van Loon

Such Stuff As Dreams Are Made On

tellwell

Tellwell Talent
www.tellwell.ca

ISBN
978-0-2288-7220-7 (Hardcover)
978-0-2288-7219-1 (Paperback)
978-0-2288-7221-4 (eBook)

We are such stuff as dreams are made on, and our little life is rounded with a sleep. *William Shakespeare: The Tempest*

For all of you who played the game with the joy and respect that became our Friday Night Baseball trademark. Special thanks to Frank and Fred who ran with the flame when my legs began to fail me. And for anyone else who might find something of interest in our journey.

Table of Contents

1

Who Are Those Guys?

If you had found yourself walking along the lane that runs along the south side of the three ball diamonds in Toronto's Coronation Park at nine thirty or so on the morning of Sunday September 21, 2014, you might well have been in a hurry to get where you were going. Not so much because you needed to get there quickly; more because of the rain which was not heavy but in no particular hurry to stop. On the other hand, had your eyes turned from the lane to the second diamond, you would have seen two men in late middle age, one with a shovel, the other with a pail. Had your curiosity caused you to pause for a moment, you might have determined they were attempting to clear the infield of the water which had collected around home plate and along the base lines. Knowing it had rained all night and was showing no clear sign of stopping, you might well have been reminded of Emmett Kelly's clown character attempting to sweep his shadow into a dustpan. You'd have stopped for an amused moment and continued on your way.

What could possibly be inspiring about two men in late middle age attempting to clear the infield of water in the midst of a persistent rain? The answer lies in moments lost to time. No power on earth can bring those moments back to the audible, visible, tangible quality of the here and now. Writers attempt the impossible. They begin with a blank page, fearing like Shakespeare's Lear, that 'nothing will come from nothing,' but Lear's 'nothing' is a better place than the palace from which everything was his to command. Sometimes by some unpredictable mixture of faith, luck and skill, doors and windows open. Sometimes we try too hard and the words fight themselves and paragraphs strain to say what could be better expressed in a word. We look to other writers for the secret, but the secret lies within. It will not reveal itself easily, sometimes it will appear inscrutable, and for certain, it will resist all attempts at perfection. We must journey diligently and patiently nonetheless. There's a song in the air. It's haunting, lovely in its way, but it doesn't want to stay there. It wants to descend and be heard.

It's my impression - one shared by many others - that the best books about sport have emerged from baseball. My favourite is Roger Kahn's, *The Boys of Summer.* Kahn was keenly aware of the juxtaposition of youth and age in the book's title, the dazzling play of third baseman Billy Cox at Ebbets Field while talking to Billy the bartender in Hoboken New Jersey twenty years later; Jackie Robinson, daring and defiant as a Brooklyn Dodger, while showing him paying the price the bottled up anger he had a world of justification to express; Roy Campanella so relentlessly efficient in his catcher's gear, taking holidays from the tools of ignorance to hit home runs, now in a wheel chair. There are other legends as well: Lou Gehrig, Hank Aaron, Roberto Clemente, too many to name. Of all the luminaries, it was Willie Mays, the eternal kid, who most sadly grew old before we had time to notice. Perhaps Willie, had he been with you that damp September morning, would have understood, would have pitched in and helped, played a few innings in center field, found joy in catching a routine fly ball, would have remembered how he felt playing stick ball in the streets as a boy, and learned once again (if he'd forgotten) the joy of the game.

You could say our story begins in the spring when legions of boys and girls wake up thinking, 'There's going to be a game,' knowing nothing in the world could be as important. But more likely it begins sometime much earlier, sometime before Abner Doubleday (so it is said) invented the game, sometime in humankind's distant past when we first learned how to play, when we took time from running for our lives to run for fun, when a spear became more than a weapon and we found the joy in throwing it straight and true, when a club changed from a thing to subdue our enemies with into something to strike a ball with. It might be instructive to look thousands of years backwards at those phenomena, but given the difficulty (amounting to impossibility) of the task, let's just say there was a phone call and the phone call led to a ball game and the ball game led to more ball games.

I don't know when it was that we realized that we had something special going, although I do know that for eight of those early years Jim Wilson postponed his weekly visits to the cottage till late Friday evening to umpire our games. This was no small compliment. Jim was one of the best umpires in Ontario and for many years a mainstay of the Senior 'A' Leagues. He often told us about the discussions with his wife, the difficulty he had explaining to her what there was about us that was special enough to delay the weekend trip to the cottage. Jim had a deep respect for the game and saw what was special about us more clearly than we did. The message came closer to home on September 20, 1998, when George Gamester featured us in his column in *The Sunday Star.*

I'd turned fifty-nine that year and the rest of the original gang weren't far behind. We seldom talked much about how much longer we were going to play. It was always somewhere between a year and forever. I was doing a lot of writing at the time, mostly musicals, with the dream of the Big Broadway hit dancing in my head. I'd had a ripple of success with four or five musicals for children along with a small splash with *Babe Ruth Comes to Pickle River*, a play about an ex miner trying to make a success of a radio station in the early thirties. I'd made a few notes about our games and sent them along via email, but it had never occurred to me that Friday Night Baseball would offer rich material. The motivation was simpler. I wanted us to be better.

When Jim was with us, we'd asked him to teach us some essentials. For the first three weeks of every season he schooled us in throwing to the cutoff man, the execution of the rundown play, smart base running, along with other basics. When he left after eight years (somewhere around 1990) his influence lived on and five years later we still could manage the rundown play with some claim to efficiency. Its execution requires four players, two on each side of the runner and smart choices about when and where to throw it. When it's done well, it's lovely to watch and I always felt proud when we pulled it off. By the late nineties, we'd lost it. At the beginning of the 2004 season, I found myself both annoyed and impatient with our inability to do the things he'd taught us. It occurred to me that I could write about the issues in a manner that would lead to discussion and that over time the information would gradually sink in. It might have worked, but the instructional exercise quickly turned into something else.

2

The Hand

June 4/04: I've been thinking it would be a good idea to send an email after each game noting our progress to date as well as a thing or two we could improve at. The infield and outfield practice seem to be working well. But while the sun is high, let's take some extra time out there - which we wont be able to do in August and September. Also, since there are more infielders than spaces available, let's try to get all the infielders involved before the game starts.

A couple of things about base running that are often overlooked, but occur regularly. Both situations occurred last Fri.

1. Man on first, shallow fly ball and it's not clear whether or not the ball will be caught. What does the base runner do?
2. Man on any base. Line drive. What does the baserunner do?

That was what it was supposed to be, a weekly commentary on baseball do's and don'ts. I got several thoughtful replies, which gave me reason to think it would help us play smarter. However, something happened the following week to move it in an unexpected direction.

June 11/04: On Friday last, there was a moment we must not allow time to steal away from us. While not all the details are clear, it can be said with certainty that it was late in the game and the losing nine was mounting a rally. It can also be stated with reasonable claims to truth that the winning side, while still far ahead, was beginning to doubt the result. At this point, reality and myth converged in a way no one in attendance is quite certain of. Some say The Hand came out of nowhere, others say it came from out of the sky, others say it was the bare, ungloved hand of Austin Repath extending itself in some unbelievably acrobatic manner. Wherever it came from, The Hand caught the high Texas Leaguer that seemed certain to fall into short centre field which (if it could talk) the ball would still be insisting that it had every right to do. Which leads to the further question as to whether or not our Austin Repath is a mere mortal, or some ageless being who descends from Mount Olympus to sport with us on Friday evenings. Further inquiries, speculations etc, welcome.

> Got this from John St James: 'Yes! Women may think that June was made for weddings, but I think June baseball inspires magic (I remember that I too had a magical Friday evening about a year ago!) But you may be on to something more here. I certainly wouldn't discount the "ageless being who descends from Mount Olympus to sport with us" theme where AR is concerned. He continues to astound. "The Hand" also reminds me of the playful parody of the Sistine Chapel image where God is reaching out to Adam's hand… with a baseball in His hand. The gods HAD to be involved last Friday night.'

Austin started playing with us sometime in the mid nineties when he was in his mid sixties. The mixture of will and magic required to complete that play got me thinking there was something mythical about us that might someday become the stuff of legend. It should have provided the impetus to keep on writing, but the excitement ebbed, as excitement often does, and it wasn't till three weeks later I wrote the next entry.

July 2/04: You never know with our gang. Barely enough guys to field two teams at the beginning, so went with six a side till others arrived. It turned into a fine game that was tied at the end of six. While all played well and with good spirit, one Steve Chadwick had the game of his career while turning three double plays.

Steve is one of those people you might never guess is a natural athlete. Medium height, slightly built, quiet. He tells me he never thought of himself as anything special when he was a kid. He just hoped he'd fit in somehow: outfield, infield, catcher, anywhere so long as they'd let him play. The pattern continued when he joined us. I remember him playing catcher in an early tournament in which he threw out two baserunners with throws so accurate the second baseman didn't have to move his glove. I suspect he'd been doing other remarkable things in his quiet way, and that they were appreciated but soon forgotten. Sometime the next year, one of our regular shortstops couldn't make it. I remembered Steve's accurate arm, and suggested he fill in. He's been there ever since - so long, it's hard to think of him as playing anywhere else. Steve Chadwick, aka Chatz, aka (apologies to Ozzie Smith) Mr Shortstop.

July 30/04: Numbers low again along with the threat of rain, but when I arrive at the park Frank Trotz is already there muscling the equipment out of his car. By six there are only ten of us. It's not looking good for a game, but the bases are in and Ken Pagel has come down all the way from Orangeville and Jim Betts has come back from retirement and we decide to play work ups. With two batters and a pitcher and a catcher, there are only six of us to play the infield and outfield. We have to decide whether to go with three infielders and three outfielders or four infielders and two outfielders. The umpire arrives and we offer him the chance to play. He is happy to accept.

After some awkward swings and some shaky defense, the pace of the game picks up. We see Ron LeSarge turn his back to the batter and run to where he thinks the ball is headed. We see him throw up his glove in what seems like a futile gesture of faith and hope. We see the ball land and roll to the fence, but our eyes have deceived us. The ball is in Ron's glove. The infield play is sharp. Frank throws out a runner trying to steal second and picks off a couple more who get too fancy. Ken makes a gallant try at what would have been a superb shoe string catch. I snare a line drive while playing first. It's that zeroed in focus where everything goes into slow motion which cuts in from who knows where, maybe from Mount Olympus, because Austin was up to his old magic again. I see it up close because I've moved to centre field and he's playing left. Fred hits a looping liner. I think maybe I can get to it, but it's a foot or so over my glove. Austin scampers over from left field, leans far to his right catches the ball a foot off the grass. Since I don't see him from the time he starts for the ball and only in those fleeting milliseconds when he catches it, I can't say how far he ran to make the play. Frank says sixty yards, so that's what we'll go with when we report it to the Guinness Book of Records.

Also should mention the achievements of John Larocque, just back from a four week bout with shin splints. John is the owner of Ring Music, a first rate guitar shop on Harbord Street. It's relaxed and homey. Guitar players often drop in to check out a guitar they don't need, but sometimes buy anyway. It's also a social thing. A chance to talk guitars with people who love guitars. Sometimes a chance to jam, sometimes with someone you connect with. Sometimes the talk moves into other categories, although it was probably a good many visits along the way when I mentioned FNB. John is a low key guy, even when he's excited, but something told me there was a kid inside him aching to get back on the ball field. One spring three or four years ago, he said, 'This year, I'm going to make the time.'

Of the many players who have joined the original crew, only a few end up staying for the long haul. John is one of the long haulers. He bats from the left side and hits ropes down the first base line. When they elevate, they become home runs. He can field too, good reactions. His base running is often overly enthusiastic, but he's a fast learner. I was warming up with him one day and he started tossing underhand and everything hit my glove. I was thinking, 'This guy can pitch.' Yesterday was a good opportunity for him to try his wares on the mound. Lots of strikes, snared a hard line drive right back at him, raced over to cover third preventing the ump from taking an extra base. (This event makes sense only if you remember that the ump wasn't umping, he was playing.)

> Got this from Fred Breitner: 'What a night of baseball it was! We all agree that Scrub is not our intent, but those of us who played, loved it – lots of movement and action as we sauntered around the field. The evening was punctuated with some of the best plays we've seen in some time: Ron's Willy Mays centre field snag and Austin's shoestring spectacular. I sometimes wonder about Austin. He must have signed into some sort of Mephistophelian pact, 'cause he just gets better and better with each passing year. If not, if indeed he is revealing his natural talent and ability, we'll be seeing him off to the Majors some time in 2007.'
>
> Also this from Frank. 'Hi All: Just thought I'd share where I am after a Friday night, which is my usual space after I arrive home, having partaken of the great food, beer and conversation. Sometimes I'm more aware of it than at other times, and tonight is one of my most aware times. I can feel all the muscles in my body, not in a hurting way, but in a wonderful awareness that they have all been used. It's as though my body says, "Yeh, what a great night!" It all works together and all feels together and it's just wonderful. It truly is, for me, like entering into another world for a time, one in which nothing matters but (God

> this sounds awful) "The Thrill of the Game". What a wondrous thing we have created over these many years and how wonderful it is that we are an assembly of some who have been with FNB for many years, and some new and some newer. That's what my body says to me after tonight's game.'

Frank joined us in the late seventies. There's nothing to say he can't catch for any of the other pitchers, but it's somehow come about that he almost always catches for me. Our energies are different. I'm cerebral, he's physical. I remember the score all week, he forgets it five minutes after the game is over. Three o'clock Friday afternoon, he can't wait to get to the park. Three o'clock Friday afternoon, I'm dragging my butt.

Aug 6/04: Jack Alvo is back. He never stopped smiling the whole time, except when we decided to stop an inning early. Good see Jim Betts again, although he will probably have told his wife and kids he was four for four against me. John Dorsey made one of the season's great catches in a season of great catches. A liner to deep centre field, still rising and somehow John, while moving backwards, got his glove up to meet it. (That might have been another moment when Jack stopped smiling.)

It's often occurred to me that we are a remarkable group of people. Like Fred Breitner, owner of Great Metropolitan Sound. He once told me he started out with a high volume quick sale outlet, realized he wasn't enjoying the territory and decided to go in for something more satisfying. He loves music, possibly even more than he loves baseball, if such strength of feeling is possible. He could have opened three high volume units for what it cost to open Great Met. It looks like passion trumping business, but not so fast. The store attracts people who love good sound, enough of them with the income to buy state of the art equipment, some of them wanting something on a grander scale which led to Great Met getting into the home entertainment side of the business which is now its biggest source of income. One more example of, 'Do what you love, and see where it takes you.' Maybe that's the secret to joyful longevity. Then again, it's probably unwise to rush to a conclusion. Meaning does not take the form of a kernel or a seed, found by digging and paring till you arrive at absolute center and ultimate truth. It exists in moments that gather around the centre with a profound, undefinable glow, reminding us we are on a journey whose meaning cannot be found in methods, theories or systems.

One small part of Fred's journey involves our problems with the volume of the music at The Big Slice. He'd made a request to Hilda, our waitress, to turn down the music. She told Fred that this could not be done without turning down the music for the customers on the outside as well. Fred arrived the following week with a device which would allow her to turn down the sound for us, and still allow the customers on the patio to have their ear drums assaulted by Fender basses and electronic drums. The device is worth $80.00 and Fred was planning to offer to install it himself. It turned out that we'd been misinformed. Hilda didn't know how to work the controls of the restaurant's sound system. A marvelous display of ingenuity nonetheless, which goes to show how much Fred values the art of conversation, especially our conversation. For those of you who haven't been there to hear us, it's tough to recapture the moments and maybe we shouldn't try, but we do, and we will.

I'm not sure when it was a group of us began going to the pub after the game, but it was so long ago, I can't remember when we didn't. My favourite was Giorgio's Restaurant on Dupont Street. There were two flights of stairs leading to the main floor. At the bottom of the second flight, just to the left, was a section with a large table and a huge window overlooking the street. There was enough room for twenty of us at the table. Frank's, Ken's, Fred's, Craig's and Gilles' kids were somewhere between the ages of six and ten. They'd sit at a table at the edge of the level above. We'd hear them laughing and see them looking over the railing at us and knew they were making fun of their dads. I'd look out on Dupont Street at the cars and the people and everything seemed right with the world.

Aug 13/04: Our guys were down by six after the first inning, but we clawed our way back, and by the fifth we had a game on our hands, the kind where each pitch, each batted ball, each fielding play can determine the outcome. But the game can be cruel and in the top of the sixth when we should have been setting ourselves up to win it, we had one of those innings that gets away from you and it's no one's fault. For a moment you doubt the existence of God (though it was a lot longer than a moment in the early days). But that's life and life is good and the game is good and if it were perfect, we'd get bored.

However, it would be wrong to continue as if the runaway inning were just an act of God, because there was also an act of George as in George Wheeler who hit my best rise ball into the trees for a three run homer. Got this from Fred the next day:

> Hello gang. Another Friday night and yet another unique experience on the field. George Wheeler showed his true colours by swatting a monster home run. We can expect the opposition to play him in the next county next week. We can also expect the umpire to keep close tabs on our newly identified super slugger, as he missed every base on his ceremonial trot around the circuit. Umpire Joe, well known for his malleable decision making and flexible strike zone commented on George's achievement, saying that he had never witnessed such a spectacle before in all his years of calling balls and strikes.

George is a natural athlete, an accomplished gymnast in his younger years. He didn't play much baseball as a kid. His sport of choice is tennis. It's interesting to pitch to someone whose training has taught him to keep the ball in play. When translated to baseball, it means he'll swing at pitches out of the strike zone and hit balls where no one expects him to. He's more a contact hitter than a power guy so he must have been ecstatic about the one into the trees. He probably felt like he was flying around the bases, that touching them would take mean coming back to earth, and earth was too ordinary a location for so remarkable a feat. No doubt he went to sleep thinking about it, and had one of those dreams you have as a kid where you can fly. When he woke up the next morning, he was slow to get out of bed because his feet would touch the floor, reminding him he was mortal like the rest of us.

Aug 20/04: The game was unfolding at a snail's pace when it unexpectedly shed its shell. Big plays to cut down base runners taking us to the fifth inning with the score one to nothing. Living that close to the edge is not something you'd want to go through every day, but a game like that holds you in its spell more compellingly, more convincingly. 'This is the world,' it seems to say, 'and we need no other.' It's an illusion, of course, but to enter into that illusion, be an actor in its development and outcome does something good to mind, body and soul. There was a sense on both sides that we were creating something beautiful out of the evening's unpromising beginnings.

(How do I say it without blowing my own horn? What the heck, Harry James did it. I pitched 6 1/3 innings of shutout ball.)

Aug 26/04: It was the hottest day of the year and it was muggy and there were mosquitos in the outfield and it was a blowout and we quit after five. By way of contrast, the innings at The Big Slice were among the liveliest of the year. We talked about our history and our friendships, once again exploring whatever it is that keeps us coming back year after year. Up north in Madsen Red Lake Gold Mines where I grew up, we practiced Wednesdays and Fridays and played Tuesdays and Sundays. I loved Toronto, but there was an empty space in my gut. I'd called *The Star* and was told that there was a lot of softball, but the teams had established rosters and newcomers were not smiled upon. I thought it unlikely I'd ever play again and had little reason to expect otherwise.

The Phone Call

The phone call came one evening in June, 1971. I was involved with a therapeutic community named Therafields, living in a house with ten other people. Our being together was based on the belief that daily contact with other individuals would reveal our family dramas and the parts we had played in them. Once we became aware of the script we could decide to step out of it. We were encouraged to speak honestly with each other and our therapists, and become involved in the community. The idea that sport could be in anyway useful in this process never came up. In fact, it seemed that it was something to be avoided, something that might lead us away from our task and pick our hard won gains off first base. Enter Bill Barnes. Bill was about sixty-five when I first met him, balding, with a fairly pronounced beer belly and a wry smile that seemed the very essence of cynicism, a smile that made you feel that just about anything you said to him might be dismissed with a raised eyebrow. As far as I know, he was never seen with a hammer in his hand or lifting heavy furniture or doing anything else that was supposed to be good for you. Occasionally, he'd get talking and he'd tell the story about how he'd had a tryout with the St Louis Cardinals and got a hit off Dizzy Dean.

The person on the other end wasn't Bill, but was clearly acting on his behalf. Would the people in 152 Howland be interested in getting together for a ballgame? (No one told us there'd been a game a year earlier which ended with a fist fight.) The call came shortly after supper and five or six of us were still gathered around the table. Their reaction to the news varied between disdain and indifference. I felt the weight of the silent objections, but underneath that weight was a longing to pitch and hit and chase fly balls once again. I think what the people at the table also saw - whether it made much sense to them or not - was a kid who wanted to play baseball real bad. For sure Rick Secord saw it. We went to a nearby schoolyard, I threw a few pitches and he agreed to be my catcher. Gilles Morin was also interested and with players from the other new house groups we scraped together a team. The game took place at Christie Pitts on a Sunday morning.

There's a scene in John Updike's *Rabbit Run* where Rabbit is playing golf with Eccles, the local minister. Rabbit's marriage is in trouble and Eccles thinks the trouble is Rabbit. He keeps asking him what he's looking for. Can he see it, can he hold it, what is this irrational thing that's so damned important? Rabbit can't answer. At the point where the question has become a pain in the ass, Rabbit sees Eccles is just as lost as he is. He steps up to the tee on the sixteenth hole and hits the ball three hundred yards straight down the fairway. He turns to Eccles and says, 'That's it.' The words jumped off the page. Yes, it's a cliché, but now and then words actually do that. Rabbit's swing was mind, body and soul together in one unshackled moment, as if club and ball had acted alone and Rabbit was merely the agent of an unseen power.

That Sunday morning the ball was flying out of my hand. Except for Mo Farge, they were striking out or hitting pop flies. Mo was from Texas, had played some serious baseball and knew enough to stay back and let the ball come to him. He kept hitting hundred mile an hour line drives down the third base line, five feet foul. I counted my lucky stars and let my body do the rest. But something happened. It wasn't my arm. It was a voice saying the person who'd been pitching shutout ball for five innings wasn't really me. The ball was climbing out of strike zone and I'd hear, 'Wait him out, he's got a lot of those.' 'Pitcher's in the air, catcher needs a chair.' The voices joined the voice in my head and the flow was broken. After the game, we gathered in the backyard of one the Admiral Road houses. Bill said I'd probably be tougher next time out. It was good to hear him say there'd be a next time, but on that June afternoon, I had no idea how many next times there would be.

There were more phone calls that year and the next. In the summer of 1973, Bill organized a tournament to be held at Nobleton a small town about fifty miles north of Toronto. About halfway through the final game, it started to rain. We went back to our cars and waited for it to stop. Afterwards, Peter Dales said he knew something special was unfolding when we didn't pack up and go home. We finished the day and our guys won and I felt like quite the fellow. (Actually, it was far more dramatic. I'd never been on a winning team all the years I'd played in Red Lake. Success was dizzying. I guess that's what happens when it goes to your head.)

A footnote to the final game is Tom O'Sullivan's line drive. Tom had grown up in Detroit where he'd played with Bill Frehan who later went on to catch for the Tigers. They were considered pretty much equal in talent but Tom had decided not to pursue a baseball career. The line drive came in the fourth inning and was headed straight at my head. I got my glove up, knocked the ball down, and threw it to first to get the out. I was a mere lad of thirty-four that year. Winters were long and summer was another country, but we didn't forget what happened that Sunday in Nobleton. In May, 1974 a group of us met on the front steps of 125 Walmer Road and made plans to play every Friday night which begs the question, 'Why Friday?' Participants of Therafields were encouraged - although it might be more accurate to say expected - to work on various building projects in the evenings (excluding Friday) and on the weekends. We were going to build a therapeutic community and baseball was a distraction from a higher purpose. Interestingly enough, Friday Night Baseball continued long after the community ended.

Sept 10/04**:** It was Chatz once again who broke the good guys hearts, fielding balls deep in the hole and making perfect throws and racing into the outfield to catch balls over his head and positioning himself perfectly (much closer to third than politically correct) to snare Frank's three line drives. Once lucky. Two unlikely. But three? At The Slice, Mark Riddle, said that Chatz fielded six ground balls and five balls in the air, which gave him eleven out of twenty-one outs. It was a somewhat harrowing for our guys watching all this from the bench. Even more harrowing was my being told by Jim Betts what I suspected, but didn't want to know, that into the fourth inning, we still hadn't got a hit off John Larocque. Thank God - although it was Jack Alvo who actually did the deed - the hit finally came.

The big over the table item was Anna's white water trip throughout the far north. Anna is Frank's daughter, a catcher like her father and her grandfather before her. I'd heard enough about her trip that I was expecting a good story, but what I'd forgotten is her passion for photography. When I got to The Slice, her album of the trip was already opened. Definitely not one of those My Holiday sessions where after five minutes you dread seeing one more picture of someone doing something that must have seemed cute at the time. Anna's album is thick. (Ask Frank how much it cost to develop the pictures.) Looking at it was like reading one of those books you don't want to put down.

What's that got to do with baseball? Our story begins there, but it reaches out from there to other parts of our lives and one feeds the other in some magical way which has something to do with The Hand, with Craig, Chatz and Fred sharing their love of the game with their kids, with John Larocque's rekindled love of the game and his life as the proprietor of Ring Music, with how we leave our daily lives for those enchanted moments on a Friday evening from which we return to work, friends and family larger and renewed. Our only sadness was the time of year.

June skies seem to promise forever. September skies are more truthful. If it's a perfect day for baseball, the fading light in the late innings reminds us we are on the downside. The sadness is somewhat softened by The Tournament. If there has to be an end, we will not fade into winter without protest. We will make a joyful noise unto the lords of the diamond and eat, drink and be merry.

3

The Tournament

If by chance you are still wondering about the two men attempting to clear the infield of the water on the morning of Sunday September 21, 2014, they were not rehearsing a scene from the theatre of the absurd, they were not afraid it might never rain again intent on storing water for the dry years ahead, they were not searching for a lost Rolex watch or diamond ring. They were preparing the field for The Tournament. Yes, it had rained all night and was showing no clear sign of stopping, but when you care deeply, when you believe in the supreme importance of a thing, you do not shrug your shoulders and say, 'It wasn't meant to be,' or 'It was God's will,' you carry on.

In the beginning, the season was pretty much a week to week thing. Numbers uncertain, but with a pattern that became clear after the first few years. Thirty or more players in May and June, a steady decline from there on, nine or ten in late July and early August at which point we'd pack it in for the year. Steve Shapiro and I (more about Steve later) thought it a shame to go out with a whimper. A couple of years later we got the players together for a September game at Riverdale park. (The score was 26 -25 and ended with Peter Roach's grand slam.) The idea of ending the season with a bang stayed with us and we began dividing the players into three teams, and playing three games. I remember all too clearly one of those early affairs at Ramsden Park. One team won the first two games. My team had lost its game and I was eager to play another, but the winner had been decided and everyone went home. I sat on the grass wondering how a day that had offered such rich promise could have withered into such profound discontent. I don't know if I figured it out then or later, but the remedy – which had never entered anyone's mind – was to have the team that won the first game not play the second game. Meaning that the winner couldn't be determined without playing a third game. Simple though it was, I had to do a lot of explaining.

Tournament, Sunday, Sept 17, 2004

This year instead of taking a picture of the team that won The Pig, we took pictures of all three teams. It was a year in which everybody won. The game also won. Witness Jack Alvo's play on Anna's soft pop into the Bermuda triangle between pitcher, second and first. I see a lazy pop to my left and I think it's not my ball. It falls to the ground and takes a high bounce. Wayne Oake at second has the best chance to make the play, but the runner is only steps away from first. Jack, who is playing short, appears seemingly out of nowhere. Knowing there is no time for a throw, he bats the ball to first with his bare hand to get the out. Everyone on all three teams applauded.

It got me thinking about who we perform for. Sometimes it's that high and mighty judge in the sky who decides on the basis of how each of us played whether we spend the week in heaven or hell. But I think more and more we perform for each other. Chatz laid down a perfect bunt in his first at bat in the final game and I threw wild to first. Next time up the bunt wasn't perfect but it was good and I got him by an eyelash. On his way back to the bench he said, 'Great play.' I should have quit while I was ahead. In the woeful inning when we'd given up seven runs and still hadn't recorded an out, I got an easy one hop grounder and threw home, but there's no force and we still haven't got an out. I hear Ken Pagel say, 'It's okay Nelles.'

Our gods are kinder these days, and all things considered the baseball is just as good. But this thing about winning and losing is so deep in our collective psyches that we can never be completely free of it. It's part of who and what we are. Something in us wants to win. When I woke up Monday morning it was different from last year when I woke up with that winning glow. This year that glow wasn't there and I missed it.

There are all sorts of stories which don't make the cut if it's just about the winners. Lorne Mitchell, with his ailing rotator cuff, who missed the last two weeks of the season so he could nurse it back to some semblance of normality, coming up to bat for the first time afraid that one bad swing could put his shoulder out of commission till this time next year, and hitting a grand slam. Luke, higher in the batting order than I would have put him, being patient and taking his walks. Joe Leonard at second after a tough year with his eyes and his rheumatism. Sluggo racing around the bases on his plastic knee. Craig who just plain loves to play no matter where or when. Ben Woolfit returning to the game after nearly fifty years out there taking his lumps in the field but hitting the ball hard each time at the plate. Peter Roach who lives in Stratford and comes down every year to join us for the day. And Ted Bradan who marches to a different drummer. Ted doesn't like playing with those old gods because they don't understand that baseball is a lot like music. I'd like to say I get it, but it's like talking to one of those eastern philosophers who come down from the mountain now and again to suggest other ways of being.

There were always withdrawal pains after The Tournament. Seems to me they've never been expressed with such simple, plaintive eloquence as in this message from Fred.

> Friday, September the 24th was unlike anything that had preceded it. I left my Yonge – Eglinton office at the usual time, approximately 5 PM and headed

west, as had been the custom since early May. But this was no ordinary departure. I had been charged with the solemn mission of replacing the master bedroom latrine lid, a task requiring a visit to the 'Taps' store on Lawrence Avenue just west of Dufferin. The 'Taps' expedition played out as expected. But it was only after completing the mission, as I fired up my trusty Saab, that I felt the full import of a baseball season that had ended too early. Indeed, I felt ready to don my running shoes and both FNB caps for yet another episode of our diamond drama, but it was not about to happen on this night.

This is not a new feeling. Friday Night Withdrawal, or FNW, happens every year. The summer that never was, turned into the summer that wouldn't quit. This edition of September 24 was a perfect baseball evening. Despite a powerful urge to continue west toward Keelesdale Park in the faint hope th would be at least one other player with the same irrational tendencies, I proceeded hesitatingly toward the Breitner ranch, arriving just in time to greet Susan as she departed to spend an evening with a friend. I began to reflect on our season and the tournament with the realization that in 2004 we had once again pulled off an amazing feat, with a deep understanding that our competition is more like a coalition, a drama in which all participants are at once in opposition and at the same time completely unified in a synergy of brotherhood and camaraderie. This is powerful stuff folks, a union that could not be ordered in advance, a true adventure of body, mind and spirit. Our very existence invites reflection, like the game itself.

> My apologies are extended to anyone who waited at Keelesdale for me to arrive.

I'm not sure of the year but somewhere along the way, we decided to meet one Friday evening a month during the off season. It was Fred who took the lead and sent out the schedule. One January evening in the early 2000's, I was driving to the Pizza Hut near the corner of Black Creek and Lawrence. The trip took me past the diamond at Upper Keelesdale where we'd played the last few summers. The field was covered with snow. It looked beautiful in the moonlight, peaceful and mysterious. I could see myself stopping by the side of the road, getting out of my car and walking over to home plate. I wouldn't have been able to see it, but I had a good idea where it was. If you had been walking along the sidewalk on the south side of street, you'd likely have seen me and wondered why I was there. If you'd asked me, I couldn't have said anything that made much sense, although if I'd thought of it, I might have referred you to Robert Frost:

> The woods are lovely, dark and deep,
> But I have promises to keep
> And miles to go before I sleep,
> And miles to go before I sleep.

4

When Winter Comes Can Spring Be Far Behind?

May 20/05: May 6 and May 13 felt like the days when I pick up my guitar and all the good notes have packed up and gone. On Friday May 20, spring arrived for real and baseball was as natural as the grass. We celebrated by creating a one run game.

Hope to see you at the reading of *We Never Came to Lose* this coming Tues, May 24 at Rowers Grill and Pub, 150 Harbord St, 7:30 to 9:00. Frank and I will be wearing our FNB T shirts.

'We Never Came to Lose' is the play Frank and I wrote about Friday Night Baseball. It was Austin who gave us the idea. The three of us of us met at Tik Talks on Harbord St Tuesday mornings. There was a lot of back and forth and a lot of wondering if were on the same page, but we managed to wrestle it to completion. The reading was fun, a splendid evening of memorable performances and an appreciative audience. Our own multi-talented Jim Betts was especially entertaining as the pitcher. I found working on the play occasionally harrowing inasmuch as it forced me to look at my capacity for dumping my discontent on my fielders. Jim's reading of Pitch pulled no punches. I met Jim in 1980 when I joined the Lehman Engel Musical Theatre Workshop. Jim was one of the more accomplished and experienced students. Why bring musical theatre into it? Maybe because of the passion and dedication required to write a show which has what it takes to capture an audience. Maybe because that same

passion and dedication is required to create a memorable ball game. Ed Kleban who wrote the lyrics for 'The Chorus Line', was in Lehman's New York workshop. Remember 'What I Did for Love?' The words are Ed's. Forget six degrees of separation. Ed is just one degree from FNB.

June 17/05: It was June baseball and it was good. Some clouds threatened at five, but they saw the good stuff and steered around us. As always, the night belonged to all of us, but more so to Gilles who pitched the best game of his career. He pitched inside, he pitched outside, he pitched up, he pitched down. Only three balls made it out of the infield. I've been joking with Gilles for the past twenty years that just as he's starting to pitch well, he goes down east to New Brunswick. This year he somehow put it all together before his departure. I asked him where it came from so early in the season.

'From my dreams.'

Nov 2/14: Yesterday, I sent this off to Gilles who had a stroke the week after the tournament. Nicole says the recovery is going well.

Jan 15/15: Got this from Gilles. 'Hi Fred and all you Friday night baseball friends: Nicole made you aware of the predicament I was in last October when I passed a kidney stone and it led to an ischemic stroke, and a hemorrhagic stroke. Wow serious stuff! I have read since that there are an estimated 50,000 strokes in this country annually. Of every 100 people who have a stroke, 15 die immediately, 10 recover completely and 75 are left with moderate to severe disability. Because there seems to be no real damage as stated by the neurologist, I feel so lucky and privileged. I was told many times at the hospital how lucky I was but I did not realize how serious it was since I do not remember a single thing. A week and a half totally out of it on serious drugs!

This Friday I have a long assessment at the hospital to determine the extent of any possible damage to the brain. Anyway, I feel fine now and hopefully the results will be very positive. I might have to do some kind of therapy to foster some new brain neurons or patterns, but on the phone they told me it was more of a precaution and they wanted to assess the progress I am doing. I am back training, walking, jogging and I have gained all my original weight back. I had lost 15 pounds during my stay at the hospital. So I should be ready for our coming 2015 FBN season.

Nelles, I would like to thank you so much for sending the e-mail way back regarding one of my best games. It did lift me up since I was so down from pitching in the last tournament where nothing worked, no inside, no riser, no outside and no movement to the ball. It was flat as a pancake and I really thought "no more pitching for me". It was a bad, bad day. As a pitcher I feel a responsibility to always be at the top of my game and sometime even if I trained hard during the week when I know I will be at the field to contribute with the pitching, it's so very discouraging when nothing is working; your delivery is off, your arm fails you and your legs are not synchronizing with the rest of your body. I felt ashamed of my performance and your e-mail helped me heal the memory of the tournament.'

Mrs Peterson, Angus, Ernie Banks, Dizzy, Pee Wee, Pierre Berton, Peter Pan

July 15/05: All week long the news was heat. An email in which I wrote, 'Any thoughts?' elicited a go-for-it response, most notably, 'Let's play two,' from Russ. At The Slice, we were on the patio again. Hot summer days often turn into lovely summer evenings. Like being at the cottage. Only the lake was missing. (Could someone look into that?) George and I talked about Edith Wharton and Henry James and Roddy Doyle. Lorne raved about a biography of Winston Churchill. Apparently, there was a lot of talk of appeasement when the war was going badly and it was Churchill who led the resistance. We ordered twice as much pizza as required and we had to chuck in extra to pay the bill. Fred! Help! (Fred was spending the evening with his daughter Catherine, who is off to Germany for the year.)

Geez, this is sounding a lot like Mrs Peterson's column in the Red Lake District News.

'The Red Lake District News' was run by Lofty Harrison and Ted Harding. They ran it off on their Gestetner and there was always lots of typos. There were columns from each of the five towns. Mrs Peterson, who wrote the Madsen column, supplied the usual fare about who wasn't feeling well and who had holidayed with far away relations. (Everyone's relations were far away from Red Lake.) She also had a flair for story telling. One of her favourite subjects was a large Collie named Angus who liked to herd people on their way home. He was always finding variations on the theme and it was fun reading about how he kept finding new ways to get people headed in the right direction. Maybe we're all a bit like Angus. Each of us has ideas about where the rest of ought to be going.

I too have my ideas about how the world should unfold, although I will add in my own defense that if Mrs Peterson were writing this entry, it's not likely she'd have noticed that the great Cubs shortstop, Ernie Banks, died earlier in the week. Ernie was an accomplished fielder at the game's most demanding position. He also hit the long ball, unusual for a shortstop in those days. He was an eleven time all-star and played eighteen years for a team that never got to the World Series. He's famous for the expression supplied earlier by Russ: 'Let's play two.' One of the tributes was a story from an ump who said that Ernie never turned back and glared when you made a questionable call. If he turned back, it was to say, 'What a beautiful day for baseball.' Did he regret never making it to the World Series? Maybe once in a blue moon. The rest of the time he was having too much fun. It doesn't show up in the record books, but the love of the game is not about records. It's about two men in late middle age draining an infield in the rain.

July 22/05: At ten to six we start counting bodies and the number is thirteen, but someone says fourteen. We've figured out how to manage with seven a side over the years, so it's no big deal. Given the Reds success in the past few weeks, it seems a good idea to have the out-machine, Chatz, play for the Greys. As I sit down to make up the batting order, I write down six names and I can't find our seventh guy. The reason for this soon becomes clear. He doesn't exist. Which means the Greys will have to supply two subs when the Reds are in the field. With a couple of guys on base, someone playing left field, someone at bat, someone on deck and someone keeping score, coaching the bases is a casualty of low numbers. The next batter and anyone else in the area can yell words of caution or encouragement as needed. Hopefully, they all will be saying the same thing.

On the bench, Jim Betts asks me what inning it is. I give him a number. 'Is that all?' John LeSarge says, 'Don't worry, Nelles. All we gotta do is make it down to the pub.' 'Okay, but with dignity.' "Nah.' 'Some dignity?' John seems okay with that. The Reds take the field in the bottom of seven with a four run lead. We get some outs, but they get some hits and John Larocque comes to the plate.

'Yes ladies and gentlemen, the tying run is at bat in the person of John Larocque, the owner of Ring Music and he looks ready to do serious damage. Here's the wind up, here's the pitch. It's hard ground ball to second. Klumak scoops it, and throws to first for the out. But wait a minute, Klumak plays for the Greys. What's going on Dizzy (as in Dean)?'

'Simple Pee Wee (as in Reese). When there aren't enough guys, the teams sub for each other.'

'That's tough, Diz. He just threw out his own player and lost the rights to the water hole for a whole week.'

'Yes Pee Wee, but no player who believes in the game will screw up just so his team can win. And whosoever believeth in the game shall not perish, but shall have everlasting life.'

Walking out to the parking lot with Walter, I hear him say he's still not a strong as he was a few years back, but he's back on third with his rights to the water hole (not to be confused with the watering hole) safely in place.

The reference to the water hole is from Stanley Kubrik's '2001: A Space Odyssey. In the opening scene one gang of apes discovers bones of the dead can become weapons. They raise their arms and beat their chests in triumph, but how did other team feel? Stay posted. At the moment, the narrative requires a shift from the apes to James M. Barrie. Too big a stretch? Okay, what about Pierre Berton? At least we're talking about a Canadian. A Canadian who lived in Kleinburg, not far from Frank and Susan's place on Windrush Road. A few days before the game of August twelfth, Frank had attended his funeral.

> "Yesterday was the celebration of the life of Pierre Berton up at the Windrush House. It was a great, happy/sad event with the Berton family and some close friends. I had the good fortune to be asked to drive Lister Sinclair up to Kleinburg and back again. What a great man! He is of the stature, both physically and intellectually, of Pierre. Truly a man of ideas. And we talked on the way up and on the way back. Did we talk! It was like being with an old friend. As we passed by Bindertwine Park on the way back home, I began talking to him about the play Nelles and I are writing about Friday Night Baseball. I started out by recounting the tournaments we had there and as we talked he moved through "Alice Through the Looking Glass" and recited some of the poems from Carroll's book and then we got onto "Peter Pan", his favorite play.
>
> I talked about the four old men who used to come to watch us at Viewmount, and Lister told me about the production in England where the actress playing Wendy was going to refuse to go on if a section of the script was not cut. It's the point in the action where Tinker Bell dies, and Peter asks the audience to help

him get her back. If they truly believe they can bring her back they must all shout 'Tinker Bell'. The actress said that the playwright was a fool, that there would be nothing but a dead silence and she was not going to be a part of such nonsense. Well they did what the playwright wanted and there was a huge shout from the audience. Then he spoke about the end of the play, where Peter is alone and returns to Wendy's house and knocks on the window. Wendy comes to the window and asks what he wants. He says he wants to fly away with her. Wendy says she can't fly. Peter says he has some magic powder. All she has to do is open the window. Wendy says it wouldn't make any difference. The lights come up as she speaks. Peter looks at her and asks her what happened. The last lines of the play are:

"Peter, I'm sorry. I got old, I couldn't help it."

Lister recited the line with the same voice and intonation as we all heard when he did "Ideas". I think I almost drove off the road, but what a trip it was."

Frank talked often about his friendship with Pierre. Many evenings of nonstop conversation aided and abetted by good Scotch, the Scotch against doctor's orders. At this point in his life he'd written fifty books. Franks wife, Susan, remembers him saying, 'I set out to write fifty books and I wrote fifty books. Fifty is enough.'

Aug 12/05: The air is thick and heavy. It sits on us like a blanket. A tall, young guy gets out of his car and checks out the infield. It's the ump. He sees what the rest of us have seen. A couple of shallow lakes, one around home plate and another between first and second. I tell him he's in for an easy night, but he'll get paid anyway. He smiles and says, 'Whatever'. From somewhere out of the heat and water I hear, "What about scrub?' I'd checked out the diamond up the hill just after arriving and the lakes were only ponds. Eleven men who were formerly scattered about in various games of catch, begin to move as one body and walk to drier ground.

The ump has marched up the hill with us. An ump is not required for scrub. No matter. It's decided he will pitch. Fred, notable for great plays at third, races in from deep right to make a tough catch look easy. Russ and I call for the same fly ball. Russ makes the catch with my glove waving at the air in front of him. And then the catch that doesn't happen, but oh the possibilities so clearly in waiting as Jim races back for a ball hammered thirty feet behind him. Everything is right, the angle of approach, the position of the body, the readiness of his glove. Just one tiny step more and he has it.

And oh, the hitting. Paul Casey's sweet swing and the ball thirty feet over my head. Wayne, with a Garry Sheffield waggle driving one into deep, deep left. Mark Riddle hitting the ball hard so many times in a row that he got tired of running the bases. The ump finally taking his turn at bat not bothering to wait for a pitch he can drive and driving it anyway. A true lover of the game this fine young man, having the option, with the air descending like soot, of getting into his car, collecting his thirty-five bucks, instead pitching tirelessly for the greater good and taking his well earned at bats with superbly swung enthusiasm. Unknown to all, Peter Pan and Captain Hook have got wind of our proceedings. When we don't play till dark, Peter is disappointed. Hook scowls with delight,

'Fakes!' he shouts. 'Fakes one and all. Such pretense, such shameless posturing, such ill feigned joy. 'Tis beer, beer and nothing more that makes them tick.' With the word 'tick' his face turns ghastly white. It seems there are crocodiles at Keelesdale. In fact, there are crocodiles everywhere for those who cannot give themselves joyfully to the moment.

For those of us who've forgotten, Hook is relentlessly pursued by a crocodile who had accidentally swallowed a sailor's alarm clock. The sound of a ticking clock, merely an annoyance to anyone else, is mortal terror for him.

At The Slice, we're on the patio. The air is no longer heavy. Joe Leonard phoned earlier in the day asking for someone to call him when the game was over so he could meet us at the watering hole. He'd been hoping the eye operation would come in August so that he'd be able to play in The Tournament. All the same, there is so much baseball among us, so many years that happened yesterday, that he's on the field with us still. It shows in our talk, which on this evening has a wonderful free for all quality without ever getting chaotic.

Somewhere between the beer and the salad, we talk about Lorne's nephew, who played with us three different times while visiting from Cape Breton. Lorne and I remember vividly the game five years ago in which he put on a display of hitting seen neither before nor since. It was my guys against Rolando's and the little guy from the Philippines was on his game. For the longest time, it seemed we were never really in it. They kept hitting and we kept not hitting - except for Lorne's nephew. His second home run into the trees, somewhere around inning five, got us back in the game. We were three or four down in the bottom of the seventh when he hit a third one into the trees to give us the lead. Sitting at the table on the patio of The Slice, I can feel the joy of all the guys who've joined our revels and I see a pillar of holy sound rise above us.

Ted and Rolando

Whenever we go back to Lorne's nephew and his three home runs against Rolando, I'm reminded that history, even when truly related, can sometimes skew reality. We've had some good pitchers over the years, but Rolando was likely the best. I was looking through some old score books one day and found 'Tournament, First Game, 1997,' along with a note at the bottom under Rolando's team.

'No hitter!'

That must have been one heck of a performance, but I don't remember a thing about it. Will tear myself away from my computer and see if I can find the score book.

Eureka!

The date was Sept 14, 1997. The score was 8-0.

One year, Rolando brought a large container of sweet and sour soup to the barbecue. We all understood it wasn't just about food, it was his way of saying thank you for a second career playing the game he loved. In the photo which accompanied the George Gamester article in 'The Star', he's in the front row smiling wider than anyone else. I drove him to the tournament several times. During one of those trips, he told me about driving along Bayview Avenue with a friend one winter night and their car breaking down. They began walking, hoping to find a gas station. It was so cold he thought he and his friend were going to freeze to death. I think the story came as a result of my asking him how he was finding life in Canada. I didn't realize at the time that it wasn't just a story about our cold winters. It was also about no one stopping to offer a ride.

I'm not sure if it was that year or later at one of our barbecues that he spoke about feeling like an outsider. It's not hard to see why. The rest of us were engaged in conversation about things we had in common, and now in the late summer afternoon without the game to embrace him, he felt suddenly alone. We did our best to reassure him. Frank, in particular, was able to find warm words of appreciation, but more was needed on a consistent basis. There was also his fear that if he threw inside, he might hit someone which meant the hitters could sit on the outside pitch. He'd sometimes tell me about talking with his wife about how it felt to pitch with one hand tied behind his back. She'd say, "Why do you keep playing?' One spring I called him several times to let him know we were starting up again. He didn't answer.

Aug 26/05: Ted Bradan is back. He pitched three strong innings and did his goalie act on a line drive smash from Russ. John LeSarge, who hasn't seen him play, can't believe it. Tom Cain dropped by to say hello just because we're such great fellows and it turned out we needed a right fielder. He got two big hits in our glorious bottom of seven. One went all the way to the fence. (Tom was born in England, never played baseball, but did play cricket. He has an easy flat swing that got him his share of hits, most of them against me.) My guys are down by seven, not really expecting to win. The next thing I know five runs are in and the bases are loaded with nobody out and we can smell it. John St J brings in the tying run and John Larocque drives in Frank from second to win it. But wait a sec. Fred has the scorebook in hand and he's saying, 'Where's the winning run. I can't find it. John, can you find it?' John can't find it either. Frank has to go back to third. Ron is at bat and you can see the intent in that unpredictable swing of his. He hits the ball into right centre, but Ted is positioned perfectly and it's a tie. No matter. There is such a splendid feeling of what we've achieved- not just one team, both teams - that winning and losing fade to irrelevance.

When I get to The Slice, there's a spot for me across from George. He's on a roll. The theme is the ten greatest movies. Tom Cain's first choice is Fellini's *Amarchord.* We all agree. Lorne probably added that he watches it once a year, but he's on the other end of the table and it was a long table. Ken raves about a movie about a cello player who comes back from the dead. I choose Denys Arcand's *The Barbarian Invasions.* The question arises as to what English Canadian movie ranks with films from Quebec and we're having trouble thinking of any. I nominate Carolyn Wheeler's *Bye Bye Blues,* but it didn't get great reviews (just good). George chooses *Apocalypse Now.* Seems to me that everyone, including the movie critics, was overwhelmed by it. The protagonist is war itself, a monster with an appetite for young men unleashed by old men safe behind their money. George was so pissed off by the cool reception, he refused to watch the Academy

Awards. Which would have been fine, except his roommate at the time was just as determined vice versa. (The Oscar for best picture that year went to *Kramer Versus Kramer*.)

The evening of August 26, 2005, Keelesdale Park, Toronto Ont. It was good. It was very good.

As I read through these reports some ten years after the fact, I'm aware of how quickly the present becomes the past. The reference to Ted reminds me once again of what a pure force he was. His last name is actually Bradanovich. I know this because I took guitar lessons from his dad who had a public presence as a member of bands in the thirties and forties and shortened the name to Bradan. I didn't do much playing for Tony. He'd sit and talk and write out the week's lesson. He'd tell me how he'd been driving or swimming while thinking about the notes on the third string and how the answer would come from the sky, as if it had nothing to do with him, that he was simply the recorder of a universal law. His approach to teaching arose from his conviction that guitar players were essentially contortionists who had coaxed and cajoled the fingers of their left hands into the positions necessary to make notes and form chords. If you've ever played the guitar, you'll know there's a eureka moment when you finally manage to finger a chord which had seemed daunting to the point of impossibility. You tell yourself, 'I did it,' and indeed you did. What you didn't do was pay attention to what notes you were playing.

Tony was fond of saying that if you wanted to know the notes in a "C" chord, and you asked a pianist, he'd pick them out on the keyboard, "C", "E", "G". If you asked a guitar player, he'd clomp his hand on the neck, look at his fingers and maybe ten minutes later, he'd be able to name the notes. It's not that guitarists are inherently lazy, it's the nature of the beast. If you look at a piano keyboard, you see the keys, neatly arranged in groups of twelve: seven white and five black. Twelve is a manageable number and after you've studied a month or two, you know the names of the notes. If you look at the neck of a guitar, you see six strings and twenty-one frets.

Each conjunction of a string and a fret is a note. Six times twenty-one is one hundred and twenty-six. One hundred and twenty-six is a helluva lot more than twelve. Tony's teaching was based on the idea that when you look at the neck of a guitar, you shouldn't just see strings and frets, you should see notes. No one had ever looked at it that way. To take something so difficult and elusive and make it simple is the essence of genius.

Writing about his dad reminds me again of talking to Ted after The Tournament in 2004 and his saying baseball is a lot like music. I'm still not sure what he meant, but I'm intrigued enough to want to take another stab at it. When the music is good, there's a flow to it. A good game has a rhythm, which holds it steady and from which surprise can emerge. Without rhythm, surprise is merely commotion. There's also the sense of being in tune. Not just with yourself, but with the other players. If the game becomes discordant, each player can play a part in restoring the harmony by getting in touch with his inner musician. It helps if you play an instrument, but there is music in all of us. It's one of our deepest and most ancient attributes. It brings us together and there is joy in the merging of voices, even in songs of pain and loss.

Ted knew all this and though he said little about it, it would rub off on you. His genius was not as evident as his dad's, but it was there in his understanding of the simple basic elements of the sport. Often when I sense discord in myself or the game, I feel his presence. You wont find it in the scorebook, but if you had been on the field with him for those fifteen years or so, or even if you had just dropped by to watch, you might have sensed there was something about him that raised the bar in some gentle but powerful manner. It was the Ted Era and his legacy is with us still. Yet another reason why two men in late middle age were on the infield with shovel and pail that rainy Sunday morning at Coronation Park.

Sept 9/05: With everyone back from holidays and getting ready for The Tournament, there were twenty-six of us, thirteen on each side. It was a church picnic, a small town circus. Austin said he enjoyed having all those people buzzing around him even though he only got two chances to hit. At the end there were so many people to shake hands with you didn't know if the next person in line was on your team or the other.

At The Big Slice, we talked about Joe. Lorne told us he'd won an important award. He'd made notes for his acceptance speech, but when the time came, his eye issues made it difficult to read them. He improvised, no doubt with the same quiet, good natured, straight forward manner that we have come to associate with him over the years. No doubt there was also humour, perhaps one of his Chatsworth stories. Lorne was uncertain as to the exact nature of the award, and advised me to e mail Russ for a fuller explanation.

He won the association of Ontario Health Centres award which is given annually to the person who has done the most to promote community health centres and generally non profit health care. It is life time achievement award.

P.S. Ben Woolfit had come to the game to invite us to his show at the Moore Gallery. I went to the opening and was mightily impressed with the rich energy of the display - deep, powerful, rich colour on every wall. Austin was there, and Lorne, and Gilles, and Wayne, and George. When Lorne and I left, the obvious thing was to take the Spadina street car, but we started walking. Up through the crowds milling around the sidewalk markets, past Darcy street where the tai chi people were getting ready to board the buses taking them north to Orangeville. As we walked on that perfect September afternoon, talking about whatever the surroundings brought to mind, some things came clear as to why our journey as acquaintances, team mates, friends, has had difficult moments. There were some pretty memorable rows. And yet there was something in each of us which never gave up. I thought afterwards about what a remarkable journey it's been and it seemed to me the walk was like that too. As if it had taken us through thirty years. We knew it had been a good road, but also a tough road, and we knew the road ahead would have its share of tough times, but being able to share that in the context of our friendship felt like a minor miracle. I chatted on the phone with Lorne about what I'd written before sending it out and he agreed it was a wonderful happening. I told him my only reservation about putting it in the email was that it shouldn't stop us from ruffling each other's feathers again. He agreed.

Tournament, Sunday, Sept 18, 2005

I never felt the end of the season so profoundly as this year on the way over to Frank's with John Larocque, Ted and Austin. Not as the member of a winning or losing team, but as someone who'd arrived at one of the major turning points of the year. It gathers and builds towards the third Sunday in September and we all feel the buzz and we all want to do well. When we get home and Mom and Dad, say, 'Did you win?' and we want to say, 'Yes'. We've learned a lot about winning and losing since the beginning, but losing can be tough. Perhaps no tougher than for the aforementioned gang of apes who lost the rights to the water hole in *2001: A Space Odyssey.* As promised, here is the rest of the story, as reconstructed in *We Never Came to Lose.*

Catch

Nice play, eh?

Pitch

Yeah.

Catch

You didn't see Second's face when he was going for that ball. He wasn't gonna miss it, not on his life. And you didn't see his killer look back at you after he finished that DP. Whole body was saying, 'Fuck you, asshole.'

Pitch

I just got a little irritated.

Catch

Bullshit. You been callin' off anything I call. You told me to fuck off when I came out and told you to relax. You yelled at Lefty for being off his bag. You been doing nothing but yelling. You know what first said to me as we're coming in? he says 'Who's he gonna yell at next? The old guys?' And you're obviously not having fun. Right?

Catch takes a handful of sunflower seeds from his back pocket. Pitch sits, head down, glowering. Catch goes to his bag, takes out a can of water, takes a long drink. Walks back and sits down beside Pitch, and passes the can to Pitch.

Pitch

Yeh. Second's working hard. He always works hard. Why do I let it get to me?

Catch

Dunno. But it sure leaves you all alone.

Pitch

(To audience.) What can I tell you? No excuse for it. But if you think it's easy being out there and watching balls sneak through the infield and bloops dropping in behind second, and watching the other guys cross the plate and high fiving each other like they just won the World Series, no way. It's something like being mugged by a gang of thugs in a dark alley - although the image comes to mind goes much farther back to an episode from the Great Ape Wars where two gangs of apes once fought for possession of the same water hole.

The date on the scoreboard now reads 20,000 B.C Two of the apes (Ginzo and Gonzo) find baseball bats. Pitch and Catch become Pokey and Sam.

Announcer

Ladies and Gentlemen, tonight we have the good fortune to be transported backward in time to the Twenty Thousandth Century B.C. where Ginzo and Gonzo will make the remarkable discovery that fallen tree branches – in particular, Maple and Ash - can be used as weapons.

Ginzo and Gonzo use their clubs to batter Pokey and Sam into submission, after which they beat their chests and throw their arms skyward.

Announcer

Victory! How sweet it is. But did you ever wonder what happened to that unfortunate band of apes who were the archetypal losing team. What did they feel as they ran off across the dry and dusty plain?

Pokey and Sam run away in panic mode making loud anxious sounds.

What did they say to each other when they huddled together to face the cold, thirsty night?

Pokey and Sam sit down, looking fearfully in all directions. They speak in ape language. The announcer holds up signs which translate the dialogue.

Sam (Catch)	Sign
Whamamamamanama?	What now?
Pokey (Pitch)	Sign
Doomadooma.	Doesn't matter.
Sam	Sign
Whymanotta?	Why not?
Pokey	Sign
Gersplunked.	We're fucked.
Sam	Sign
Ainapainadover.	*(Side one)* It aint over...
Tilladoomadover.	*(Side two)* Till it's over.

Pitch and Catch revert to their roles as ball players.

Pitch

With all this stuff about winning and losing, in case you're wondering what we play for...

Catch brings out a large, unattractive - dare we say ugly - piggy bank.

Catch

We play for this. For want of a better name, we just call it The Pig.

Pitch

At first it was just a joke. But it wasn't too long before the capper to the season was being in the picture with the winning team and holding up The Pig.

Catch

Pitch has a Ph.D. But what does he think about when his head hits the pillow. Shakespeare? Jane Austen? Mordecai Richler? Nah! He thinks about The Pig.

Pitch

The Pig, The Pig, my kingdom for The Pig.

It's The Pig that's on our minds when Fred and Frank and John and Lorne and I gather at my place in the first week of September. Our goal is to assemble three teams any one of which could win the elusive porker. We got it right this year. All three games could have gone either way. In the last inning of the second game, with the tying run on base, Ted struck me out with a change up. He told me about it after how, he knew it was chancy, but there is an element of the poker game in all things. If you can make a pitch like that with the game on the line, you deserve to win. It's called rising to the occasion, which leads me to Nicole's great play to get the first out in the bottom of the fifth. She was playing second base and Lorne was pulled away from first by Walter's ground ball. She had to come a long way to pick up the ball and her momentum carried her across the bag. Walter did some sort of magical spin to avoid a serious collision, but they both went down. It's taken me awhile to absorb the picture of Nicole hurling herself into position to make the play. I've been too scared to think about it much. But what desire! What courage! (Hey Dakota, that was your mom who did that.)

Another big part of the win was Anna throwing out two base runners. Austin, without telling anyone, had decided the previous night that he would wake up twenty years younger and played two fine games at second base and got some key hits. Wayne made a sweet play on a ground smash down the first base line. John Larocque pitched smart in game two, though I suspect he felt best about getting the game winning hit. Gilles told me he's going to the gym in the winter to work on a drop ball and a change up. I felt like saying,

'Geez, Gilles, do you really think that's necessary?' 'Hey, if you love to pitch, you wanna keep getting better, don't you?' 'Yeah, but I just turned sixty-six?' 'Hey, Robertson Davies didn't publish his first best seller till he was fifty-eight and kept going into his eighties.'

The Barbecue is an extension of The Pub. At the Pub, you might know you had a bad day at the plate and that you didn't make a couple of plays you should have or didn't have the big pitch when you needed it. Somewhere way back when, we learned that walking off the field and going home to contemplate our bruises was not the way to end it. It's a celebration, not a ritual sacrifice, and that's why The Barbecue came to be. We never come to lose, but we're friends. It's at the barbecue that I tell Russ he had one heck of an at bat when he got the big hit with two strikes in game one. He tells me about the cold feet and the fear in his throat when he choked up on the bat for the first time all year. We put ourselves in those situations because there is something about the game that teaches us about life. It's not always fair but it's wishing on the moon to think we'd love it if it didn't test us, if it didn't take us to the edge, knowing that in any one of those situations we could succeed or fail and that our only choice is to give it our best.

The Dregs of Winter, Upper Keelsdale, Jim Cottrell

Feb 26/06: It used to feel strange to be thinking about baseball in January in the days when it felt like forever between one season and the next. Back in 1987, we needed something to remind ourselves that spring and baseball had not been banished, never to return. It didn't start out that way. It started because John St J's brother, Jim, had taped the sixth game of the ALCS (the Angels and Red Sox) which turned into one of those unforgettable games that comes along once every ten years. We must have had a good time, because we got together again the next year and likewise ever since. There was a significant change when Fred moved from Castlefield Avenue to Richmond Hill. I always got a ride up with Lorne, and for the first five years or so we kept getting lost. I remember the nights driving along 16th Avenue between Leslie and Bayview not realizing that Spadina was named differently on the south side. This year, the weather was not the best, and when we arrived, there was no one there but John and Fred wondering if anyone else was going to show, but soon Frank, Steve and Mark were followed by John D., Craig, George, Sluggo, Wayne, Jack, as well as our umpire in chief, Jim Cottrell.

After Jim Wilson left, we struggled to find a replacement. I remembered George Dempers from my years in the TASL. He called a good game but was inclined to chat nonstop between innings. It slowed down the game which was plenty slow enough already. Jamie Crammond referred us to Jim Cottrell. In 1998 during the Viewmount years, a pop fly came down in the playground area narrowly missing a baby carriage. It wasn't till later that we speculated about the outcome had the ball and the carriage met. It also brought into full awareness of what we'd always known. That Viewmount was a community park. Along with the playground was the endless parade of citizens on their way home from work. One of us would warn them of the dangers, but it was their park, not ours. Someone mentioned there was third diamond at Keelesdale Park. I don't know if we'd have got it without Jim's letter.

Ontario Umpires Association
Jim Cottrell, President
September 23, 1998
To: Ms. Rita Shahani
cc: Mr. Fred Breitner

Subject: Keelesdale Diamond #3

Ontario Umpires Association has been supplying umpires to the Walmer Road Men's Softball League for the past six years. I would like to point out that of all the leagues for which we supply officials, this league is by far the most educated and responsible.

The background of the players and executive is that of professional people, entrepreneurs and educators. This alone does not give them a clear path to heaven, but their approach to the game of softball is unique and refreshing. The enjoyment of playing and having the opportunity to expend energy and display one's ability in a competitive situation without being offensive is one of the main reasons this league has prospered.

Should you give this league a permit for the diamond, you would elevate the standard of individuals using your facilities. They have always displayed proper conduct and respected the park and their fellow players. The behaviour pattern is exemplary.

People's reaction and behaviour exposed during an athletic contest are the true indicators of their upbringing and value systems. By now you are wondering where I am going with these thoughts, but in all the years we have been umpiring this league, there has not been one ejection, not even one admonishment.

Not only would your diamond be treated with respect, but you would be dealing with a group that would be refreshing and reward you with a positive experience.

Jim Cottrell

5

June Please Stay a Little Longer

Friday May 27/06: We had men on second and third and less than two out and someone (who?) hit a long, hard liner to centre. Frank who was coaching third was waving the runner round third. Elsewhere, Craig was running towards the ball, then stretching flat out with the ball in his glove. Back at third, Frank was still giving the go sign as the ball popped out of Craig's glove. Between innings, the ump said he'd done four games and Craig's effort was the best play he'd seen all day. Later at the parking lot, he said we'd given him hope for the days and years ahead.

It's all too easily escapes notice what a good umpire brings to the game. It wouldn't be fair to expect them to be Jim Wilsons, but we've had a few who did their jobs with amused disinterest, although some were not disinterested enough to refrain from condescending remarks about age and proficiency. (Frank was the one who'd hear it all. He'd sometimes talk about it later and how steamed he was about it.) Some of them were good natured but ineffectual, one who shall remain unnamed, who went about his duties with a casualness that left us feeling we were being supervised by an absent minded adolescent. The mediocre ones made us more appreciative of the good ones, many of who'd played Senior 'A', had retired, but were still younger than many of us. They set up behind the plate in a manner that did justice to the game and its traditions and brought out the best in us.

Friday June 16/06: First time I've started writing before the game, but watching the World Cup gets the juices flowing. However, the thought came to me while watching Holland vs Ivory Coast is that it's the norm to think we play against the other team. Seems to me it's much closer to the truth to say that there's a sense in which we play with them. That is, we play with them against some more elusive and inevitable opponent. Fear, for one. Anger, for another. To say nothing of time and loss.

Every once in a while, a game comes along which reminds us of these things so strongly that we understand what we always knew. As in the sixth game of the 1975 World Series. The Red Sox against the Big Red Machine. Bernie Carbo's home run to tie it and Carlton Fisk's homer to win it in extra innings. The Reds went on to win the seventh game and the World Series, but when the last Red Sox hit a routine pop fly, Fisk (or was it Pete Rose?) said he wished the ball had stayed up there forever because it was too beautiful a series to end. Maybe Rose because Dwight Evans, the Red Sox right fielder, remembers Pete saying, 'Dewey, can you believe this game? This might be the greatest game I've ever seen or played in.'

We've had games that achieved splendid moments, but this wasn't one of them. A missed strike three call got me squawking and it was like nothing was going right and nothing was going to go right from then on and it would be a mercy when it's over. A moment of redemption arrived in the bottom of the fourth when I got an out with the first pitch, turned to Fred and said, 'Could be a three pitch inning.' There was an easy out on the next pitch and Nicole snagged a line drive on the third one. Three pitches, three outs. On the way back to the bench, Bill D said, 'I know what he's going to write about this week.' Far more noteworthy was Gilles pitching with the winning running one third telling the prophets of doom to piss off because he had work to do. Which he did. But don't let anyone tell you it's easy.

It was a merry crew at The Slice. Ken was sitting next to Frank. Ken being the only person at the table who has openly admitted to voting for Mike Harris, and Frank who leans to the left but not leaning away from Ken, who marveled briefly at the fact they remain good friends. A lot of the world's problems were solved at that table. Unfortunately, no one was there to write it all down, so we'll have to do it again next week.

June 23/06: Did anyone see the game between Portugal and the Netherlands Sunday afternoon? All kinds of yellow cards and four red ones. A game that lost the true spirit of sport. 'An ill tempered game' as Dick Howard described it. Everyone (especially the referee) was glad when it was over. In the meantime, it was June baseball on Friday night up at Keelesdale. Jim St James was with us, on holiday from Edmonton. He and I (with coaching from brother John) rehashed the doomsday play in the last inning of a tournament in the early eighties which we never fail do on the few occasions Jim comes to town. (The game ended with a ground ball and three chances to get the last out and we messed up all three.) At The Slice, we talked about Bindertwine Park - our likeliest candidate for the Friday Night version of *Field of Dreams.* Frank remembered that on our first morning there, a deer wandered into centre field, smiled in our direction and wished us a good day.

(The doomsday loss was a monkey on my back for long time. It happened circa 1982 in the last inning of championship game. Pitchers are supposed to have short memories, but that episode replays itself with cinematic detail every time I think about it. Maybe the deer was telling me to let it go.)

We squeak in one more game before June leaves us. I have an enduring memory of some of us (Ted was there) coming out of the

Pizza Hut at nine thirty a few years ago looking west from the hill on Lawrence, with the sun setting ever so softly behind the trees behind Black Creek Drive. There was a feeling that if we kept looking with enough heartfelt yearning, it would stay that way.

Fri July 7/06: Just fifteen guys, but with a will to make good things happen. Among them, Sluggo with a nagging injury from over extending during beach volley ball and Wayne who was rumored to be in Indiana. Ken played the game of his of his life at third. Big two out plays on two or three tough ground balls to end rallies. He must be practicing on the side. I wonder if the boss knows.

The boss is none other than Ken himself. He owns a construction company. Now and again he'll talk about a couple of million or so on the line and if things don't work out, being on the hook for huge bucks. Not for the weak of heart. It helps if you love what you do, which he does - to the point where he can get lost in it. He loves us too. He comes down from Collingwood – a two hour drive each way. His wife, Martha, also loves us. She knows we're good for him. His greatest joy is seeing the expression on my face when he pounds the crap out of my rise ball.

Footnote: I'm walking along St Clair just before sitting down to write this. Naturally, a lot of red white and green out there, a lot of whooping, a lot of honking with Italy prevailing against France to win the World Cup. I was thinking about how well France played and feeling sad for the great Zidane. One of the Italian players said something to his face along the lines of your mother wears army boots. Maybe it was his sister. Whatever. The intent was to make it nasty enough to provoke the head butt which drew the red card. One of those ugly moments when sport is no longer sport. Just as I'm turning the corner to walk up Rushton Rd, I see a guy standing in the middle of the sidewalk with a flag, but it's red, white and blue, not red white and green. I realize it's not the Italian flag, it's the French flag. Right in the middle of Italy, Italy, and more Italy, there's a French guy waving his country's flag. I stop and I tell him

France played a wonderful game. They made things happen, they took chances. 'Are you French?' 'No.' 'You are now.' He gives me a miniature flag with the red white and blue stripes. The Italian fans got a big kick out of it.

July 14/06: We thought we should have been hammering John L's rise and sink ball all over the lot, but ended up on the other end of the only regular season shutout since the days at Eglinton Park. It was 1-0, then 3-0. John hit a monster shot deep - and I do mean deep - to right field and it was 5-0 and that's how it stayed. On another night I could be writing about Walter's catch of a hard liner at third or Frank's throwing out Ron by eight feet to end a tough inning or how well I pitched. The line drive that got me in the forearm didn't make me feel any better, but I got the out. Thanks to Ron for having an ice pack on hand.

Looking back, I see that John's pitching and hitting deserved more acclaim. I suppose the sting of watching him dismiss us with such ruthless ease dulled my appreciation. Later that week I got an email from Jim Betts wondering how I was doing after being hit by the line drive, along with his intention to write a poem about it.

The Ballad of Nelles Van Loon

It was Friday night
In a blazing light
All the baseball world in tune
And the game was on
Six innings gone
When the great Nelles Van Loon
Strode to the mound
To the roaring sound
Of ancient mythic cheers
And prepared to pitch
(The praise of which
Is sung by balladeers).

It had been a game
(OK, somewhat lame)
And the score was lots to little
But it ain't the score!
No, what matters more
Is a concept far more brittle
What matters most
To the Baseball Ghost
Is the passing of the flame
It's not how much
Rather - in the clutch -
It's how one plays the game.

Now the great Van Loon
Has been know to croon
A jazz tune now and then
But when on the mound
He'll make not a sound
For he's in his ball-game Zen.

And his legend's told
How in days of old
He would pitch like Nolan Ryan
And the outs would mount
Too high to count
Just like lambs before the lion.

Even Satchel Paige
Succumbed to age
But not, it seems, Van Loon,
For it appears
Even twilight years
Have not stalked him too soon.
For on this night
What a soaring sight
'Twas there for all to witness
When to much concern
A tragic turn
Appeared to test his fitness.

A ball he'd pitched
Seemed to be bewitched
As the batter smacked it hard
Like a pistol shot
Came hard and hot
And caught Van Loon off guard.
But the ball knew not
That it would be caught
Thanks to Loon's uncanny skills
(The end result
Of those difficult
Years of infield drills.)

Though no longer young

And though the ball it stung
And a few blood vessels burst
He bid pain adieu
And bravely threw
That batter out at first.
Though he tried to stay
On his feet that day
The pain it did resound
And like a fallen oak
His spirit broke
And he toppled to the ground.

But despite the pain
And the muscle strain
There can be no wisp of doubt
Though bruised and battered
All that mattered
Was getting that last out.
And next Friday eve
You can well believe
To all pain he'll prove immune
And he will rebound
And be on the mound
The very very
Legendary
Nelles Van Loon.

Getting hit by a line drive is a pitcher's worst fear. Sometime in the '80's when we were at Ramsden, I took a shot from Tom Christopher just above the ear. (The same Tom Christopher who hit two of my best risers onto the roof of the warehouse behind left field a few years earlier.) When he saw I was still standing, his comment was, 'I got all of that one.' Later in the game, I struck him out. Probably because he was concentrating on not hitting the ball anywhere near me. All the same, I enjoyed hearing

Milt McCrystal say, 'Don't get mad, get even.' There was another line drive a year later while playing in the Toronto Arts Softball League that got me just above the heart. I didn't hurt, but I coughed up some blood. I stayed in both games, but I was a nervous wreck on the mound for ten years or so, despite wearing a batter's helmet with a face mask. (Baseball fans who've been around long enough will recall that Herb Score was carried off the field after Gil McDougald's liner struck him between the nose and the right eye. The date was May 7, 1957. He was never the same again.)

Aug 4/06: Talking with Mark and Lorne on the way back to the parking lot after The Slice, still feeling that lingering sense of loss, trying to make sense of it all, I realize I am talking too much. Looking for order in a universe with an order all its own. Often we hold on to old fictions. Different words are required.

Walter, Chuck Knoblach, Tiger Woods, Richard Wagner

Aug 18/06: Got a phone call earlier in the afternoon from Walter's wife, Maureen telling me he'd had a stroke. We did our best to be the boys of summer with the shadow of our mortality floating in and out of the evening light. I had a chance to speak with Walter very briefly on the phone. He is very tired at this stage. I sent flowers on our behalf (which he will get on Monday) along with a baseball. I wrote some encouraging words on the baseball.

At The Slice, John spoke briefly about Sandra's struggle with M.S. and how humour has helped them get through many tough times. Frank, Ben, Fred and I had a long talk about bad backs while hoping that Ted can get the better of his sciatica. We also talked about whether Lorne's dash for home was a bonehead play or an inspired gamble and whether Sluggo should have got an RBI.

From Lorne on Tues: Maybe I made a run for it because I could taste the cold beer and I had been stranded at third with one out earlier in the game. For my efforts I have a pulled hamstring with some tearing in the muscle that created a pretty big bruise on the back of my left leg. I'm seeing the doctor tomorrow and I expect he'll tell me that I won't be doing any running for a while. I'll be there next Friday though (I have the equipment) and hope I can get a sub-runner.

From Russ: Lorne, its never a bonehead play if it works. If it works it's called being aggressive

From Bill D: As the creator/destroyer of the game ending play, let me add my two cents. First, my identity does not have to be protected. It was ME who made that play. It wasn't pretty. It was ugly, very ugly. I remember the whole play in slow motion. I have also been reviewing the play in my head many, many times. If there is an afterlife and Hell is my ultimate destination I imagine it might be spent watching reruns of this play for all eternity… The only question remaining in my mind is whether I have emulated Bill Buckner more so than Chuck Knoblach. I will tabulate your votes. At the end, Chatz was the only guy whose hand I can remember shaking. Chatz the OTHER shortstop who everyone wants on their team, the guy who makes all the plays. As we shook hands, he said, 'Great catch, lousy throw!' I enjoyed the comment actually, I appreciated the spontaneous candor. He didn't try to console me with "tough break" or "nice try" kind of talk.

We are planning to go to the cottage this Friday afternoon. But not me. I'm driving up after baseball. I don't want to have to wait two weeks to get back in the game. That's a great thing about MLB players who play six days out of seven. You can celebrate greatness one day and humiliation the next. In either case, tomorrow you start tabula rasa all over again.

From John St James: Dear Knoblach-head. Get off your case already! First of all, you made a great pick-up on the ball. If you don't field that cleanly, Lorne scores anyway. Second, being off-balance and having to do a 360 just to get ready to throw… well, there are some major leaguers who would have trouble making an accurate throw. The point is, things that happen at the end of a game can be magnified beyond their proper significance.

Take care, Bill, and have fun on Friday.

I feel pretty sheepish reading Bill's email eight years after the fact. No doubt the black cloud over my head didn't make it any easier for him. Thanks to John St J, the wisest and kindest among us, for helping Bill put things into perspective. He's a good shortstop, one of the few among us who can field a tough ground ball and make a strong, accurate throw to first. All the same, I loved his straight ahead account of how it feels to screw up. (In case you've forgotten, or were born after the fact, Chuck Knoblach was an all star second baseman with the Minnesota Twins. He was traded to the Yankees from which time he was unable to make an accurate throw to first on even the most routine plays.)

Sept 1/06: Moments I attempt to rescue from time's relentless swath. Austin beating out a well executed bunt by an eyelash. Frank's eyes lighting up the horizon as he spotted a chance to throw out an overly adventurous runner (mission accomplished). Sluggo racing round the bases on his plastic knees while running on behalf of Lorne (he of the badly torn hamstring). John Larocque helping himself with two sparkling defensive plays. Bill D navigating his sore back through a good game at short. Anna, back from co-leading a rigorous canoe trip though the NW Territories, hitting the ball harder than when she left.

A baseball thought I shared with Frank on the bench around the fifth inning. We often hear of athletes being in a zone and how that always translates into a remarkable performance. Seems to me that's rare. What happens in most cases is that an athlete goes in and out of his rhythm. Gets it, loses it and works to get it back. A lot of the time, it's staying focused enough to get by with your B game that makes the difference. Case in point, Tiger Woods in complete ownership of his swing at the PGA, and a week later grinding his way round the course and winning via determination as much as skill. Back on our planet, I remember John Larocque being completely out of sync in a game in late July and managing to hang in and give his team a chance to win - which I seem to remember it did.

Sept 8/06: I pitched well. Funny how success gives you less to talk about than failure. At The Slice, Austin claimed the conversation was too full of wishy washy reminiscence. All of a sudden, we were talking about Mozart and Beethoven with me putting in a claim for the Ninth as a leap past Mozart and Fred pointing out that the ones who've heard it all always come back to the wunderkid from Salzburg. Somewhere along the way, we got talking about doctors and why a doctor would leave his practice to work for a drug company which led to Mark Riddle explaining that nothing beats research. Turns out Mark works in a small but productive lab which comes up with many astounding molecular redistributions.

Have I mentioned how we found Mark? It was through George Gamester's article about us in 'The Sunday Star.' With all the stuff about how remarkable we are, there was a phone number. Mark was the only one who called. He's our young guy, a mere lad of forty. He hits the ball a ton, has a gun for an arm and can play all nine positions. At some point along the way, he began to realize what brilliant conversationalists we are and started coming along to the pub to listen. It wasn't long before he realized he is at least as smart as the rest of us and became a regular contributor. (Probably smarter. He's a brilliant chemist with several patents under his name.)

Sept 15/06: At The Slice we were on the patio again. With no one there knowing anything much about opera and less about Wagner, we managed to talk about the Ring Cycle and related matters for a good half hour. Mostly, of course, we talked about the two guys who do know something about Wagner - John St J and Fred - who were at the new opera house taking in the performance of the third of the four operas which make up that epic work. We speculated that at some point - probably during some endless blob of recitative - they would most certainly think of us. From the Ring Cycle, we went to *The Lord of the Rings* and how many times each of us had read it. However, not all the talk was whole hearted. Lorne kept insisting that John and Fred had abandoned us for the rinse cycle.

Tournament, Sunday, Sept 24, 2006

This was our first season with the rights to the lower diamond at Keelesdale. Funny how it seems so completely ours after just one season. No more lugging the equipment from the parking lot to the upper diamond with the creek just behind us swallowing up foul balls and the rising outfield and the Eglinton West traffic too close to the field for comfort. The traffic was a constant worry. Pop flies sailed onto the street on a regular basis narrowly missing cars, trucks, buses, vans, cyclists. Except for the one that didn't. The potential for disaster was not lost on Fred who chronicled the event as follows.

The foremost risk of playing at Keelesdale Diamond #3 was that the right side of the field was immediately adjacent to Eglinton Avenue. The fence along the first base line wasn't high enough to contain all foul balls, especially by right handed hitters, and the cage around the batter's box was similarly in-adequate. Occasionally a ball would leave the yard, landing on the sidewalk or even worse, on Eglinton Avenue. The ball in question cleared the fenced easily, spiraling onto a very busy Eglinton Avenue. The first impression was registered by a car which made contact traveling eastbound, sending the ball hurtling towards Keele Street. A westbound car ran over it. It rattled around under the car like a pinball, eventually squirting out the driver's side, making contact with another westbound vehicle which sent the scarred ball back to where the action began. Finally, an eastbound pickup registered the final indignity. The ball arrived at the street gutter where it rolled slowly down the gentle slope of Eglinton Avenue.

Having watched this incredible medley of contacts with the realization that FNB just won the insurance lottery, I decided that this ball deserved to be enshrined in the FNB archives. I ran down the hill and rescued this special memento of FNB's sojourn at Upper Keelesdale. It resides presently on a coffee table in my living room, in a beautiful vase created by Frank.

We didn't think much about insurance in the early days. Over time I came to understand that we had third party liability insurance with the city. I also came to understand, by way of a discussion with the fire marshal about residential fire regulations, that while insurance companies generally settle without protest on smaller claims, in the case of a million dollar liability suit, they are apt to scour the territory for loopholes. Whatever else happened in that particular game, none of it was as important as winning (as Fred so aptly puts it) the insurance lottery.

This summer we had the lower diamond at Keelesdale and it was good. The weather was also good. Not like the previous summer where it was brutally hot in early June and pretty much stayed that way till the end of July. There were some fine games in June, with Gilles finding his curve and another pitch to go along with it, pushing me to get better control of the riser and the drop. When he went to New Brunswick in late June, we kept hoping Ted would return, but his sciatica refused to respond to treatment. John Larocque stepped in to pitch the only Friday night shutout in recent memory. (Rolando and Donnie Crawford pitched shutouts in The Tournament, but none in the regular season.) The last two weeks of July and the first two weeks of August were more than good. In former years we'd often feel lucky to have seven a side. It was also the year of the return of Mike Marino, the best natural hitter in the history of FNB.

It was also a year with more than its share of heart break and struggle with the death of Russ's oldest son, Joe's battle with leukemia, and Walter's stroke. Joe and Walter came by with Susan and Maureen to watch some ball and say hello. Joe is looking good. His hair is growing back and he is mighty pleased about it even though everyone agrees he is still in Yul Brynner territory. Walter told us he was given a velcro glove by one of his therapists and can catch a velcro ball with it. He has good movement on balls to his right, but not to his left. Seems to me that same wanna that he displayed at third when going after hard hit ground balls is there in the way he approaches his exercises. It was also a year without Jack who has been plagued with a pulled calf muscle. He came to the tournament as a DH along with Ted who coached third base for all three teams. Lorne - badly pulled ham string - played first base and hit well as always, but needed a runner. He's still paying for the two triples he hit a couple of weeks earlier after telling us he needed to take it easy.

This year, as always, The Tournament was good. It was a perfect day for baseball till the rain came at five, and by then we were celebrating at Frank's and Susan's.

GAME ONE: Team 2 against Team3. Their guys went ahead 2-0 on Mark Riddle's homer which followed Wayne's two out bunt. Don't remember all the details after that, but I do remember their half of the third. Two bunts, two walks, one run in, the bases loaded, nobody out and Mark R at the plate. Somehow got Mark to hit a chopper back to me. I was going to take the easy out at first, but Frank was bellowing, "Home! Home!" They ended up getting three and we felt pretty fortunate to get off that easy. The fortunate feeling no doubt had something to do with the rally that put us ahead 6-5. They scored one in the fifth - a solo shot by Mark - and that's how it ended.

GAME TWO: Team 3 against Team 1. I could see things taking a capricious twist right off the top. Two of Gilles' pitches were so badly mishit that they ended up in no man's land. Had me thinking there had to be some pretty wicked stuff on the ball. Nothing seemed to go right for Gilles's guys and John L's guys couldn't do anything wrong. By way of illustration, John Dorsey's drive to deep centre. John has good wheels and when he got to third, Ted waved him home. In the meantime, Craig had retrieved the ball and thrown it to Jim Betts who made a perfect relay to Steve who threw a strike to Mark to catch John by half a step at the plate. I scored it 8-7-6-2 and wrote "Big Play!" beside it.

GAME THREE: Team 2 versus Team 3. Both teams failed to score in the first and it was 2-2 in the third and it had that good feeling that goes along with a pitcher's duel. We got things going in the top of four and in the top of five and it was 10-3 when we went out to protect the lead in the bottom of the fifth. Don't remember all the details and don't particularly want to, but Team One needed a win real bad after the blowout in the second game. When they got the momentum going in the bottom of the fifth, you could hear that hungry hunter feeling in their chatter. They were all set to serve us up on a platter at the barbecue. I could feel that familiar urge to panic. It's like a script in which you screw up beyond belief. What you have to do is say, 'Buzz off script! I'm gonna write my own story.' Sometimes the script gets you anyway, but we squeaked out of it and the other guys enjoyed knowing they'd given us a big scare.

Winning feels is better than losing and no amount of nice talk will change that. All the same, I liked the message of George's post tournament comments:

> I just biked into work and I was thinking about how grateful I am to have had the chance to have a 2nd baseball career, and in that regard I want to thank the main organizers for keeping it all together, especially Nelles, Frank and Fred. Often I find the game frustrating, but I realize that it likely results from my not grooming the right attitude to this particular sport, which I've started to realize is to accept and go with the flow of the many things that are beyond control - the often unpredictable bounce of the ball, the limits of my own skill and reflexes and that of my

> teammates and opponents, etc. etc. I actually enjoyed playing the game more than the year (two years ago I think) - when we won the trophy - even though this year we lost every game.

Dec 26/06: We agreed at The Slice that this report would be our letter to Joe.

Hello Joe: We are here - Ken, Nelles, Frank, Walter on one side and Fred, Austin, Lorne, John St J on the other. We are talking about Walter's wonderful physio-therapists. They asked him what his goals were for the coming year: one was to play baseball in the spring (I forget the other) so they started throwing a bean bag at his left hand and he was successful in catching it 70% of the time. Lorne told us that when you were going into remission this summer, you were thinking about playing in The Tournament. Hope you weren't also thinking about stealing third. From there to religion and spirituality and how great the temptation must be at times to give up, though there has never been a sign of that from you. Austin wants you to know that he felt the need to get a haircut this morning so as to make a good impression in the letter.

Love from all.

I knew Joe's work had something to do with health care, but I didn't know he was the inspiration and the energy behind the creation of community health centres in Ontario. After the idea, came the task of selling it to the government. What a slog that must have been. It was his passion for social justice that kept him going. He didn't talk much about his work. Along with his passion for justice was a passion for festivity. I learned this about him back in the 70's when we spent a week together along with five or six others in a mansion which had once belonged (so it was said) to Gloria Swanson of Hollywood fame. There were twenty or so bedrooms and a huge living room with a raised dining area. Joe went shopping every day to buy food for the evening meal. He was also the chef and wine steward. The dinners went on for a couple of hours.

The property manager ate and talked with us. He said we were the happiest gang he'd come across in all his time on the job. It wouldn't have happened without Joe. Apparently his business meetings at Lamp were conducted in the same spirit.

Feb 24/07: Winter days, too, are precious. Baseball will arrive in due time. We are building our dreams from snow, grass, beer and friendship.

Steve Shapiro, John Dorsey, Rob Johnson, Lorne Mitchell, Peter Roach, Milton McCrystal, Nelles Van Loon

Tournament Champs 1978 Rob Johnson, Milton McCrystal, Tom Cain, John Dorsey, Peter Roach, Steve Shapiro, Bill Davidovitz, Lorne Mitchell Nelles Van Loon

Tournament Champs 1982 BACK Tom Christopher, David Bolland, John St James, Fred Breitner, Doug Jones, Steve Shapiro FRONT Don Crawford, Tim Bryson.

Tournament Champs 2002 Russ Ford, Joe Leonard, John Larocque, Anna Trotz, Jim Betts, Gilles Morin, George Wheeler, Doug Densmore, Harvey Bradley

Tournament Champs 2003 BACK Harvey Bradley, Lorne Mitchell, Fred Breitner, Nelles Van Loon, Craig Donovan, Dez Oku, Phil Klumak, FRONT John Larocque, Frank Trotz

Tournament Champs 2004 BACK Peter Roach, Wayne Oake, Steve Chadwick (with son Eric) Austin Repath, Gilles Morin, Walter Weary, FRONT Mark Riddle, John Larocque, John Dorsey

Tournament Champs early circa 2001 Mike Marino,?, John Dorsey, Russ Ford, Wayne Oake, John Larocque, Ted Bradan, Eric Hellman, Ron LeSarge, Fred Breitner

Tournament Champs 2008 BACK Phil Klumak, Nelles Van Loon, Fred Breitner, Craig Donovan, Bill Davidovitz, Ben Woolfitt FRONT Frank Trotz, Jack Alvo, George Wheeler

Tournament Champs 2009 BACK Ron LeSarge, Luke Donovan, Alex Bierk MIDDLE Phil Klumak, Marc Hershoran, Gilles Morin, Lorne Mitchell, FRONT John St James, Steve Chadwick

Tournament Champs 2010 Doug Densmore, BACK Gilles Morin, Alex Bierk, John St James, Steve Chadwick, Mark Riddle FRONT Jack Alvo, Nelles Van Loon, Frank Trotz, Austin Repath

Tournament Champs 2011 BACK George Wheeler, Fred Breitner, Warren Quinn, Luke Donovan, Marc Hershoran, Craig Donovan, Eric Hellman, Ump FRONT Anna Trotz, Steve Chadwick, Zak

BACK John St James, Mark Ridddle, Walter Weary, Justin, Peter Roach, FRONT John Larocque, Mike D (dynamite ringer) Mike Marino, Steve Chadwick, Richard Veldhoen

Tournament Champs 2013 Wayne Oake,?, Craig Donovan, Fred Breitner, Eric Hellman, Anna Trotz, Warren Quinn, Stephen Breitner

Tournament Champs circa 2002 Walter Weary, Gilles Morin,?, Ted Bradan (with original Pig) Bill Davidovitz, Peter Roach, Jack Alvo, Wayne Oake, Joe Leonard, Ken Pagel

Frank and Susan's backyard at Kleinburg after a tournament
(probably late 1990's) - Joe Leonard at front.

Another after tournament barbecue at Franks and Susan's in Kleinburg.

A later version of The Pig. The original was dropped and repaired, but a second mishap shattered it beyond restoration.

There was always a cake compliments of Frank's daughters Sarah and Anna and later the Harbord bakery.

6

Alumni, We Never Came to Lose, Charles Darwin, Mad Dogs and Englishmen

May 4/07: The return of spring is always something of a miracle in these northern climes, but this year more so after a dreary April, as if our field of dreams knew we were coming and was looking her best just for us. Although the shades of our ruin mingle with the trees, we are still the children of summer.

May 11/07: Something about the here and now which becomes the then and was. The difference between actuality and memory, how quickly the former becomes the latter. All the ball players with us before I started writing these accounts. Howard Gerhard (good catcher, hit for power), Perry Gerhard (Howard's twin brother), Jason Gerhard (Perry's son), John Le Sarge, John's sons, Mike and Greg, Tom Christopher, Tom's son Danny, Sluggo's brother-in-law Rick Traugott who went to the Dodgers' spring training camp, Milton McCrystal a rock at third base for twenty some years, Jim Conlin who played semi-pro hardball and made me pitch to his glove. And the ones we met at the park. The kid from Newfoundland with serious heat and a wicked knuckle ball. (What was his name?) Dave Le Chaz and his pal Jay, from Ramsden days, along with Randy whose dad used to yell at him from the side of the hill behind first base. One day we invited the dad to join us. He was on the heavy side and not in good shape, but the desire was still there. I still see him rounding second, hell bent for third when he stumbled and fell. He picked himself up, dusted himself off and never yelled at Randy again.

Also the guys I played hockey with, Ted McGee, Craig Doyle, Kevin Adams, Nick Power. The ones I got to know in the Toronto Arts Softball League. Jamie Crammond, Nelson Smith, Warren Quinn, Rick Czepita, from the Amigos; John Jarvis from The Bullets, Doug Jones from the Eagles; Bruce Hack (as umpire) from Agency; Donnie Crawford. Donnie was with us close to ten years, maybe longer.

I met the players from the Toronto Arts Softball League after an early tournament in which a fourth team lobbied for inclusion and ended up winning. The leader of the challenging team had approached us about recruiting two pitchers. Since they played a version of slo pitch and had no one to compete against the likes of me, it seemed unreasonable to say no. (Beware of Greeks bearing compliments.) One of the ringer pitchers was Jamie Crammond who invited me to play with The Amigos the following summer. I ended up playing in the TASL for five years and met a lot of good ballplayers some of who joined us on Friday nights. That's where I met the great Warren Quinn. More about Warren later, except to say that he plays the game with a balance of deep respect and fierce intent seldom seen in our league or any other.

I joined The Amigos in 1982 and FNB goes back to 1975. I didn't start writing these reports till 2004. That's nearly thirty years with no written record. I've tried to work around the issue by interjecting reminiscences and observations to give the impression of dealing with all our history, having to trust memory to capture Bill Barnes's change up, the only pitch he had, which dropped at the foot of the plate and looked so juicy it was hard not to swing at it. And Milton McCrystal back in the Jesse Ketchum days, whose long drives narrowly missed taking out school house windows. (I've already mentioned Milton, but he was so accomplished both in the field and at the plate that once doesn't do him justice.) Bob McKenzie, a big part of the picture back then, a good pitcher, a tough hitter, a true lover of the game who'd be with us still if the drive from Pickering wasn't hadn't become too demanding. And many others, their exploits lost in time, although one comes to memory as I write, Remo Brassolotto, accomplished catcher, powerful hitter who played the game with enviable grace and skill. No doubt many others as well who've had their shining moments in 1978 or 1986 or 1995.

May 18/07: Not one for the ages, but it was good to be out there anyway. Lots of people - other people - at The Slice. It was hard work making deft conversation. However, I did hear George (just two bodies away on my right) say that the news about tomato sauce's preventive powers against prostate cancer has been called into question. Lorne added to the list of past greats. The high energy guy from Red Lake (Pete McCarthy), Austin's friend Eric Hellman who moved to Vancouver, Peter Handley, Rob Johnson, David Fisher, David Greisman, Tim Bryson, Paul Pernette, a catcher named Monty, Steve Shapiro.

Steve was one of our founding members. A superb organizer, a star at Ontario Housing before Mike Harris axed the budget. He told me a revealing story about Harris's first election win. One of his workers was rhapsodizing about Mike being the tough guy who was going to cut his taxes and show the poor that life wasn't a freebie. Steve told him he'd end up without a job. 'Oh no, Steve, Mike is a good guy. He'd never do that to me.' After the axe fell, he came to Steve in tears. What do you say to so perfect an example of an uninformed electorate?

Without Steve's help, I'd never have got the sub list working. Back then we didn't have the convenience of email. He always called in early April when I was still in hibernation. Thirty or so phone calls in April, more phone calls every week to deal with cancellations, another thirty calls in September for The Tournament. He moved to Ottawa in the mid eighties. I kept saying, 'Don't go, Steve. Don't go.' He explained, but

I wasn't listening. I figured the least we could do is make him the first member of the FNB Hall of Fame.

May 25/07: When it was all over I had given up seventeen runs. John Dorsey noticed at one point that we had an outfield made up of Mark Hershoran, Luke Donovan and himself - that is to say, Mark, Luke and John. This revelation made it clear that our misfortunes arose from the absence of Matthew. Matthew, wherever you are, we need you.

At The Slice Frank talked about *We Never Came to Lose* which will be part of the Fringe festival in July. Frank has assembled a cast made up of his students from the Etobico School of the Arts. I heard them read on Sunday and they are a dynamite crew. Stay posted for further details. Also learned that Mark Riddle is a gourmet cook. He has a recipe for Lobster Risotto that tastes like more. Lots of work though.

June 1/07: Gee but it was good sitting out on the patio at The Slice after the game. It had been one of those smoggy days with a forty per cent chance of showers and to have had a fine game and be together in the cool of the evening with the beer and pizza a good talk was an unexpected delight. The cast of *We Never Came to Lose* came to the game to check out the action and ended up at the pub with us. The place was next to overflowing, but the waitress got it right: ten small greeks and eight caesars. Lorne went inside to make sure the beer found its way through the crowd. We talked about the music of the sixties, the lack of specificity in the talk of politicians and the inequities of the justice system. But that was just John St. J and George and Ken and Phil Klumak and me. Who knows what brilliance flowed elsewhere? The game was even better. Four to three at the end of five. Somewhere along the way the gang from *We Never Came to Lose* cheered Frank as he crossed the plate.

July 13/07: Got a call from Fred on Thursday telling me he'd had a bad spill on his bike. No one sounds sadder than Fred when he calls me to say he can't make the game. Come Friday, it was getting close to six and the bases still hadn't been put in. This led to the question of where they were. Frank didn't have them because he'd taken time off from the equipment gig while directing *We Never Came to Lose.* The question went around the diamond as to who had them. I had a sinking feeling it was Fred. I called his cell and got him on the 404 fifteen minutes away from his house and an hour away from us. Loving the game as he does and knowing how much it means to all of us, he was mortified at the news, but there was clearly not much point in holding him to the task.

As luck would have it, we had the bats, three or four balls and a couple of helmets as well as one set of catcher's equipment. Lorne had some whatevers in his trunk that looked like towels and we used them as bases. After the game, the ump paid us the compliment of offering to play with us on the Fridays he isn't umping.

At The Slice it was perfect patio weather. Lorne had read my missive about my days with the U of T track team and talked about the summer down in his Cape Breton home when he went to camp and won the hundred yard dash so convincingly that they brought up a fellow from Sydney to put a watch on him. On a dirt road and with no spikes, Lorne ran 10.1 which fits with his memory of 6.4 for the sixty yard dash. He's not sure how old he was at the time, but it was either fourteen or fifteen As I remember it, the world record for the hundred yards at that time was 9.3, though someone ran 9.1 in the early sixties. So at fifteen, with no training, no spikes, on a dirt road, Lorne was within a second of the world record. 'Hey kid,' said the man with the watch, 'You just ran 10.1. That's fast for a kid your age. Make sure you tell your coach about it.' When he got home, being a good Presbyterian in a family of good Presbyterians, Lorne said not a word to his mother and father. Summer faded into autumn and Lorne went back to school, where there was no track coach, and studied tough talk, smoking cigarettes and chasing girls. (The beer came later).

P.S. Some of you saw *We Never Came to Lose* on Fri at 2:15 and Sat at 10:30. Chatz and Eric were there on Fri and Bill and Walter were there on Saturday. Thanks a bunch to all who came earlier, but it was really flying in those last two shows. Looks like we'll be doing some rewriting, but speaking for myself, I think Frank's direction was brilliant and the ESA gang was dynamite. As I sat there Saturday evening with Bill D on one side and Walter on the other, I loved every single moment. There was a real ball game up there. For the record, the members of the talented Etobicoke School for the Arts gang were Sebastian Heins (Pitch), Jake Zabusky (Catch), Sam White (Ump), Caitlin Feeney (Anna), David Simkins (Lefty), Adriana Disman (Assistant Director), Dakota Arsenault (Stage Manager & Sound Design), Reilly Grunberg (Lighting Design & Sound Design), Luis Lopez (Scoreboard), Sophie Traub (Production Manager), Philip Bowser (Promotional Material), Katie Toth (Publicity).

July 27 07: It was the week of the Jamaican Carnival. We tried valiantly to make a game of it, but the guys setting up the sound system liked doing their tests loud and long. As we left, the sound crew was bombarding the park with what Fred told us later was 'pink noise' which incorporates the ten octave range of sound audible to the human ear. To which Mark R added that the crew had succeeded in annoying us in all ten octaves. Six of us showed up at The Slice where Fred gave us the fuller explanation of pink noise. The record is somewhere around 180 decibels. Putting the issue in perspective, to a listener in the third row of Roy Tompson Hall, the TSO at full throttle comes in at about 100 decibels. 103 would double that. 106 would double 103. 180 is so loud it would deafen anyone listening for a tenth of a second. Chances are someone was crazy enough to check it out which led to Fred's favourite topic (after cycling, Wagner and Yogi Berra), the Darwin Awards. Apparently, the only recipient of the award who has lived to tell about it is a gentleman who launched himself into the sky in a lawn chair attached to forty helium balloons, his sole means of controlling his flight being a pellet gun with which he reasoned he could shoot holes in the balloons as required and thereby bring himself back to earth. It seems that in his zeal to experience the wild blue yonder, the gentleman had underestimated the sky power of the forty balloons. This error in judgement led to him heading upwards pretty much like a rocket and he was at eleven thousand feet in no time. An airline pilot saw him and contacted Air Traffic Control. I imagine the conversation might have gone something like this:

'Hello Control. We have a fellow in a lawn chair up here and I'm not sure what to make of it.'

'How did he get the lawn chair into the plane?'

'He's not in the plane.'

'Where is he?'

'He's up here at eleven thousand feet about four hundred yards starboard.'

'We're crazy busy around here, 707, so if this is a joke, it's bad timing.'

'No joke. He's really up here.'

'In a lawn chair?'

'It's yellow with aluminum tubing.'

'I'm not computing 707. Is there something you're not telling me.'

'He's got a gun.'

'I'm still not computing, 707.'

'One more time, Control, there's a guy in a lawn chair up here and he's got a gun and we would appreciate some advice. Oh, oh! He just shot out one of the balloons.'

'Balloons?'

'It's okay. He doesn't seem to be interested in us.'

'What balloons?'

'They're attached to the lawn chair.'

At this point, I imagine there was a pause as the full picture began to form in the Flight Controller's mind.

'He's really up there?'

'Yup.'

'In a lawn chair?'

'That's right.'

Not knowing whether to laugh or put greater Los Angeles on high alert, the controller elected for the middle course and got the Air Force, I guess it was, to send up a plane which dropped the guy a rope which he tied to his chair by which means he was returned safely to earth and lived to tell his story. Apparently, his lifelong dream was to be an airline pilot, but his vision was not up to the mark. He was heartbroken, but undeterred and his answer was the lawn chair.

Dare to dream.

Aug 24/07: Last week it was the wind. This week it was the heat. Hot and humid. The kind of day The Weather Network tells you is not good for the health. The kind of day you long for air conditioned clothing. The kind of day where you step outside and think about Noel Coward and mad dogs and Englishmen. But there we were, seventeen of us, at Keelesdale. What else could have brought us there? It started out like another one of those crazy ones. Seven - two for the other guys after two innings, but it tightened up after that and ended up a one run ball game.

Sept 14/07: The rain started just as we were taking the field. We headed for shelter hoping for a break in the clouds. We got our break, but didn't get past the first out. For the record, Phil Klumak hit his first FNB home run, but the rain started as he rounded first and by the time he crossed the plate, the crowd was heading for the exits.

Phil joined us circa 2005 via Jack Alvo. He's a criminal lawyer and occasionally talked about his work. Not for the weak of heart. He's friends with Doug Gilmore and asked if he should invite him out. I was worried we might not be up to Doug's level, but it's hard to imagine any forty year old more formidable than our own Mark Riddle. I wish I'd been more relaxed about it. I could have told Doug that of all the players who were said to be giving a hundred and ten per cent, he was the only one who actually did it.

Tournament, Sunday, Sept 23, 2007

The Tournament always has that feeling of the apes at the water hole about it. Everyone wants to win The Pig and you can feel the adrenaline all the way up to College Street. I don't enjoy the pressure, but I can bring something reasonably close to my A game and there's an exhilaration that comes with going with the momentum. It's our version of the World Series. Sometimes the Series goes to a seventh game and with pitching (if Casey was right) being seventy-five percent of baseball, it's the two pitchers out there for that final game who probably didn't sleep much the night before.

Seventh games. The one that comes immediately to mind is the Twins and the Cardinals, 1991, 1-0 in ten innings. Jack Morris was the winning pitcher and sad to say I don't remember the other guy who pitched just as well and would have been the winner if Lonnie Smith hadn't got crossed up running the bases. Okay, so maybe I'm a sucker for legends and maybe it's me who puts the pressure on myself and maybe it's my own damn fault, but passion and common sense have always been an uneasy pair. As far as tournaments go, my best game was probably the final in 2003 when I went out to pitch with a sore arm and a slow drop ball. And yeah, I did enjoy it - after it was over. And yeah, it was fun thinking about it all winter. *(The other pitcher was John Smoltz.)*

On the other hand, this is Canada eh, and we sort of know - except for hockey - that winning isn't everything. All the same, there's something about the way we get ourselves out there on that Sunday morning in late September and chat and toss the ball and sort out last minute changes that's special. We have two umps instead of just one and they're usually the ones we like and who get a kick out of us and they bring that extra element of ceremony to the proceedings. Somewhere along the way, Frank will ask two or three people not playing the first game to go back to the house to get things set up for The Barbecue. It would be a good chance for me to relax, but I usually find a way to hang around the adrenaline.

We play each other tougher and louder and it isn't the real world any more, it's a place we've gone that gives us the opportunity to forget our mortality. But even gods can die and some of us will feel like we've died along with them. But no one dies and no one gets to live forever, it's something we invent. Why we partake of it, no one will ever fully explain, but after it's all over, and we are mortals once again, we are more alive than when we started and we eat and drink to celebrate the wonder of the day.

The Barbecue is easy. With the baseball behind us, all we have to do is find our way to Frank and Susan's place. There are kids and dogs and hamburgers and beer and best of all, friendships some of which go back more than thirty years. For whatever reason, we don't seem to be getting tired of each other. And I never get tired of cutting the cake and saying my few words. This year after I said my bit, Joe stood up and reminded us of life and death and the health system. But mostly about how it was feeling connected to his friends that got him through the toughest six months of his life. I had spoken to him on the phone one day and he told me that the odds of surviving the operation he'd undergone are fifteen per cent. 'And that,' he added with a chuckle, 'is for healthy people.'

The words about the pressure aside, I enjoyed this tournament more than any other in memory. I woke up at three Sunday morning and realized square on how much I fear going out there and screwing up, but somehow knew that I'd pitch well and enjoy the day. Even thought I might manage to enjoy the day if I pitched badly. Ended up with a wish no one would get hurt. Maybe I didn't wish hard enough. On the second play of game one, Jack made a spectacular diving stop of a ball far to his left and got the force at second after which he lay there motionless. He wasn't moving because he knew he had to relax and figure out how to get up without doing further damage.

What I wouldn't have fully understood if I hadn't talked with him several times during the day was how much it hurt not to be out there with us. I also realized that he didn't have any idea of how far he'd come to snare the ground ball or what he looked like, stretched flat out while making the toss to second. One of the best infield plays I can remember, though nothing can top his miracle play in Tournament 2005 where he raced across the infield and tapped the ball to Lorne at first. Those two, along with Craig's over the shoulder catch in deep centre while on the dead run (back in the Bindertwine days) make up my list of the three greatest plays in FNB. Although if the category is dodging death, I would include 'the-light-was-fading-fast' play at Eglinton park in the eighties.

Lest I forget, in the last game, Chatz raced to his left, managed to get his glove on the ball and threw off balance to Richard (Quinlan) at first who dove far to his right to take the throw and get the out. That play was made by two guys on the team that lost both games. It was Vince Lombardi who said, 'Winning isn't everything, it's the only thing.' As far as I've been able to learn, he wasn't really that kind of guy. He loved his players and when they reminisce about Vince, that's what they talk about as much as the two Super Bowl victories. In all this talk about winning and losing, I'd like to be the guy who goes out there, expecting to win, who brings his A game when everything's on the line, and who knows how to accept defeat when victory isn't in the cards. I work at it, but these days, come the time to protect a one run lead in the bottom of the seventh, I'm looking out to the bull pen.

So yeah, there is something about the guys who come up with their best game when the going gets tough. Like John Larocque who doesn't have the stuff I have, but for two years now, he's been getting guys out on a pretty regular basis. For a while, I thought it had something to do with having Chatz and Fred on the left side of the infield, along with Mark behind the plate. But he had none of those guys and he kept his cool and threw the ball where he wanted to and was the winning pitcher in both games. It's tempting to think that because he makes it look so easy, anyone can do it. It looks easy, but it's not. (I've come to believe that the well thrown pitch comes from a still, inner place. Not sure I've ever been there, though it's one of those things that if you were thinking about it, it probably didn't happen.)

So it was John's team who won The Pig, except that this year, we had Three Pigs because of *We Never Came to Lose*. The second night of the play, when Pitch reached into his equipment bag to show the audience what we play for, The Pig wasn't there. The lead-in line is, 'In case you're wondering what we play for…' Without missing a beat, Catch reached into the bag and pulled out a catcher's mask and said, 'We play for this.' That night when Frank got home, there was a big black and pink pig on his porch. The next night when he got home, there were two more pigs. Which altogether makes not one pig, not two pigs, but three pigs. So this year, there was a Pig for all Three Teams. This winner-take-all thing never seemed right to me. What I was thinking at the picture taking ceremonies, was first of all give credit to guys who came up with what it takes to win, because winning is healthy and we should all do more of it. But so is being out there and playing hard when things aren't going your way.

As for our guys, I think we had one heck of team and I liked the way we played and we can all be damn proud of Our Pig, if only we can remember which one it is. They are all resting comfortably at Frank's place if anyone wants to check them out. (Correction: I heard through the grapevine that Bill D. decided to take the winning pig to his place. No doubt it will be on display, with his wife's blessing, in a prominent place in the living room.)

The Pig dates back to the late seventies. Tom Christopher brought it to one of the early tournaments. It was his son's piggy bank. It was big and borderline ugly. I don't think Tom thought anyone would want to take it home. 'The-light-was-fading-fast' play happened at Eglinton park sometime back in the eighties. It was late summer and there were no lights and it was, to say the least, unwise to continue. I'd lost my release point and had moved to first base. The tying and winning runs were on base and the batter lay down a near perfect bunt. I'll leave the rest to the characters from 'We Never Came to Lose.'

Catch runs out to Pitch acting like he has a very important message.

Pitch

What?

Catch

Lissen, what do you think has been the greatest play in the history of Friday Night Baseball?

Pitch

You came out here to ask me that?

Catch

Never mind. It's just, I was thinking, it's just on my mind that's all. And I can't concentrate till I get it outa my head. So, what was the greatest play ever?

Pitch

Will you get back behind the plate?

Catch

No, really, lissen, I can't concentrate until I get this outa my head.

That questions runnin' and runnin' round like an infinite home run. So tell me.

Ump

Okay fellas, let's keep it movin'.

Catch

This is important, eh.

Ump

Whatever you say, but come seven thirty, I'm outa here.

Catch

Never mind him. I'm not going back there until you tell me.

Pitch

It's gonna be fast and when we're done you get right back down behind that plate, got it?

Catch

Yeh, yeh. Go

Pitch

There's a play that still possesses the power to transfix,
It was early September, nineteen eighty-six
We were at our old stomping grounds at Eglinton Park,
It was the bottom of seven and it was getting dark.
I'd pitched a good game, some might say great
But my arm had arrived at a weary state.
There were men on first and second and only one out
And seeing as losing isn't what it's about

We called in the relief with all due speed
With the hope we could protect our one run lead.

All
And the light was fading fast,
The light was fading fast.

Catch
Pitch moved over to play first base
Not exactly a familiar place.
The guy at the plate was a guy named Kerr
And we all knew the damage that he could incur
'Cause he hit line drives that were particularly vicious
So to play in close was clearly not judicious.
Fred at third had an arm like a gun
And now and then he'd throw a curveball just for fun.

All
And the light was fading fast,
The light was fading fast.

Pitch
Well we all were expecting the guy named Kerr
To swing with force and hit a ball that was a blur,
But old Kerr had a wily streak
When you were thinking straight, he liked to think oblique,
And the last thought sitting up at the front
Of our minds sure as hell was not a bunt.

All
And the light was fading fast,
Yes the light was fading fast.

Catch

The bunt was perfect, heaven sent,
But Fred at third had read the intent,
He raced in and grabbed it and let the ball fly,
With the arm that had the power to terrify.

All

And the light was fading fast,
The light was fading fast.

Pitch

Well I was on first as you know
And I'd seen Fred race in and make the throw,
But what I didn't see as night began to fall
What I didn't see in the flurry of it all,
What I didn't see I clearly recall,
What I didn't see was the ball.

All

And the light was fading fast,
The light was fading fast.

Pitch

By what strange mixture of luck and skill
I didn't know then and I don't know still,
But a slice of a second before I might've been dead
I saw that ball coming straight at my head.
I caught it and maybe I should've stopped to pray,
To give thanks I'd survived to play another day.
But I saw the tying run race to home plate
And a throw with a prayer would've got there late,
I threw to Catch without a trace of delay
And he made the tag for a double play.

All

And the light was fading fast,
The light was fading fast.

Pitch

That was back in nineteen eighty-six,
We were younger then and no longer get our kicks
From playing in the dark at Eglinton Park.

Catch

But though the light is fading still
It aint over till it's over, we haven't had our fill.

Pitch

We hit and catch and throw and run.
Some games lost and others won.

All

Though the light is fading, fading, fading,
Fading, fading, fading, fading,
Though the light is fading, fading, fading …

Ump

Play ball!

Maybe not the greatest play, but when you consider the stakes, it's right up there. If Jack or Craig or Jim don't make those plays they live to tell their grandchildren. If I don't see that ball, if I'm thinking, 'I don't see a ball, so I guess it isn't there,' if I'm not telling myself, 'there's gotta be a ball somewhere', if I don't hold up my glove in position to catch the ball I don't see, I would not have been around to win number three hundred and along with it my shot at the Hall. Hey, if Lorne can hit .407, I can win 300. Sure, there's a minor issue with documentation, but consider the math. Thirty years, twenty games a year of which I was the winning pitcher in at least ten which adds up to three hundred (300). I don't exactly remember what game it happened in, but it was a big moment and I sent off an email to John St J about it. John reminded me that Greg Maddux didn't stop at 300. Neither did Warren Spahn.

I was about to send this off, but had been wanting to write something more about Joe and not finding the words. He had a fall and broke his hip a few days after The Tournament. My mind went back to The Barbecue and his words about health care and friendship and I wondered what had happened to poetic justice. Naive of me, I guess, but it was such a wonderful moment for all us and I didn't want the news of the fall messing it up. Neither did he and Susan. But it is what it is.

7

Earlscourt, Coronation, Amicos, Famous in Huntsville

May 2/08: It was not a baseball day. Chilly and rainy. But our new park, Earlscourt, was waiting and we could not disappoint her. At The Slice, the talk was off and flying right from the start. Just when I thought I was content to sit and listen I found myself behaving as if everything depended on my next sentence. A poet once wrote that it was a red wheel barrow that everything depended on. It had raindrops on it and the poet became famous for it.

Checked out the poem and was reminded it begins 'so much depends' not 'everything depends.' Still close enough to debunking the need for spectacle. After all the years, perhaps I understand. A moment when you see the simplest of objects, suddenly beautiful in the light and the rain, and you don't need to chase after the seven wonders of the world. Should you chose to do so, the pyramids will be nothing more than sand and stone if you resist the beauty in simple things.

May 16/08**:** At Earlscourt at six o'clock, the sun is shining directly into the eyes of the pitcher and the centre fielder which we didn't realize last week because of the overcast sky and we went back to Keelesdale. I was counting heads and saw a body (face turned away from me) which I couldn't identify even though it looked familiar. It was Walter (aka Lazarus) throwing and catching very nicely. He got his bat on the ball with authority as well. (Austin, if you're reading this, there's your miracle.) On the downside, Slugo and Chatz are on the DL. Sluggo's elbow, Chatz's leg.

May 30/08: The rain that looked certain to descend didn't, but the likelihood amounting to near certainty pressured Fred to cancel the ump. The catchers called balls and strikes, the pitchers called the bases and there was not even the hint of an argument. It was low key, but one day not too far down the line, the apes will reappear demanding exclusive rights to the water hole, the game will lure us once again into its drama. For a magical moment we will feel that winning will lend us a sprinkle of immortality and we will want to taste it, although perhaps not as much as we want that first taste of beer. Which segues nicely to The Slice where ten of us entertained each other with wit, wisdom and well chosen banalities for another very fine hour and then it was over for another week. But not really over. We carry away something undefinable which we store up against The Great Nothing.

June 13/08**:** I haven't written much about our difficulties finding a satisfactory venue after losing lower Keelesdale. Let's just say there was much frustration and uncertainty. In the meantime, Frank was making our case to City Hall resulting in the news that we had been allotted a diamond at Coronation Park. Our first game there was a sweet one. Both Gilles and I pitched well and before we knew it, we were in the seventh. Them prevailed over Us with a one run victory, but I was happy with how I'd pitched and the feeling stayed with me all week.

After the game, we headed west and north to Amicos. We had the upstairs pretty much to ourselves which allowed the conversation to be heard all around the table. Aside from a prolonged discussion concerning the rights of dogs - led by George on one end of the table and Walter on the other - it was endlessly interesting and eloquent. An unexpected bonus of Walter's presence arose from his finding a woman's cell phone earlier in the week, and arranging to meet her. She was thrilled to get the phone back and rewarded us with a free pitcher of draft. The rain began just as we left. It was torrential.

In case you've grown to like us so much that you want to drop by, from this time forward, the watering hole has shifted from The Big Slice (St Clair and Dundas) to Amicos, aka Sam's (Queen St West, a long stone's throw east of Roncesvalles.) An Italian restaurant with a big table next to the front window set just for us.

June 27/08: Somehow we went from thirteen guys last week to twenty-five this week which meant two rovers and twelve players in one batting order and thirteen in the other. Don't remember much about the first two innings, but I do remember the hard hit ball that cut my upper thumb - a nasty gash that wanted to keep bleeding. I went to get the cut cleaned and patched up and Craig came in to pitch. In the top of the third, we scored four runs. The cut had been neatly bandaged and the mound was calling to me to go for win number 315. (Let's be honest. It was probably just 314.) I started the inning by striking out Jack with a drop ball on the outside corner. Then, as if to avenge his father, eleven year old Stevie came up and worked the count full and proceeded to foul off five good pitches before earning a walk. A great at bat. I've seen my share of games where at bats like that have been quiet turning points in big games. Example one, Derek Bell's base on balls in the second game of the '92 World Series which set the table for Ed Sprague's game winning homer. Example two, Ed Sprague's base on balls in the final game of the '93 series which lead to Ricky Henderson leading off the bottom of the ninth.

July 4/08: In George Orwell's *1984,* the powers that be erase history and rewrite it the way it suits them. I've always had a deep respect for history and have a pretty good sense of the diabolical implications of the totalitarian assault on truth. However, at the end of the game, I felt like tearing out the score sheet, burning it and replacing it with another documenting my four hit shutout.

(Nov 8/20: I will consult with Donald Trump as to the ways and means.)

July 11/08: A perfect night for baseball. Twenty-three degrees, hardly a cloud in the sky, a sweet breeze coming off the lake. The numbers were down and we played seven a side and subbed one outfielder. Our guys had lost four or five in a row and we were hurting a little. It felt good to finally win one.

At Amico's, there was an awkward moment when it came to light that someone had eaten George's garlic bread. After the disappointment, he pulled an apple out of his bag, along with some almonds and walnuts, and his digestive track was all the happier for the misfortune. John Dorsey told us about his last gig in Huntsville. Eight hours and seventy-five songs. Year after year, they keep inviting him back. He says there will not be another CD, but if he changes his mind, the title has got to be 'Famous in Huntsville'.

July 25/08: It was a long game which ended in a 23 - 23 tie. The fans enjoyed Alex's big night at the plate - three home runs, a double and a triple – but it wasn't a classic. I pulled a thigh muscle running out a miserable little spinner and took a shot off the lower shin. What's going to happen when we all need someone to run the bases for us?

Aug 8/08: I've been thinking about Bill D's remarks about my loving to win but losing with equanimity. I don't always see myself in such a kindly light, but I like the challenge of pitching to big boppers like Lorne and Fred and Jack and Mark and Alex. I could just say that Alex (he of the three home runs, a triple, a double and fifteen RBI's a few weeks ago) and I had a couple of great battles. At the end of the evening, he instructed me to tell the whole story.

In the first at bat, he fouled of two inside pitches way, into deep left field. I managed to get him to hit a weak foul out of reach of

Wayne at first. As I picked up the ball I told Wayne I couldn't see how I was going to get him out. 'Don't let him get his arms extended.' Frank was on the same page, and when I got set to make the pitch, his glove was up and in, just off the black. The pitch was right where the glove was and I got the K. That was enough to make my day. I stepped aside to let John LaR and Wayne and Alex take over. In the last inning, it was going to be either John LaR or me. I was happy to rest on my laurels, but somehow it ended up me.

Don't quite remember the sequence of pitches, but I managed to get a strike. A pitch or two later, he hit a foul ball which carried so far, it baffled Fred, who among other things, is a good outfielder. I tried the inside one a couple of times and didn't have the same feel as earlier. So there we were. Three and two and the moment of truth. Once again, Frank put the glove up and in, just off the black. I was surprised – maybe the right word would be 'amazed'- to see the ball end up in Frank's glove. I heard Wayne say, 'I think you took a little off that one.' I'd love to say I did it on purpose, but it just came out of my hand that way. I might be able to throw it again if I pitch another fifty years, but I'm not counting on it. Still, one savours what there is to be savoured because the hitters will have their days. Makes me think of Ted Williams. His eyes were so good, he could read the spin on the ball and determine if it was a curve or a heater. I wonder if he'd have read the change up I threw to Alex.

A thought to build a dream on.

Greg Maddux, Jamie Moyer, Steven Hawking, A.E. Housman, Anna

Aug 15/08: We got to Amico's just as the rain started. A rainbow graced our proceedings, signaling better days ahead. Somehow, we got talking about pitching. Something I heard Tim McCarver say to the effect that even big league pitchers can't always throw the ball exactly where they want led to Fred talking about Greg Maddux. We agreed that Greg made his pitches more often than most and that his control was the key to his greatness. He was never overpowering, even in his twenties. Mark went from Greg to Jamie Moyer. Unknown to us, Greg and forty-five year old Jamie were in a 1-0 pitcher's duel as we talked. John St J emailed me with news the next day. I wish we could tell the story to Greg and Jamie. I bet they'd get a kick out of it.

Aug 29/08: Our guys had a big edge till the bottom of the seventh by which time I had given way to Chatz and had replaced him at short. We got an out after which the hits kept coming. A sentence started to form in my mind which might have been the opening for this week's blurb had events continued that way much longer. 'Tonight, I discovered the meaning of eternity in the top of an endless seventh inning.' My part in the saga was muffing an easy ground ball which would have been the second out. It was part of the big momentum swing, one of those things that can sweep you up like a tornado. We could hear the energy multiplying on the other guy's bench with each new arrival on the base paths. We got the second out and third out came soon after. A big relief, but few things are either all good or all bad. If the inning had continued, we'd have discovered the meaning of eternity and impressed the heck out of Stephen Hawking.

Sept 5/08: Short of players once again, but Sandy was there. Sandy is our sixty-two year old rookie. We met him at Mitzi's Sister's. (Amicos is on holiday.) Gilles is back from New Brunswick, though he probably felt like heading back after the disastrous two out rally. Nice to see I'm not the only pitcher who occasionally throws his glove on the ground. Sometimes I think I write better when I lose. Is one of the purposes of art to make sense of what we have lost? 'These fragments I have shored up against my ruin.' (Thomas Kyd, *The Spanish Tragedy*, for anyone who cares.) Art as a means of coming to terms with life, finding beauty in the midst of truth, creating order out of chaos. A conflicting opinion from A.E. Housman: 'Malt does more than Milton can / To justify God's ways to man.' Which segues with unexpected ease to Amicos where we were the usual merry crew.

The TV set was on and normally we don't pay much attention, but it was the Jays, the Rays and Roy Halladay. Close ups of Roy. Is it possible for anyone to be more intense? BJ Ryan, was also intense, but didn't pass the message on to the ball and it was the usual BJ Ryan grind out save.

Sept 12/08: The numbers looked good on paper, but the icons at The Weather Network were the ones with clouds and rain. Two o'clock came and there was no rain. Three o'clock came and there was no rain. Four o'clock came and there was no rain. When I left the house at five, there was no rain. And so it continued all the evening through as if the Baseball Gods did battle with Mother Nature (always daunting to say nothing of dangerous) on our behalf. Our guys hung on for the victory, but everyone had reason to feel good because it was back and forth all the way with some nice defense and good hitting.

We are getting fond of Amicos. We have the room upstairs all to ourselves and the conversation has clearly benefitted. We can hold forth uninterrupted by Muzak and the echoing din of lesser talk. We can relax into more intimate chat, we can tease someone at the other end of the table, we can finish each other's sentences and not miss a beat. Just a couple of problems. It's a bit dark up there, and the compressor for the ice machine is always on. Frank has promised to speak to Sam about the light, but we are stuck with the compressor.

Sept 19/08: Got an email from Frank earlier in the day titled, 'Anna'. I thought, 'Oh, oh, something has come up in her busy life and she isn't going to be able to make the Tournament.' In fact, she was letting us know she was going to join us Friday evening. At Amicos I learned she's taken one of her weeks off so she could be there on Sunday. Turns out that she's been playing with us for thirteen years and it's become one of her annual traditions. Thirteen years. It doesn't seem possible.

Anna and Sarah came to the ball park with Frank in the early years. They were entertained by our endeavors, if at times puzzled by occasional displays of ill temper. One spring when we were at Ramsden, they arrived with baseball gloves and Frank spent the first five minutes or so playing catch with them. One of them – they're twins and I hadn't yet learned to tell them apart - zipped the ball back towards her dad with serious intent. After our brief stay at Ramsden, we relocated at Viewmount Park, by which time Anna was eager to play. Although it's probably truer to say she had a fierce desire to play. There were scenes, as I heard later from Frank, at the house after the game, where she raged about boys her age who had never shown any particular interest who got to play while she sat idle and ignored.

When we got together to set up the teams for The Tournament that year, Frank made the case for including her. Her natural position was catcher, but she ended up in right field. Late in her team's game against my team, a fly ball came her way. I still see her maneuvering herself in position, taking a step forward, realizing the ball was hit farther than she first thought, taking a step backward, but not far enough to make it an easy play, reaching up and back and the ball falling into her glove. (The glove was her catcher's mitt.) Sarah and Christina and Julia Pagel were seated behind the backstop. Sarah had brought along her trumpet. The catch was celebrated with an enthusiasm never heard before or since in our long history. The next spring, Anna was Anna the catcher. She's had many shining moments, but the one that comes to mind involved one of the players who have come and gone. I don't remember his name, but he was fast and loved to steal a base. We called him Rocket Man. One day Anna threw him out trying to steal second. Next time around he told himself, "I'll show her.' She threw him out again. Although young, fast and eager to impress, Rocket Man was smart enough not to try it a third time.

Tournament, Sunday, Sept 21, 2008

I did a Tai Chi set in Humewood Park at about 10 P.M. Saturday and another one in front of the house before breakfast Sunday. There was a temptation to think that the bargain was, 'If I do the Tai Chi, my team will win The Pig,' but that became, 'I'll do the Tai Chi because I want to do my best.' All the same there were some cozy little traps beckoning along the way. 'We've got a seven run lead, so I can give up five and be saved by the mercy rule.' 'If we lose the last game, each team will have won one and lost one and we'll have a three way tie and everyone will win The Pig.' 'Here I am pitching the top half of the final inning and there is no mercy rule to save us (especially me, i.e. the pitcher) from the onslaught.'

GAME ONE: Team One vs Team Two. It stayed close for a couple of innings, but somewhere around three or four we scored five. Gilles struggled with his control early on, but got stronger as the game went on. They had rallies going every inning, but we kept getting the outs when we needed them. Two force outs to get the lead runner at third in the second. Some fine grabs by the rover (Sandy) who always seemed to be in the right position. A game ending double play on a fine catch by Damian (Russ Ford's son) who made an equally fine throw to first to catch the runner trying to get back.

GAME TWO: Team One vs Team Three. This one also started out close, but Team Two pulled away for the win. Gilles relaxed and found his A game, and the hits were few and far between. It made me realize we were lucky to have hit against him in game one. The best moment came in the fifth. With Team Three appearing to be headed for the big inning which would get them back in the game, Sluggo hit the hardest ball of the day, a long line drive to distant left field. I remember seeing the ball rocketing towards Lake Shore Blvd and the rover (was it Richard?) making a move in the ball's direction. Behind him, partially screened by Richard was Jim Betts, back turned to home plate, and running in the ball's direction, as if hoping to chase it down and hold Sluggo to a triple. It never entered anyone's mind, least of all Sluggo's, (and probably not Jim's either) that the ball might be caught. Then, as if out of nowhere, there was a glove, the glove and the ball met, and for a moment - as our imaginations captured it and held it for our amazed and grateful contemplation - we saw the white ball in the brown glove against the backdrop of the outfield grass and the late summer sky.

GAME THREE: Team Two vs Team Three. Team Three came into this one eager to atone for its loss in game two. They showed they meant business by scoring three in the top of the first. They hit me hard and often. I remember especially Jack's screaming line drive to left. Now and then, I reached back for a little extra and each time the little extra became a missile to the outfield. The message was clear. Don't try and throw the ball by these guys. It was back and forth after that, the lead going one way and then the other. It ended with us protecting a three run lead in the top of the fifth. I remember Fred looking as if there was no way I was going to get him out. Which I didn't. I also remember going three and oh on Dorothy - the only time all day when I let the pressure get to me - and having to come over the plate and watching the ball sail over second for a base hit. I also remember telling Frank we had to pitch outside and stay away from their power, after which John LaR took an outside pitch to the gap in left centre.

I don't remember who was on base with the winning runs, but I do remember Richard Quinlan coming to the plate, the same Richard who'd smoked an inside pitch over third an inning or two earlier, and I remember Frank setting up outside and the pitch heading exactly where I'd directed it and seeing it come off the bat, well hit but high with plenty of loft. I remember thinking that the ball would be caught and turning to see it come down into Craig's glove and Frank tossing off his mask and walking out to the mound, smiling, hand outstretched and it all seemed a bit magical.

Talking with Gilles after it was all over. He was all smiles, knowing how well he'd pitched in the second game after relaxing and allowing himself to have some fun. Gilles and I go back a long way - to the fall of 1970 when we both lived at 152 Howland Ave. It's always been his way to take the yoke and help others and forget about himself. That same feeling was with him in the first game – worried about letting his team down, putting too much pressure on himself, a prisoner of his loyalties. Somewhere it changed, probably before the first game was over. And after that he was a different pitcher: not only more effective, but a lot happier. He talked a bit about how much he loved the game and how pleased he was about giving himself a chance to enjoy it.

Iden Ford, who played with us for several seasons back in the early eighties, has lately taken up photography as his livelihood. He looked very purposeful and professional out there and the results reflect his efforts. One great shot of Frank (from the side) in his crouch getting set to catch one of my rise balls. (Just got Iden's Web Site address. Seventy-nine photos which tell the story of the day in pictures.) Iden's partner, Maureen Jennings, was also there. Maureen and I first met at Ryerson when I joined the English Department in 1966. Maureen has won both recognition and significant dollars as the writer of *Murdoch Mysteries.* We got an account of what's up with her latest which had us eager for more.

John St James was Iden's contact on the subject of the photos, but there has been an unfortunate spin for John who is somewhat worried that Iden has a photo of the fly ball that may link him forever with José Canseco. If you've got it, Iden, burn it. At the very least, don't show it to John. On a more serious note, it was one heck of a big relief to see John unhurt and smiling when he came back to the bench. John combines a boyish affection for the game with a capacity for viewing our efforts with honesty, compassion and humour. He also imitated the great José in the manner one would hope with some solid base hits.

P.S. Oct 13 (Thanksgiving Monday). Got a call from John. I wondered if he was wishing I hadn't mentioned his José Canseco moment in right field. I was pleased to hear him say he didn't mind the Canseco bit and that he thought the report was my best. What also came out in our brief chat was something too inanely sweet to be missed. When the ball came off John's noggin, Jack who'd raced over from centre to cover, picked it up and threw to second to nail the runner trying to advance. The first words to come out of John's mouth were not, 'Oh the shame!' Or, 'They'll never let me hear the end of this.' The first thing he said was, 'Do I get an assist?'

The Canseco moment refers to the fly ball that bounced off his head for a home run, May 23, 1993, when he was playing right field with Texas. The replay shows him following the ball onto the warning track. He stumbles as he leans towards the wall, causing his glove to drop and his head to move to where the glove had been. The ball hits him on the head and bounces into the stands. The centre fielder comes over trying to appear sympathetic, but he's having trouble controlling the grin that says it's the funniest thing he's ever seen.

Joe

Sunday, Nov 30/08: As most of you know, Joe died on Monday. I've been thinking I'd like to write something to share with the people he played ball with. Our lives have moved closer together over all the years and the loss of someone who was so much a part of it all is part of our journey. As I was walking along St Clair this morning I saw some handwriting on a blackboard outside a flower shop. I took a quick look, was immediately taken by the power of the simple words, but kept on walking. I felt the need to stop and have another look just to make sure I'd remember it: 'In the depth of winter, I finally found within myself an unconquerable summer.' It reminded me of Joe and his struggle and the setbacks which left him discouraged, but never destroyed his capacity for hope. There was also his huge capacity for love, though he wasn't remotely interested in being a saint. Saints don't curse and smoke cigars and drink good scotch. (Joe could curse in paragraphs without ever repeating himself.) Was it the Irish who invented the wake? Maybe they just perfected it. In any case, I get the feeling he doesn't want me to tip into sentimentality and suggests I stop and pour myself a double scotch.

Jan 3/09: It was a long scotch. What I want to add came to me during the holidays as I was thinking about friends and family. All through those difficult days, Joe kept reminding us how much Susan's love and care meant to him. Next to that was the support of his friends - the visits and the phone calls and the prayers that kept him going. Both Joe and the holidays reminded me of the quiet joy we find in simple moments with friends. They are with us even when they are far away.

(One Thursday afternoon I walked over Joe's place to read him the first chapter of 'Sunshine Sketches of a Little Town.' His left leg was soaking in a pail of water and Epsom salts to ease the discomfort of the psoriasis. The nurse was due a half hour later to change the bandages from his operation. For a moment, I was drawn into his ordeal, a sympathy bordering on pity that led nowhere helpful and was rescued by the account of Josh Smith freeing Judge Pepperleigh from the clutches of the temperance folks. Joe smiled the whole way through.)

8

Eric Hellman, Warren Quinn, Fydor Dostoyevsky, bp nichol

May 1/09: It was chilly down by the lake but good energy. Two infield practices and thirty minutes or so of scrub with everyone getting two hits - everyone but Frank who refused to get out of his catcher's gear. Everyone including Eric Hellman who played with us for fifteen years or so before heading out to B.C. a few years back. He looks fitter than when he left. By way of contrast, there was a lot of rust. Bending and throwing were the villains of the piece. Everyone our age needs an exercise program. Go back to Frank in the eighties when he struggled out of his squat in the middle of the fourth inning and said, 'I can't do this anymore.' Sciatica. It's not just a word. Neither is exercise. Why Frank is still catching in his sixties.

I got a lucky with the Bathurst branch of the Toaist Tai Chi Society just a fifteen minute walk from my reclining chair, but the big thing is forming the habit. Just five minutes a day is a good start. Should be easy, but it's not. Find yourself a few good stretches and do them first thing in the morning before the day starts ganging up on you. I believe in stretching and the movement of the life blood through the tendons and the muscles and the arteries. (That includes the brain.) I believe in stretching and the elimination of the toxins that tie our muscles in knots and make us look bad when fielding ground balls.

July 7/20: Taoist Tai Chi is not just a set of exercises. It's an art. Like Mozart. So simple a child can understand it and so deep you never get to the end. I learned somewhere along the way that it's not just the stretching, it's also the turning. The more you know, the more you realize you don't know. I'm both fascinated and perplexed by Bruce Lee's observation that the intangible represents the real power of the universe. Maybe it's like a light in the distance. You're not sure if it's really there and the harder you look the more you wonder if it's a figment of your imagination. It will resist the attempt to be seen and named. It will reveal itself in precious moments, but only if you let it go.

Friday May 8/09**:** It was strange standing out there on the mound with my team behind me and the other guys getting ready to hit, knowing that when I threw the first pitch, the game would be on and the season would begin. As if there were some sort of invisible connection stretching back through the winter to the final out last September. Our baseball lives. Seven innings every Friday from May till September that take us to a place you can't go unless you enter into the game and its rules and rituals and traditions. I could have waited a little longer, I could have decided not to throw the ball at all. I could have decided to simply stand, ball in hand, as if etched onto Keats' Grecian urn, a moment captured in eternity. But with Frank crouched behind the plate, the fielders in place, and the ump calling out, 'Play ball,' there was no possibility of delay.

Around the table at Amicos were Charles Darwin, Fydor Dostoyevsky, Bertrand Russell, Arthur Koestler, Albert Einstein, B.F. Skinner (briefly), Jesus of Nazareth, Samuel Beckett and the Pope. Hope I didn't forget anyone. The topic was the relative claims of religion and science. The Pope did not fare as well as the others. Nor would have B.F Skinner, had he dared hang around for more than a sentence or two. Perhaps correct scientific method deserved more respect, but it was hard to resist Arthur Koestler's brilliant description of the eureka moment - especially with the beautiful slave girls attending to Archimedes in the bath. And it was difficult not to listen raptly to Einstein as he declined his laurels and spoke instead of how his discoveries served to make him humble in the face of the universe and its mysteries.

Along with Chuck, Fydor, Bert, Art, Albert, B.F., Jesus, Sam and Benny were Fred, Wayne, Frank, Mark, Lorne and I, making sure the beer didn't go to waste.

May 15/09: The game featured the return of Warren Quinn. I met Warren back 1981 when I played with the Toronto Arts Softball League. I was the closer. Warren used to wait till the bases were loaded to give me the ball. I got a few starts here and there and got knocked around a few times, but wont forget the night we played the Bullets. I'd spent the afternoon putting up some shelves in a friend's apartment. There was concrete and steel behind the drywall and a wiser person would have given up. I persisted and arrived at the park feeling too tired to pitch, but decided to give it a go. It was a mixed league with three women on each side and we had a pitcher named Lisa who pitched to the women on the other team. Neither one of us allowed a hit and we called the game after five innings. I didn't find out till later that it was the only no hitter of any kind in the history of the TASL.

May 22/09: We had one of those first innings that make you wonder if the baseball gods had got bored and decided to piss around. At least three excuse-me's that didn't make it out of the infield and three or four bleeders that no self respecting batsman wants on his resumé. We found ourselves back on the bench having given up five runs without getting an out, but we got ourselves back into it and it was tied after four. Warren's home run was the big blow. At the end of the game he was still smiling from the sweetness of the swing.

May 29/09: It was one of those games that drew you into to the struggle no matter how indifferent to victory and loss you might have been at the start. In the bottom of the seventh, Sandy made a running grab of George's soft liner behind second base, but the second out was long in coming. Our lead of four had shrunk to one, and Fred was at second representing the tying run. So easy to lose faith, so tempting to look for alibis, so difficult to simply focus on the task. Would the second out ever come? Like *Waiting for Godot*. Maybe tomorrow, maybe the next day, maybe never. I knew I had enough left in the tank to throw hard to one more batter. A nasty little squirter between the mound and first. Lorne pounced on it cat like and raced back to the bag to end it.

At the pub we talked about the game. Four big plays their guys made to keep it close. Two pin point throws from Mark at catcher to nail two would be thieves; Chatz' amazing snare of Warren's liner, hit so hard that it turned him in mid air; and Fred's equally reactive grab of Jack's vicious liner down the third base line. But that was just part of the talk, which was wild and woolly. Four (or was it five?) on each side of the table, each ready to hold forth at the drop of a hat. Fydor and the Grand Inquisitor dropped in to question the capacity of human nature to handle freedom, but they left early. Pascal ('Nothing human is foreign to me') also came by, but sensing the mood belonged to Falstaff, he swallowed his tongue and waved us a quiet good bye. Merriment won the evening and no one, apart from the Russian and the Frenchman, was the sorrier for it. Having caught the mood myself, I couldn't keep my eyes off Austin's plateful of spare ribs, which he generously shared with me. The TV came on briefly. The Jays were leading the Red Sox in game one of their three game series. As we descended the stairs, Fred and Frank spoke of a sweep.

June 5/09: Made some notes on Saturday. It's now Thursday and the feeling of the game is starting to fade out of memory. The words can't bring back the game. What I'm doing right now is something else, though I'm not sure what to call it. It's a lot to ask of words. To request them to create the illusion that we have been transported through space and time to the moment itself. Easier done with a camera. But when the words are the right words, there's a feeling that a moment has been rendered timeless, as perhaps was the case in the case of Austin's miraculous bare-handed grab of the elusive pop up which had seemed to have spun his body out of any opportunity for success. As for my notes, they presented themselves as follows:

> Marks' bomb 100' over my head in right. The outfield chatter that preceded it. Jack sneaks into the infield to get the assist on the last out. John's catch. Luke's catch with girlfriend in attendance. Chatz looking oh so smooth and efficient at short. Warren's pitching. George's triple to right. My three pitch first inning. Alex's home run, adjusting his hands to move up to the ball. Another one run game. Bill D finding it hard to believe we'd won. Strange that the unvarnished facts have a simple power for which I can claim little credit. And now on Thursday, I feel I'm taking a bit of risk in thinking I can improve upon them. Maybe I'll start with Bill D. Bill, Jack and I were standing in front of the bench ready to pack up and Bill said, 'Did we actually win that game? I can't quite believe it.' Jack grinned and said, 'I think so.'

It's starting to come back to me now. Warren had gone into to pitch and I was standing in right field where I had a good view of things unfolding. Many of the details escape me, but the ones I remember were not unfolding well. I saw Jack move from one of the rover positions to fill the hole between first and second. There was a tough lefty at the plate. I don't remember the ball's path, but do remember Jack down on one knee, struggling to get control of it, an expression on his face, tense and anxious, making me fear he could try too fervently get it firmly in hand and knock it out of reach. There are no words to express my feeling of relief when he recovered in time to rise, throw and get the out. I assume Bill had seen pretty much what I saw - perhaps with the added element of it appearing to be a miracle which might be rescinded by the gods for reasons unknown. There was also Luke's racing catch of a low liner with his girlfriend in attendance. And for a moment, perhaps longer, how like a god did he feel himself to be?

Something also about Mark's long drive to right. At the end of the evening, he asked me what it felt like to watch that ball sailing over my head. Shock? Disbelief. Perhaps better to remind myself of the words of bp nichol. A warning to writers not to drown in emotion: 'The surface will take you there.' The surface in this case being what I saw. The ball hit so high and so hard it seemed to bear no relationship to me at all. Looking up to see it sailing through the air like a high flying bird and wondering if it would ever come down. There is a rumor that our guys won the game, but you will have to consult with Bill and Jack.

By the way, I guess you all got the email from John St J explaining that the words I had attributed to Pascal a week earlier belong to the Roman playwright, Terrence. Needless to say, I was somewhat dismayed to see my attempt at erudition exposed to the light of reality. I might have read a page or two of Pascal's *Pensées* in second year university French. As for Terrence, not a word. Embarrassing for me, but redeeming for John. 'It was the moment when my university degree in the classics stopped feeling like a total waste of time.'

there is no desire for speech

there is no desire to spell

each gesture
against the chaos
must be made well

there is stillness in the heart of the power
as there is stillness in the heart of the storm

between the w & the d
the in side of
the mind

          /
          's a quiet place
From which the power unwinds

bpnichol

Ernest Hemingway, W.B. Yeats, The Sunshine Boys, Mickey Mantle, Joel Horlen

June 19/09: When your team scores eighteen runs, you figure victory is a foregone conclusion. Not this time. At Amicos the talk turned to Ernest Hemingway. John St J mentioned the *Old Man and the Sea* and the old man's defiance in the face of time and age. There was something of the same defiance in Hemingway himself. It was okay for Dimaggio to retire, but it was different for writers. Writers had to keep hitting literary home runs. The home runs were things of wonder, but they were not lightning flashes, they were the result of each day's work, finding the words and knowing they were good, discovering joy and satisfaction while quieting the chaos. When he couldn't do it anymore, he was defenseless in the face of his demons.

Mickey Mantle's father died young, as did most of the men in his family. The Mick made it into his sixties, but was haunted all the while by his family history. But what a ball player he was! And who'd have suspected the fear that lurked behind the boyish smile. He loved Casey, a gentler father than his own, and certainly a more long lived one. Remember the congressional investigation as to whether or not baseball should be treated as a business? And Casey's elegantly inarticulate saga as to the ifs, maybes and wherefores of the case. And how, when it was Mick's turn, he stopped chuckling long enough to say, 'I agree with Casey.' Remember also the tape measure home runs, the speed afield, and the open sore on his thigh that refused to heal.

I seem remember John St J telling me that whenever Mickey saw himself in reruns, he could only say it felt like he was watching someone else. Strange, but perhaps not so strange after all. Age takes away the gifts of youth. Yet here we are, not simply defying time (though there is something of defiance in it also) but also enjoying it and never so sweetly as in June. Perhaps there is something about baseball that touches these varying tones and rhythms of our existence more deeply than any other sport. It's there in that wonderful poem of Bart Giamatti's: words to the effect that baseball begins with the romance and magic of spring, teaches us to love it in summer and leaves us in autumn when we need it most.

From John the next day: 'Yes, Nelles, I think it was me who mentioned The Mick's statement in retirement. I had to look it up again, and it's much sadder than your paraphrase of it:'

> I was sitting here the other day, and I tried to remember what it was like to hit a home run and win a game. And I couldn't remember. It was like the whole thing happened to somebody else.

June 26/09: Warren looked so bad warming up, I felt sorry for him. I shouldn't have. He pitched a fine game in what - though the score didn't say so - was as close to a pitcher's duel as we've had in a long time. So much better played than last week's it was hard to believe it was the same group of guys.

At The Slice, we managed to keep the talk flowing along the lines of one conversation. Must have been great stuff. Wish I could remember what it was. But we all remember the gift Frank got from the students and staff at the Etobicoke School for the Arts. A scrap book impressive for both its size and the obvious love and care put into its creation, with photos and comments from every student and teacher in the school. As most of you know, he will miss the next couple of weeks or more. He underwent a long and difficult surgery at Sunnybrook to remove the troublesome growth near his eye. He is due home from the hospital today. He's likely pretty tired, but I'm guessing in a day or two he'd be glad to hear from us.

Found these lines from W.B. Yeats inserted for no clear reason, but too memorable too erase:

> An aged man is but a paltry thing
> A tattered coat upon a stick, unless
> Soul clap its hands and sing, and louder sing
> For every tatter in its mortal dress.

It comes to me as I write that the lines might well apply to the four old men who sat behind the third base dugout at Viewmount Park. Frank remembers their 'teetering energy' and that they lived in the Seniors residence on the hill behind the park. It seemed they never stopped smiling. Lorne remembers them well.

> 'We called them The Sunshine Boys. They loved watching us play and cheered at hits and plays often. One night one of the guys (boys) brought his grandson over to the dugout and introduced him to us as if we were the Blue Jays. The Sunshine Boy was beaming with pride and the grandson was very polite and respectful. It was a wonderful experience but I don't recall being asked for an autograph.'

July 17/09: At six we were just fourteen and Shoeless Joe and three of his pals did not come walking out of the cornfield. Ron was the man of the moment, agreeing to catch for both teams. Chatz and Fred said they'd be glad to follow Ron's example. Eric (Hellman) still isn't ready to risk his sore thigh by going to bat, so was already slated to play first for both teams. It worked out so that there'd always be nine guys in the field. On the other hand, the batting orders were significantly abbreviated: six batters on their side, five on ours. This led to some deep philosophical speculation at Amicos about the possibility of having all nine guys playing for both sides.

July 24/09**:** At Amicos, we talked (again) about Lorne's nephew and the game at Keelesdale about six or seven years ago where he'd hit three home runs, the last two into the trees. Maybe at some point, we'll be meeting at Sam's or The Slice or whatever restaurant has replaced Giorgio's and we'll tell the same stories over and over. But it wont be boring because there'll be variations, there'll be some sense of arrangement and sequence, something like a symphony where themes appear and reappear. But one theme that was new was Lorne telling me I'd struck out his nephew twice.

Aug 14/09: Jack made a throw from deep centre field to cut down the runner trying to score. It was the first thing we talked about at the pub and I got my chance to tell my Roberto Clemente story. It was 1973 and there was a close race between the Pirates and the Expos and the Mets. My Ryerson pal, Craig Dowler, his wife Mari and I went up to Montreal to see the series between the Expos and the Pirates in mid September. What we wanted most, other than seeing an Expos sweep, was seeing Clemente throw someone out from right field. It didn't happen. Not that there weren't opportunities, but on the three or four occasions a base runner might have taken an extra base, Clemente waved the ball above his head as if it were a hand grenade and the base runners froze in their tracks.

I met Craig in my first year in the Ryerson English Department. I wasn't expecting to find a fellow baseball fan in a collection of academics. It was the fall of 1966, the year the upstart Orioles swept the heavily favoured Dodgers in the World Series. Neither of us thought a team with Sandy Koufax and Don Drysdale could lose four in a row. Craig was a lifelong follower of the Chicago White Sox. On Saturday Sept 9, four teams, Boston, Minnesota, Detroit and Chicago had been tied for first. Craig thought his White Sox stood the best chance on the strength of their pitching. They'd lost both games of a double header on Friday eliminating them from the race. Craig was furious because they hadn't pitched Gary Peters, a tough lefty. Word has it he went to his car, pulled his sweater over his head and stayed there all night. I spoke to him on the phone this evening. He said it was okay to tell the story and refreshed my memory. He'd gone to his car to hear the games. The reception was iffy, but in and out of the static came the news that the White Sox hadn't scored a run against lowly Kansas City. He came back into the house, got into bed and pulled covers over his head and stayed that way till dawn. It was his wife, Mari, who first told me the story. They were newly married and she was wondering what she'd got herself into. (As of this writing, they are still together.)

It came back to both of us as we talked that the pitcher Craig thought the Sox should have used more often was Joel Horlen. (Aka Joe Horlen.) He led the team with a 2.06 ERA and had thrown a no hitter on Sept 10 against Detroit after a crushing loss. He pitched twelve years in the majors. ERA of 3.11, 116 and 117 won and lost, with a team that didn't score many runs. How many good players pass from memory? How many Blue Jays fans under the age of forty have ever heard of Jimmy Key? As for hiding under the covers all night, I remember the rainy evening in the fall of 1985 when Jim Sundberg's windswept fly ball snuck over the right field wall to end the Jays' hopes of their first World Series. I was depressed for a week. Then came 1987, needing to win just one game in Detroit and losing all three. Something ominous in 1981 also which I feel fortunate to have forgotten.

Aug 28/09: It was satisfying to pitch to Frank, back behind the plate after the second Frank Op. (The purpose of operation was to extend the eyelid so he could close the eye.) Warren brought along his son, Gavin, who looked anxious in his first two at bats and then smacked a solid liner into left third time around. Warren also invited Rick Czepita who played with the Amigos back in the early eighties when I was playing in the Toronto Arts Softball League. He was steady as a rock and made the big plays. I liked playing in a league where there were playoffs and a championship, but I could see FNB stretching far into the future I knew it was my baseball home.

Sept 4/09: Standing out in right field in the bottom of the sixth on the wrong end of a blowout, it didn't feel like much of a game. Things had gone badly in the top of the first, with four solid bases hits in a row. We'd had a chance to come out of it before we got to the dreaded merciful five, but George had hit a low and away drop ball down the first base line, an inch or so past Lorne's glove and I threw my glove into the dirt, and into the dirt again, and then into the screen. It was childish, selfish, infantile, but I left the anger in the dirt and went on from there to pitch three good innings.

Sept 11/09: Got a call from Frank this morning wondering what year we started. There's more than one answer to that, but I'll go with the tournament in Nobelton organized by Bill Barnes. Bless your baseball loving heart Bill. Maybe you'll smack a double into the gap off Dizzy in the Great Beyond. Which reminds me of a joke Bill told a friend who repeated it to me.

Sunny and Dusty are good friends who played a lot of baseball together. In their later years they'd sometimes speculate as to whether or not there was baseball in heaven. They're headed into their forty-seventh season when Dusty gets a cold which turns into pneumonia and he passes away a couple of weeks before opening day. Sunny is broken up about it and gives up the game because it's not much fun without his pal. One night he's walking by a dark alley and he hears someone whisper his name. It's Dusty.

'Oh my god, is it really you.'

'Shhh. I'm not supposed to be here. I'm due back any minute or all hell will break loose.

'So what's it like up there?'

'There's good news and bad news. First of all there's baseball. It's God's favourite game and he makes sure the parks are well taken care of and everyone plays by the rules.'

'What's the bad news?'

'You're pitching Friday night.'

Tournament, Sunday, Sept 20, 2009

Gilles had some control issues after his summer down east, but gutted it out, making tough pitches under pressure and hung in to lead his team to The Pig. I was concerned about how he was going to manage to pitch two games after most of the summer off, let alone pitch well enough to win. He'd pitched seven innings on the chilly Friday evening two days earlier. I doubted the wisdom of his deciding to spend all day Saturday at the gym, but he got stronger as the day went on.

Warren wasn't the pitcher we saw all season long. We learned after it was all over that he had been up all night with a case of stomach flu. But the real story about Warren is what he's meant to our summer. His love of the game and his ability to play it well radiated from him all summer long. Without him, we'd have been okay. We'd have put in our innings and headed out for beer and pizza and celebrated summer as we always have. With him, it was a memorable season.

It was also the year of Eric Hellman's return. Eric joined us some time in the eighties and kept getting better and better as he moved into his forties. It was a sad day when he decided to head out west, but it seems to me he said something along the lines of, 'I shall return.' Now he's back and no doubt will keep on getting better. It was also the year of the Frank Op: his disappointment about missing six weeks behind the plate and his happiness at finding his vision return to normal and the return to his home behind the plate.

It was also Sandy Douglas's first full season. He's nifty fielder, he can take the pitch the other way or pull it for power, but that's what you see in the highlight reels. What you don't see his love of the game which burns with an undistinguishable fame and lights up the diamond when complacency threatens. He arrived at the barbecue with a small keg of Heineken from which I had the first glass. Somewhere during our revels he asked for our attention and told us he couldn't imagine finding a better group of guys to play baseball with. It was a wonderful compliment and we were all touched by it.

Early in the week, we got Iden's photos via e mail. Bottom left, kneeling, big friendly smile, shades placed jauntily over the brim of his cap, pumped fist, John St James; to his left, also kneeling, right hand placed affectionately on The Pig, Steve Chadwick (aka Chatz); second row, looking pleased but weary and still wearing his catcher's gear, Ron LeSarge; next to him, wearing shades, one foot resting on The Pig, looking like a sure bet to win his next case, Phil Klumak; to his left, wearing shorts, a white tee shirt and a hey-mom-look at-me smile, Marc Hershoran; next to Marc, smile partially obscured by the big white mustache but eyes alive with the joy of hard won success, Gilles Morin; one over from Gilles, Nova Scotia's answer to Ted Williams, Lorne Mitchell; back row, wearing his Red Sox Jersey, smiling but looking away from the camera perhaps in the direction of Fenway (more likely Vansessa), Luke Donovan; and finally Alex Bierk looking like a big, lovable, happy kid. And at the bottom:

IDEN FORD PHOTOGRAPHY
2009, Friday Night Baseball Champions

We missed John Larocque this season, but he assures me he'll find a way to delegate responsibility on those busy Friday retail afternoons at Ring Music so he can be with us next year. Lost to the DL were Bill D (back) and Ben (rotator cuff). Fighting nagging injuries were Sandy (knee), Jack (back), Mark R (thigh), Eric (thigh), Russ (knees). And probably a few other aches kept secret from the press. Reminds me of the following passage from *We Never Came to Lose.*

We see Pitch winding up and throwing. We see Catch in his crouch. We hear the crack of the bat and Pitch recoiling from the line drive that thuds against his thigh.

Ump

Time!

Catch *walks out to the mound.*

Catch

You okay?

Pitch

I think so… but couple of inches higher and I'm in big trouble. How's your hernia?

Catch

Okay - but if it pops out, I might have to ask someone to run for me.

Pitch

Well Second's kinda slow, Third's got a bad back, Centre's got a plastic knee, and Lefty has shin splints.

Catch

I thought it was his shoulder.

Pitch

That too.

Catch

Jesus, we gotta do something' about all this.
Drops to one knee. All follow.

Catch

Oh great Lord of baseball, Hear me.
Deliver us from the torn rotator cuff,

Others

Deliver us, O Lord.

Catch

From the frozen shoulder,

Others

Deliver us, O Lord.

Catch

From cataracts and glaucoma and all eye ills,

Others

Deliver us, O Lord.

Catch

From the dreaded lower back pain and excruciating sciatica.

Others

Deliver us, O Lord.

Catch

From the broken and/or sprained ankle,

Others

Deliver us, O Lord.

Catch

From the live drive on the shin,

Others

Deliver us, O Lord.

Catch

From the foul tip on the end of the finger,

Others

Deliver us, O Lord.

Catch

From the calcified hip joint,

Others

Deliver us, O Lord.

Catch

From the strains of hernia,

Others

Deliver us, O Lord.

Catch

From the pains of arthritis,

Others

Deliver us, O Lord.

Catch

From high blood pressure, heart attacks and strokes,

Others

Deliver us, O Lord.

Catch

From weariness, hopelessness, and despair,

Others

Deliver us, O Lord.

Pitch

And above all these, from the fear that the meaning of our life on earth is equal to the square root of diddly squat,

Others

Deliver us, O Lord.

The Barbecue seems to get a bit sweeter every year. For me there's less moping about not winning The Pig, and more simple joy in being there and taking in all the good feelings. At cake cutting time, Frank told the gang that Wednesday had been my birthday to which Fred added it was my seventieth followed by 'Happy Birthday'. Funny how it's easier dwelling on the drop balls into the dirt and the based loaded walk than writing about the good feelings.

Fred had already been making the rounds by way of determining when to schedule our first monthly get together. As if to say, 'Yes, there is a season, and the season comes to an end but the season of our friendship continues.' It's an amazing bit of chemistry: how the game brought us together and how our connection has deepened over the years and if you stop and ask which is the more important - the game or the friendships - you'd say the friendships.

But that's the short answer, and though it's also the right answer it glides over the diamond shaped field with the grass and the backstop, empty now but alive with games past and yet to come. I see those fields on the edges of the towns as I ride the train or drive along the highways and whenever I do, there's a feeling that goes along with them. Something to do with the games of my youth. Waking up in the morning, knowing there was going to be a game and knowing also, without having the words to explain, that I'd be stepping out of black and white into technicolour. That maybe I'd make a long running catch in the outfield and hit Ron Buckler's best fastball into the gap to drive in the winning run. Howard Stansell would come into the warehouse where I worked in the summer holidays and we'd talk about how the team was doing and somewhere along the way he'd say, 'That was a fine piece of hitting young fella.'

In fact, there really was a Howard Stansell. His son, Lloyd, started playing first base with the men when he was fifteen. Howard bought Lloyd a first baseman's mitt - a trapper - and it was the first time most of us had ever seen a thing so much to be wished for. Lloyd wore it when the boys from Madsen won the softball championship at the Red Lake District Public School sports day. It seemed to me he never missed a throw all year and it was the same when he started to play for the men. Lloyd never missed a throw and Howard never missed a game. Howard couldn't talk baseball like Mel White the local barber, but when he said, 'I heard you hit two home runs last night,' it was like being on the front page of *The Winnipeg Free Press.'*

It's a bit like those technicolor moments on Tournament Day still. Wanting to do well and knowing the other guys notice when you do. Something about getting the clutch two out hit, throwing a three two rise ball over the outside corner for a called strike, fielding a hard hit ground ball and throwing a strike to first. It's what we fell in love with in the beginning and what we love still. And now when we don't do those things as well as we used to and we realize some wonderful alchemy has transformed our love of the game to affection for one another, we can never forget, never underestimate this thing of wonder, this splendid creation of the human imagination, this gentle expanse of grass and clay where we grow young again under a summer sky.

9

Kidney Stones, Tommy Lasorda, Pavlov, Don't Hit the Ball to Chatz, Bill Wambsganss, Goose Shit

May 14/10: Seems to me there was something in my last blog to the effect that it was still early and we should be careful and because of the possibility of injury, extraordinary effort was neither called for nor appropriate. Maybe Fred didn't read it. The game had just begun when he snared a scorching grounder and initiated an around the horn double play. John St J made a difficult running catch on a tricky fly ball that got caught up in the wind. Wayne made three fine plays - one an over the head grab of a would be Texas Leaguer. John D made two running catches in centre field. Chatz made a couple of acrobatic plays at short. Luke threw a rope from centre field to nail the runner at the plate. Bill D made a nifty play to move over from second and cover first to take the throw that ended the game. When it was over, I was proud, as we all were, of what we had achieved on what - in my memory - was our best opening day. As for the score, except for a four run fourth, there were very few runs and to the rest of the game's beauties was added brevity. Nothing unnecessary or redundant, just the essence.

P.S. Anyone else notice Jamie Moyer (47 years young) becoming the oldest pitcher in Major League history to pitch a complete game shutout?

May 28/10: It was good to be back after a harrowing encounter with kidney stone removal. ('Harrowing' is putting it politely. When the doc finally got the big one out he said, 'This is like the gravel you find in your driveway.') Frank couldn't resist asking how it was hanging. It was hanging okay, but not fully back in the flow. I wasn't either and elected to play the outfield. Craig was well on the way to shutting us down in the seventh till someone hit a lazy pop up somewhere between first and second which no one made a move for. I'd made it from first to second on the error and as Craig went through melt down, I thought I was watching a movie of myself. It was all there. The cursing, the kicking of the dirt, the slamming of the glove into the ground, the aura of disgust and betrayal. Afterwards Sandy kidded him about it and wondered why he hadn't used my line about pitching my ass off. Yeah, I know. You're supposed to take a deep breath and relax and throw quality strikes and pick up your team mates. I'll finish this thought and tie it all up with a bow sometime in the next ten years. Maybe.

June 18/10: Anna was back and moved into the catcher's spot like she'd never been away. Frank called for a two strike change up in her second time at bat: 'Et tu papa?' It was interesting, once again, to see Sluggo coaching third and getting a wee bit conservative in late middle age. He actually gave the stop sign a few times.

June 25/10: Anyone see the Yankees Dodgers game Saturday night? It was the first time the two clubs had met since Joe Torre left the Yankees. To celebrate the occasion, Joe Buck's associates invited Reggie Jackson and Tommy Lasorda to the broadcast booth. For Tommy, it's still yesterday. He's still angry about the times the Yankees beat the Dodgers in the World Series. Reggie was more relaxed, maybe there's a grace that comes with winning or maybe he's just a more easygoing guy. Joe asked Tommy what he said to his guys to inspire them in '81 after the Dodgers lost the first two games. It was simple and to the point: 'I'm sick and tired of losing to those guys.' They also had Billy Crystal up there. Had forgotten he produced and directed *61*, the wonderful movie about the summer Mantle and Maris chased Babe Ruth. Crystal talked briefly about his long friendship with Joe Torre. Said he has a lot of friends who've played in the big leagues but that Joe is the most human. Something about that. In friendship, we exercise, develop and celebrate the never ending adventure of our humanity.

During the game I had a conversation with Tim McCarver who said A.J. Burnett was wild.

'He's not wild, he's just missing his spots.'

'I played twenty years in the majors. Who did you play for?'

'I played Friday Night baseball for forty years. '

Tim was duly impressed.

I'm noticing more material about the major leagues than I remember. There's a voice in my head saying, 'Stick with FNB, what more is needed'? I don't have the words. Maybe they will come. But I remember watching Orel Hersheiser in the NLCS in 1988 digging deep within for one last pitch. He stepped off the mound and circled behind it. Something about his body language that said he'd gathered the universe into one powerful moment. I could say I had a strong feeling he'd make his pitch, but it was more like I knew. (I'd been thinking it was Game 7. It was actually Game 4. The Mets had loaded the bases in the ninth and Dodger's manager, Tommy Lasorda called the bullpen to see who was available. He didn't know Hersheiser had decided to go there on his own. Bringing him into the game was risky. He was a starting pitcher, had already pitched in Game I and would be needed to start future games if the Dodgers were to have any chance of beating the powerful Mets. It wasn't Game 7, but everyone, the players, the writers, the commentators said it was the game that decided the series.)

July 2/10: It was so perfect an evening for baseball that when I got to the park, John St J suggested that given our affection for the sweet month we consider it the last Friday in June. Austin (playing second for both sides because he isn't ready to swing a bat) was involved in ten outs. Not quite equaling Chatz's eleven a few years back, but a sterling accomplishment for anyone, let alone a seventy-four year old. The final out came with the tying run on second, a hot grounder to Fred who scooped it up and threw a rope to Lorne at first. Reminds me that Fred told me he had polio as kid. It affects both his feet and the angle of his body when he throws. He also has a frozen disc in his neck from a car accident in his twenties. Yet here he is at sixty-five or thereabouts making the difficult look easy. Despite all the scoring, I felt good out there. Even managed to strike out Mark R who speculated that I'd probably write a couple of paragraphs about it. I could, but I wont.

I got this message from Jim Betts after one of Chatz's big games at short. It's dated Nov 22/14 which can't be right, and my efforts to locate the original have yielded nothing. It came after the poem about me, so am placing it here.

I will probably not be able to make it on Friday, but it will depend on when I leave Kingston that day to bring my mother home. As penance, therefore, I have written more doggerel.

Don't Hit the Ball to Chatz

Friday nights some young old boys
Gather in a park
And play out some old rituals
Until it gets too dark.
Bats and balls and banter,
And some nights even blood,
Bonding boys in baseball shirts
Caked in sweat and mud.
Some nights it's an artful game
Fluid and poetic
Other nights, to be quite frank,

It gets a bit pathetic.

Even so, through good and bad
There are things one expects
Some universal truths in life
Like taxes, beer and sex.
Friday nights, week in week out,
There's one constant pet peeve
The anguished cries from N. Van Loon,
"Don't hit the ball to Steve."
For there›s an eerie vortex
Where laws of physics don't apply
'Twixt second base and third base
Where ground balls go to die.

A quiet man patrols there
A sly smile on his face
Defying age and gravity
And things like time and space.
A mighty blow is struck at home
A ball streaks up the middle
And somehow a corollary
Is writ to life's great riddle,
For just as weird as "How do they
Get the Caramilk in there?"
Is the universal query

"How can that be freakin' fair?"
For hit the ball to left or right
It simply doesn't matter
If Steve can see it, then my friend
You're one done dead duck batter.
Screaming liners, pop-ups,

Even shots that take bad bounces
He flicks his super-hero cape
And suddenly he pounces.
He's some odd combination
Of a Jeter and Nijinsky
And maybe throw in Ripken
And a hint of Eric Hinske.

But nonetheless,
To have success
In your future at-bats,
Best learn to soon
Obey Van Loon
"Don't hit the ball to Chatz!"

July 9/10: Some explanation for the wives, friends and relatives who I am told read the blog along with the rest of you. When we don't have eighteen players, we improvise by playing either eight a side or seven a side. Eight is okay, because the team at bat provides a sub to the team in the field. Seven a side is workable, but subbing one player means the team in the field is short an outfielder. (If you're confused already, this is just the beginning.) In order to avoid a situation where two fielders have to cover the entire outfield, we get together with the ump. The conversation usually goes something like this:

Us

Hi there Ump. When we play seven a side, right handed batters have to hit to left field, and left handed batters have to hit to right.

Ump

So second base becomes the foul line marker. Easy enough.

Us

If it were half the field, yes, but we play two thirds of the field. Three outfielders equals three thirds, two outfielders equals two thirds.

Ump

If you say so.

Us

See that tree over there? That's the foul line for lefties.

Ump

The one next to the red Honda?

Us

I think that's a Mazda.

Ump

Looks like a Honda to me.

Us

It's the old Mazda Three Series.

Ump

Too late now. Traffic's moving.

Us

It's the tree to left of the light standard. See that bird? It just landed on it.

Ump

I don't see a bird.

Us

Okay, you pick a tree.

Ump

What about the one that great looking girl just walked by?

Us

That's it. *(Calling out to the girl.)* Thank you!

Ump

Don't think she heard you.

Us

Thank you!

Ump

She's waving.

Us

(Louder) Thank you!

Ump

What about the foul line for righties?

Us

See that tree over there? Etc, etc, etc.

Six o'clock finds us counting heads. With some players warming up, some talking about their holidays, some putting their shoes on, and some in the process of arriving, counting is not simple. On this particular night, the six o'clock count was a pretty depressing twelve. Frank said he'd catch for both teams and Austin, still not ready to test his back at the plate, said he'd do the same at second. After the first half inning, Frank realized it was too hot for double duty. Wayne agreed to catch for the other guys and even with the roar of the Indy cars so loud that it sounded as if they were driving through the infield, it was a pretty simple adjustment. Just as our guys are heading off the field to take their swings, we see John Dorsey. I'm thinking, great. We just lost Wayne, so John can play for us. Not much later, as we're making up the batting order, along comes Alex. I write his name down into the cleanup spot. As we go out to take our turn in the field, I see John D heading for the bench. He's somehow ended up on the other team. Just as I'm getting ready to pitch to the lead off hitter, I see Chatz walking through the outfield grass, glove in hand. It's beginning to feel like 'Who's on First?'

In the top of the fifth, every time I looked over at third, it was someone else. One other thing. We couldn't find the score book so I drew up some makeshift lines on a piece of paper. Our guys used it to keep track of our first inning at bat, but when we came into hit at the start of the second inning, I saw that someone had found the real score book and had kept track of their at bats, but not ours. One more other thing. What with the noise from the Indy and the confusion around the numbers, we had neglected to let the ump know about the two thirds rule. We had to stop to explain it to him in the middle of the third or maybe it was the fourth when someone dropped a blooper behind first. It was a crazy beginning, and I wasn't expecting much of a game.

Not so fast.

It was 2-0 for our guys after three. 3-2 for their guys after four. There was a flurry of scoring in the fifth, ending with a tight one run win for them. As only fitting, given his wondrous gifts, it was Chatz who fielded a ground ball and made a clean throw to Lorne at first to get the final out.

At Sam's there was a table for six on the patio, but there were eight of us, so it was back upstairs. Wayne mentioned that when he was a young man, he'd read Arthur Koestler's *The Act of Creation* and been deeply impressed. I'd also read it and we were off the races. Koestler's question. Does a salivating dog represent the limits of human potential? It's a question the behaviorist psychologists don't bother to ask. Easier to trundle along with the same old stuff. But a brain working along Pavlovian principles doesn't respond the way Newton did when the apple hit him on the noggin. The Pavlovian Newton responds by getting pissed off, or by thinking it's an omen, though more likely by deciding it's a bad idea to sit under apple trees. Koestler's Newton, on the other hand, has a eureka moment. All of a sudden, seemingly out of nowhere comes the answer to a question which has been eluding him for years.

Gravity.

From there, we went to humor and comedy and the comic hero and why we love Charlie Brown even though his team never won a game. But at Coronation Park, on the evening of July 16, 2010, everyone won.

Aug 6/10: Have I mentioned my story about Shakespeare's sonnet, "Shall I compare thee to a summer's day?" A few of my grad school pals were having coffee one noon hour way back when. Someone referred to Sonnet XVIII and quoted the second line leaving out the last word. "Thou art more lovely and more…" He asked us to fill in the blank and no one could come up with the answer. The missing word is what June is. Not chilly and damp, not muggy and hot. June is not about extremes. June is temperate. Like us. Neither hot under the collar, nor cooly indifferent to victory and defeat. We're easy, we're fun, we're temperate.

Blessed as we were by the weather, it could hardly have failed to be a satisfying game even with seven against eight and the two thirds rule for balls hit to the outfield. While jotting down some notes and trying to put it back together in my mind, I first thought of the scores: 2-1 after one, 5-2, 6-5, 6-6 at various points along the way, 8-8 after six. A close game, one which drew us into belief, unlike the two or three in July that felt like the rock of Sisyphus before they finally got rolling.

Aug 6/10: What a game! What a game! Probably the best of the year. Lots of credit to our guys at the top of our order: Sandy, Alex,

Frank, John L, and George who got the rally going. Somewhere in there I got my only hit of the day and was on second base with the score 9-8 and saw what Warren was throwing to Sandy. Two hard drop balls on the outside black and another hard one inside at the knees. Wicked. I was thinking on my roost at second that if anyone could handle Warren's newfound heat, it was Alex who lined a tough pitch to left centre to drive in the tying and winning runs. A game both exciting and heart wrenching, so memorable that I had to get right to it before the usual observations about numbers and weather.

In August, the ground is harder. The spikes we use to secure the bases bend under the hammer. I found out another way. I took a tumble at first trying to avoid being doubled up on my anemic grounder to the pitcher. I figured from looking at the scratches on both knees, left hand, elbow and shoulder that it was a five point landing. The next day I realized I had some soreness near the left ear. Good thing I was wearing a helmet because my head took the brunt of the fall.

At Sam's we were downstairs near the floor-to-ceiling front window which had been opened to the sweetness of the August evening. Sad to say, we've never managed to get June to stay a little longer and that goes for August too. We just travel from Friday to Friday, from game to game and dwell in the moments, all the more precious as time goes on.

Aug 20/10: The usual delays that come with the beginning of the Canadian National Exhibition *(aka the CNE or the Ex)* had us slow getting started, but by 6:10 we had fifteen, plus Taylor and Brock - two young guys spotted by Chatz playing catch on the next diamond. We got to witness Taylor's arm, his fleetness afoot and his prowess at bat. As Mark noted later, three guys like him in the outfield and anything in the air would be an out. His buddy, Brock, had a shining moment. With men on first and second, he snared a low liner on the dead run. It had looked certain to drop in for a hit and both runners took off for the next base. In the meantime, Brock kept running towards second to double up the lead runner after which he tagged out the runner who'd strayed off first. I remember reading in *Sport* magazine that along with a pitcher throwing a perfect game, the unassisted triple play is among the rarest of baseball occurrences. Bill Wambsganss executed one in the 1920 World Series, according to Wikipedia, the only one in World Series history.

Last, but not least, was the play of Walter. And where Walter is there is also Hunter who spent the first couple of innings howling behind the first base side of home plate, which is to say, the side away from our bench. Walter was hoping he'd settle down, but he was so damn excited by all the great baseball that he couldn't contain himself and he ended up in the dugout. Never has getting from one end of the bench to the other been such an adventure. I guess he was doubly wired because of Walter's astounding effort backing up Eric at first. It began with a hard hit ground ball that rolled up Eric's arm. Walter had run over to cover and reacted in time to snag it and flip it to the somewhat amazed Eric for the out. That might have been the moment when Hunter's howls went over the top.

Walter remembers lying in bed at the Trillium Health Centre in August 2006, looking up at the ceiling, unable to sit up. He mentioned his interest in baseball to his physio therapists, and they began throwing him a bean bag. 'Hey, you said you like sports. Catch it. Get your arm out here.' One day they decided to shift to soccer. There was young guy who was overdoing it. Walter's arm shot up and thumped a nearby physiotherapist in the chest. Not exactly the wished for result, but first you gotta wanna. Without wanna, nothing changes. Wanna and play are best pals. Hunter never tires of opportunities for play. Walter calls him his therapist.

Sept 3/10: I was at the Taoist Tai Chi centre on Bathurst south of St Clair and looked out the window to see heavy rain. It was early afternoon and I thought, 'No game tonight.' But the skies cleared and a warm wind dried the streets and I headed down to Coronation Park. Crossing the field, I could see Lorne Fred clearing away what I assumed was water from the infield. It turned out to be goose shit. Till now, the geese have just patrolled the outfield. We always thought it was out of respect.

A scary moment with Craig on the mound when I hit a hard liner that caught his left arm. He was lying on the ground as I ran down to first. Russ had the presence of mind to throw me out which seemed important at the time. The good news is that Craig was okay. A bruise, but no break. We were back on Frank's deck one last time. Someone said, 'Did we remember the beer.' Someone else said, 'It was the first thing I brought in.' (Name the voices.)

Tournament, Sunday, Sept 19, 2010

The number keeps getting larger. Remember *2001, A Space Odyssey*? The twenty-first century was the stuff of Science Fiction. But here we are at the beginning of the new century's second decade. Maybe we're characters in a Ray Bradbury novel, but let's assume it's all really happening, that what must have seemed beyond the scope of our imaginations in the late seventies, that we'd still be looking down at the ground and still be playing the game and playing it well nine years after the turn of the century is not the stuff of Science Fiction, is actually taking place, is really happening.

It's Sunday, September 19th, 2010, the bottom of the fourth in the final game. Our guys come to bat five runs down and put up a four. We've been swinging hot bats and our guts are telling us we can win if we can shut them down in the top half of the fifth. As I leave the bench and head out to the mound, I'm aware of that part of me who doesn't want to be there, who'd rather be watching, and I know there's no room for that guy. It's the feeling of the ball in my hand. That's what I need to go with. Getting my feet planted, letting my weight connect with the ground. But what I remember is nowhere close to the feeling, the journey that has taken me to the moment where there is just the ball and Frank's glove and the game on the line. I haven't thrown my best riser all day. I'm afraid I wont be able to get under the ball and it will go into the dirt, but I've got a feeling that I should give it a shot, see if it's there. It is. But I go three and two on the first hitter (I think it was Phil) and I have to decide whether to throw a soft one over the plate or give the hard riser another chance. I don't like the idea of tensing up trying to throw the soft one, so it's the riser. It works.

Next man up is Walter. I know his being here is something of a miracle, but at this moment there is no room for merciful thoughts. He's still dangerous, he can still slash the ball down the line. I go to three and two and it's deja vu all over again. I throw the riser. It's a tad high, but too close to take and I get the strike out. The next batter is George, a perennially pesky hitter with his tennis player's knack of making contact with anything close. I see the ball take a high hop in my direction and it's an easy play to make the throw to first.

In the bottom of the fifth. Gilles gets on base and Chatz doubles him to third. Jack hits a pop up to Eric in foul territory behind first. It's a tough play and Eric falls stretching to make the catch. The coach (was it Sluggo?) sends Gilles home with the tying run. In the meantime, Chatz has moved up to third. Alex takes a couple of pitches and drives a low liner into left centre. Frank says, 'There it is.'

To get to the final, we had to win the first game. First off, it needs to be understood that the first game is the toughest. It starts at 10 A.M. when the body is at its least flexible state, when the cup of coffee has only partially alerted the brain to present reality, when the sun hasn't had time to burn off the dew and any ball hit to the outfield grass comes back wet. It's that much easier in game one to get off to a bad start, that much tougher to get over the shock of a mercy rule first inning. The nightmare beginning is a dreaded thing. You do your best to keep it in the back of your mind, but it looms, it lurks, it hovers.

Don't remember the inning, but let's say it's the second. The leadoff hitter gets on. Russ comes to the plate and hits a rug burner just to my right. It's a bad feeling. Ground balls just out of the pitcher's reach almost always get through the infield. I look back and see Chatz, perfectly positioned to take the ball. He steps on second and throws to the first for a double play. Instead of two on with nobody out, it's none on and two outs. An inning or two later, Lorne comes to bat with runners in scoring position and scorches a liner down the first base line. It seems certain to clear the bases, but Mark somehow gets his glove on it and we're out of the inning.

Iden was there with his camera and for the third year in a row we have a visual record of the tournament. Two photos stand out for me. The one with Frank and I meeting in front of home plate to discuss strategy. It appears the chat is friendly. In days of yore, it would have been, 'You catch and leave the thinking to me.' But it's tough to top the shot of Sluggo's hairy belly. It's not in your face, it's a distance shot, tasteful, peaceful, inviting deep reflection. A wide expanse of grass, trees and skyline. And tastefully understated, way out there in centre field, Sluggo taking in the perfect autumn afternoon.

It's Sunday, September 19, 2010. The boys of summer are as follows:

TEAM ONE: P Warren (sneaky curve ball) Quinn, C Luke (has been to Fenway) Donovan, 1B Lorne (never sleeps the night before the tournament) Mitchell, 2B Peter (all the way from Stratford) Roach, SS Russ (no knees, no relation to Doug) Ford, 3B Fred (Yogi fanatic) Breitner, CF Craig (forever young) Donovan, LF Richard (husband to Dorothy), RF Ken (all the way from Orangeville) Pagel, ROVER Ron (say that again please) LeSarge.

TEAM TWO: P Wannabe Tony award winner, Nelles Van Loon; C teacher, potter, chef and dog lover, Frank Trotz; 1B brilliant chemist and dedicated wine taster, Mark Riddle; 2B Austin (74 years young) Repath; SS magic hands, Steve (aka Chatz) Chadwick; 3B gifted artist and long ball specialist, Alex Bierk; CF fullback and centre guard, Doug (aka Sluggo) Densmore, LF bird watcher and hockey dad, Jack Alvo; RF late bloomer, John (aka Big Red) St James, ROVER gutsy Francophone and gifted artist, Gilles Morin.

TEAM THREE: P the steady and tenacious John Larocque, C the wise beyond his years Wayne Oake, 1B the easy going and intense Eric Hellman, 2B the miraculous Walter Weary, SS the widely read George Wheeler, 3B the irrepressible Sandy Douglas, CF the multi talented Mark Hershoran, LF shaker and mover, Tim (?) RF criminal lawyer and dedicated hockey dad, Phil Klumak, ROVER chip off the old block, Stephen Breitner.

10

Ron

Friday April 29/11: Mixed in with the game and the talk was the sadness about the passing of Ron Lesarge. Thought about him playing short and third last summer. Feels like he's still with us somehow. To help make the point, Steve brought (compliments of Ron's wife) his glove and his jersey to be put in the equipment and used when needed.

Ron had a severe hearing issue. Chatz's job at short was to position the players. Ron would turn his hearing aid off when he got fed up with the instructions. No one was ever able to get him to understand not to swing when the count went to three and oh. Coaching third when he was running the bases was like trying to hail a cab in the desert. I lost my cool trying to get his attention back in the Eglinton Park days and felt badly afterwards. We talked it over and he didn't hold it against me. We talked about other things too. He was an accomplished carpenter as well as an all around handyman. I hired him several times to work on my house and was happy with the results. He'd come to understand that impatience destroyed the flow of good energy, but the rough and tumble of everyday life was difficult for him, probably more so the bumpy flow of a ball game. There would be days when he was in another world and days when he was zoned in like a laser. On the rare occasion he was called on to catch, he would sometimes be able to see where the batter was going to hit the ball before it was pitched. He'd tell me about it. His voice was different then. He'd look me in the eye and tell me where to pitch the batter. I was never sure if he could see what he was telling me. Looking back, I think it quite likely. He had a sixth sense that told him when the vibe wasn't good. When the coast was clear, the laser was still there. He was a sweet guy with a big heart.

Frank Op 2, Paris, Cat Bite, W.P. Kinsella, The Kraut

May 13/11: Our guys had the winning run on base with two out in the bottom of the ninth. We didn't score, but one run games are always fun. Mentioned to Fred that Warren will soon find out what a good hitter Mike is. Turns out he'd already noticed. He'd seen him line my riser sharply into left centre. Amazing the way he adjusts his arms and hands without losing the weight shift. John St James is off to Paris with Sandra for two weeks. Our hearts go with them.

May 20/11: I was feeling a bit groggy from an infected gum. Decided not to pitch and pretty much butchered the outfield. It was painful, but a good lesson. Be kind to your fielders, Nelles. At Amico's we talked hockey - hoping Vancouver would win the Cup, but none of us comfortable with the violence. Lorne had been reading about Eric Lindros. Every time he went into the corner, the terror of another concussion. Moved from there to discuss ultimate fighting. Why not more points for skill? Because that's not what the folks want to see. Depressing, but thought about the wonderful moments - the ones that restore your faith in sport. Like the gold medal game, 2010. The puck against the boards in the U.S. zone. Only Crosby sees the possibilities. Fights for the puck passes to Iginla in the corner, streaks towards the net calling, 'Iggy, Iggy.' We too are streaking. Through the merry month of May.

June 3/11: Susan thought Frank Op 2 would keep him out for the season, but he was back behind the plate having missed just one game. There were more of us than usual at Sam's. Our Friday night talk is sometimes like the Indy 500. Jockeying for position, racing to the finish, getting your story front and centre, and it's you with the great looking gal and the champagne on page one of the Sports Section. Like the guy in the Dos Equos ad: 'His words carry a weight that would break a less interesting man's jaw.' Sometimes something creeps into the space between the cars. It often goes unheard, but sometimes it asserts itself against the roar of the engines and our attention is held by something other than flash and speed and the desire to see our name in the papers. John St J had his heart set on thanking us for our support (both emotional and financial) for his and Sandra's holiday in Paris, but had to quiet the engines to get our attention.

I see him across the table, smiling, boyish, bursting with the wish to thank us for our support and tell us as best he could what it felt like to spend those days in Paris with Sandra. As his words settled over the table, I began to see the Boulevard St Germaine and the sidewalk cafés and the bridge that crosses the Seine on the way to the Louvre. Indeed, all of us who'd been to the city of light found ourselves contemplating once again the mystery of its gifts. Judging from the glow in the photos, maybe it's the way it quietly opens us to the possibilities of life. John says the glow is still there. Hopes he and Sandra are able to take the lesson of Paris and bring it back to our own wonderful city.

It came out also that the subtext to the adventure was the risk that Sandra's M.S. might carry more weight than the joys of Paris could bear. There was a long wait in the airport and another long wait in Quebec City, but Paris dispelled the shadows. The joy was there at Sam's also. John paid the tab. Unnecessary but appreciated. Such an evening. Yes, it's the Indy from time to time and someone takes a corner too fast and bumps someone else against the wall. It's the excitement of the moment. As if the fate of the universe hangs on you're being able to finish your story. It can't be scripted, it has to find its way. And find its way it did, with thanks to John and Sandra, on the memorable evening of June 3, 2011.

June 10/11: By the bottom of the sixth, our guys were too far behind to care about making a comeback. Maybe this was on our minds when the rain came, although it was more like a drizzle, but it was wet and so is beer. We headed up to Sam's an inning earlier than usual.

Sam's and Amico's are one and the same. Sam is the owner. He hires just one waitress who ends up being worked off her feet. We do our best to make it easier for her.

July 15/11: Another hot day, but a bit cooler down by the lake. After the game, a woman saw us making merry at Sam's and asked us, among other things, what the score was. I told her it was 124 to 119. At the end of the third I yelled at Frank who was just doing his best to get me through the inning. Pitchers are sensitive souls. It's the artistic temperament. Painting the corners and all that. Alex, who actually is a painter, said this was the worst game he'd ever had. He didn't let that stop him from smiling and having a good time and encouraging me to pretend I was twenty-five.

P.S. John Larocque was back with us after a harrowing adventure with a cat bite.

The infection moved up John's arm so quickly that the doctors were talking about amputating. John plays bass guitar. Amputation would mean, among other things, no more baseball and no more bass. He went home sick with worry. Couldn't sleep, got up, had a beer, went back to bed. When he woke up the infection had receded. Yet another example of malt doing more than Milton to make sense of it all.

Aug 5/11: A perfect day for baseball. Especially sweet down by the lake. I felt stiff and sore all week. Dragged myself to the ballpark, but got there early enough to do some Tai Chi. Earlier in the week Frank had mentioned that last week I'd had more velocity in the warm ups than in the game. More powerful when relaxed. Same thing in Tai Chi. How many times do I have to remind myself? Turned out to be my best game of the year.

Don't know how it was I got talking about The Kraut. Austin, Fred and Wayne seemed interested, so I kept going. I met him when I was in first year university at U of T in the fall of 1958. He was working at the Promenade Music Store on Bloor St. They had a booth where you could go and listen to a record to make sure you liked it. It was my first year in the big city. I knew something about jazz from listening to Glenn Miller LP's and the jazz offerings of the Columbia Record club, but the big city was full of people who knew a lot more than I did. The Kraut was always smiling, always excited about some new record that really cooked and swung like crazy. He told me about a record featuring Stan Getz called 'Long Island Sound'. I bought it and played it so often I wore it out.

The rest of the year, I'd drop by the Promenade Music Shop when I thought I had a few dollars to spare and buy another record. 'Things Are Swingin', Peggy Lee with the Jack Marshall ensemble was one of them. Somewhere on my way through university, the Promenade Music Shop went out of business and I started going to the A&A record store on Yonge. Their LP's were cheaper {$3.49), but they didn't have a room where you could listen to them and they didn't have The Kraut to steer you in the right direction. One day, I walked into the A&A and there he was. A bit heavier and balder, but still smiling. This time, he put me onto Charlie Byrd and an LP called 'Jazz at the Riverboat.' Charlie was unique because he studied with Andres Segovia and made a career out of playing jazz on the classical guitar. I fell in love with the sound, bought my self an inexpensive nylon string guitar and pretended I was Charlie.

Four years later, Charlie put out a record called Jazz Samba with Stan Getz on tenor sax. It was a blend of American Jazz and Brazilian

Samba featuring the songs of Antonio Carlos Jobim. I listened to the album all summer and learned the most difficult of the songs, 'Desafinado'. On the liner notes Charlie had high praise for Jobim and for 'Desafinado' in particular, which he claimed was as complex as Mendelssohn. I swear I was the only musician in the city who knew it off by heart. Some years later, a prominent fake book printed the song with four bars missing. Was I the only musician in the world who was playing it correctly? Maybe, maybe not, but it all goes back to The Kraut.

About ten years later when I was teaching English at Ryerson, it was my habit to celebrate the end of the week with an LP. At that time the A&A and Sam the Record Man were side by side just north of Yonge and Gould. I preferred the A&A and considered Sam something of an upstart. One Friday afternoon, I wandered into Sam's and there he was. A bit heavier and balder, but still smiling that wonderful smile. I couldn't begin to remember all the LP's he steered me towards this time round. Bill Evans, Herbie Mann, Jimmy McGriff among others, but I vividly remember one encounter where he'd dug out a record from under the counter. On the cover was a picture of King Curtis, 'But it's not him,' said the Kraut, 'it's Miles.' He spoke to me with the tone of a man who was sharing a powerful truth with one of the very few people in the world capable of grasping its secret significance. There'd been a mistake and Sam was about to ship the LP's back to the record company. The Kraut thought Sam was crazy. He thought he should be telling everyone it was Miles and it would sell like hot cakes.

'Some people don't get it. It's not what's on the cover, it's what's inside. It's his best period, after the bebop with Charlie Parker and before the far out stuff with Gil Evans.' For my money, The Kraut was right. I'm still listening listen to those cuts, though this time around I've downloaded them from itunes.

How long was he at Sam's? Five years? There was always a knowledgeable person in the jazz department after that, but there was never anyone like The Kraut. I'd walk into Sam's thinking maybe he'd show up again. I think perhaps he got rehired, but for whatever reason it didn't last long. I'm guessing he was too much a music lover and not enough of a salesman for management's taste. Strange if that's the case. He sold me more LP's than the rest of them put together.

Life went on without him for what seems a very long time. So long, in fact, I'd forgotten about him. But one Friday afternoon, long into my career at Ryerson, when beer with my colleagues had replaced LP's as my end of the week celebration, I saw him at the Library Pub on the corner of Victoria and Dundas. In those days, they had a juke box which played jazz. All the great ones: Barney Kessell, Benny Goodman, the Count, the Duke, Ella, Billie Holiday. I was deep into some discussion about the woes of the world with my pals, when I saw him. He was sitting alone and there was a sadness about him I hadn't seen before. I was relishing the conversation, but sensed that something important had to be honored. I excused myself, and sat down beside him. I'm not sure he remembered me, but when I told him about the LP's he'd steered me towards, complete with details, the smile came back.

I saw him at The Library twice. The second time, there was a sad story about his wife and another story about an unspecified illness. In-between, was the story of himself as a young man in Germany after the war and - of all people - Dwight D. Eisenhower. It concerned jazz. In what way, I don't remember, but whatever had happened was monumentally important to a young German trying to find his way in the world. I think it had something to do with The Kraut listening to a record player or the radio, and Eisenhower hearing the music as he walked by. I think it must have stuck the chord of home with the war weary general and he'd stopped to listen. When it was time for him to get back to his duties, he thanked the Kraut and told him was a fine young man and wished him good luck.

There was also a story about Woody Herman. I don't remember the details, but it had something to do with Woody complimenting the Kraut on his taste and judgement. There were other well known jazz musicians as well. They knew him and were always glad to see him. There was something about his love of good jazz that seemed to come down from the sky like the blessing of angels. I felt it and I think they must have too. The last time I saw him was at the Rex Jazz and Blues Bar about ten years ago. By then it was clear that whatever illness he'd referred to was approaching its final stages. I reminded him again of all the great music he had put me in touch with. It was close to Christmas. There was some talk of presents and he told me I was his present.

We went on to talk about the people you encounter - sometimes only once, sometimes more often than that, but not people you connect with on a regular basis who affect us deeply and powerfully and whose impact is not felt or understood till years later. That's close to what I was feeling, but not really. I guess it's one of those stories you never really finish. You can just scratch out some details and hope they somehow catch what's between the lines.

By the way, The Kraut told me once that his name was Gunther. I apologized for forgetting and he told me it was okay, that everyone called him The Kraut. He was okay with that. That's how he wanted people to be remembered. It just came to me that he worked in Eisenhower's office and it was Ike who named him The Kraut.

I was talking with a man doing what he loved - listening to jazz - for what might be the last time. And between the lines, the thought that after forty some years, our days, too, are numbered. Ask not for whom the bell tolls.

One Helluva Game

Aug 12/11**:** I pitched one helluva game. Afterwards, Eric said he was looking forward to reading about it.

'I can't write about myself.'

'Hey, it's okay to gloat.'

So here goes, but where to start? The mindset, I guess. I knew early on that the body was willing. The mind is something else. All those crazy 'what if's'. The fourth - where you cross the halfway point - was a big one. Got through it. Also the fifth. I've done my job. Five great innings. Why spoil it? Sandy is always game to pitch if needed. But I knew I'd be taking the easy way out. It was the top of the seventh I was dreading the most. The open inning. No mercy rule. The sky can fall and there's no one to stop it. (The mercy rule states that when the batting team has scored five runs, the inning is over.) There were a number of things I could have said to Frank as we got ready to take the field. 'I hope my back doesn't tighten up.' 'Even if we lose, it's been a great game.' 'Too bad I lost the feel for the drop ball.' What I actually said was, 'It'll be great to win it here and not have to bat in the bottom of the inning.' I reached back for a little extra - risky because you can start overthrowing - and it was there. The last batter was Eric. Pesky, determined hitter. I had two strikes on him and Frank set up outside. Sometimes I can get the ball to curve if I rotate the wrist, but if I get it wrong, the ball slips out of my hand and goes into the dirt. This time, I got it right. Eric got his bat on it, but it was moving away from him and he hit a soft liner to Marc H at short.

Success brings its own set of demands. It's okay to feel like you're the winning pitcher in the seventh game of the World Series as long as you keep your feet on the ground. When the guys say you pitched a great game, you can hear them. They're telling you it was really you out there. Although having my feet on the ground didn't stop me from spreading the word. I was at Julia Grandison's wedding the next day and found a couple of opportunities to let it be known. Better still, was my Sunday morning Tai Chi class with Judy Millen. Tai Chi stresses humility and Judy is big on humility, so I wasn't thinking I'd walk into the practice hall and blurt it out. But Judy gave me a correction (I get lots of corrections from Judy) which I somehow used as a seque to, 'I pitched a helluva game on Friday.' Later she invited me to say more and I talked about what I'd discovered about the similarities between the tor yu - one of Tai Chi's two basic movements - and the pitching motion. I demonstrated my rise ball in front of the class and you could almost see it smack into Frank's mitt.

There's more. My new neighbour, Heath, pitches in the B'Nai Brith league. On Monday around supper time, I saw him on the way out the door carrying a bundle of clothing.

'Hey there Heath, is that your baseball uniform?'

'Just my dry cleaning.'

'I pitched a helluva game on Friday.'

The day after the game Warren sent out an email saying I'd almost pitched a shutout and that he was eagerly awaiting the novel. It's not there yet, but it's somewhere in the mix. The themes are baseball, self worth and friendship. Plot is tricky. For the moment, suffice to say that the plot has got to be based on an action and the action has to lead to a climax. But even if you've got something that looks like a plot, you've got problems if you don't know what you're writing about. I dug out my copy of a book called *Playwriting: How to Write for the Theatre* by Bernard Grebanier, and discovered a crucial point I'd completely forgotten: that when we ask what a play is about, we are really asking, 'What is the play's *action* about?' Not sure I can run with it, but food for thought.

Speaking of food for thought, the evening at Sam's was particularly lively. The thoughts came rapidly and the points of contention were many. Western culture. Oriental culture. The relationship between culture and creativity. The place of the 'eureka moment' in the scientific method. At one point I lost my cool and thought to myself, 'Losing your cool is not the reason you pitched well.' Somewhere along the way, the excitement gave way to something calmer and at the moment of parting, we were in possession of a rich and rare collective wisdom. However, had there been no baseball, we would not have been at Sam's delving into the mysteries of the universe. So back to the game.

I arrived at a quarter after five to see Frank doing his back exercises. I told him he was too old and the exercise wouldn't make any difference. 'Screw you, pal. There are beautiful women all over the world who think I'm thirty-nine.'

Mark Riddle was the next to show. Warren spotted his limp. 'Don't know how it happened. I got out of my seat on the street car and I felt this pain around the knee joint and lower thigh.'

'Maybe sciatica.'

'It's not sciatica. Sciatica is a sharp pain and it starts up here and it goes all the way down the leg.'

'How's the shoulder?'

'My therapist gave me some exercises, but they hurt.'

Which brings to mind the phone call from Sluggo. It looks like the bad knee will end to his season. You know Sluggo. The football mentality. If you see a wall, run through it. When he says his knee hurts, it hurts. Which brings to mind the conversation I had with Fred about Sammy on the way home. Sammy is Fred's dog. He tosses frisbees with her every morning. She makes the over the shoulder catch on a regular basis. As Fred talked, I could see her playing shortstop. Why not? As the rotator cuff issue continues to crunch its way into our proceedings, more and more of us can play only the positions which don't require a strong and accurate arm: first and second base. Do the math. Nine guys a side. If five are playing first and four are playing second, who's left to play short? Okay, Sammy can't throw, but maybe we could assume the throw. Or maybe Fred could teach her to get the ball and race the runner to first. Given that our legs aren't what they used to be, she'd get her share of outs.

Had a dream last night. It was the last inning of the game and I had to go out and pitch the top of the seventh. The guys on the other team looked mean and determined. When it was time to take the mound, I couldn't find my helmet. I looked all along the bench and it was nowhere to be seen. Somewhere, in that quagmire we call the mind, there's this thing that's raining on the good stuff. When I get around to writing the novel, avoiding the rain would be the easy way out. But the rain wouldn't be the whole story, just a chapter or two. As for the question of what it would be about after all the hurts and disappointments and the aches and pains and the sadness about Joe and Ron, maybe it's the joy we continue to find in it. With apologies to Bernard Grebanier, that's not an action, it's a feeling, but it will have to do for now.

Another One Helluva Game

Aug 26, 2011: If Warren had been writing this, Eric would have given him permission to gloat. I have a strong memory of sitting on the bench in the third inning, looking at the score book and seeing nothing but X's. We were not only being shout out, we were being no hit. Warren was hitting his spots and the defense was performing with flawless ease. He deserved the shutout, but let him do it against someone else. Coming to bat in the bottom of the fourth, we could feel how relentlessly the momentum was carrying the play, that if we didn't break it now, we never would. Chatz answered the call by leading off the fourth with a double. I was coaching third when someone (Alex?) hit a low liner to Marc H. left. Marc has a strong arm, but something about his body language and the position of the ball had me thinking I should send Chatz home. The throw was low and a bit off line. The relief was palpable. But any way you tell it, Warren pitched one helluva game.

Almost forgot it was Chatz's sixtieth. The champagne arrived on Frank's deck as we sang happy birthday.

Sept 2/11: The day began with drizzle at about four and alternated with more serious stuff till almost six, leaving us with the question of what kind of game we could manage with eleven players. Frank stayed behind the plate and Warren, Craig and I shared the pitching. The play of the day was Walter's nab of a Texas Leaguer. I had a good view of it because I was playing right field. The ball was hit far enough that I thought I might have a shot at it till I saw Walter moving back and turning at the last second to catch it over his shoulder. I asked him about it later. He said that he had to tell his legs to move. The stroke means they don't do it automatically anymore.

During the week, a sadness from early years. Things I longed for and never got. An ache that never goes away, but a chance to fill the emptiness with baseball, beer, and conversation.

Tournament Sept 19, 2011

Seems to me this was one of our better seasons. There was the return of Mike Marino. He was solid behind the plate and a joy to have on the field. It was the year we helped send John and Sandra to Paris. It was the season of Warren's two almost shutouts and my 'helluva game'. May and June were as spirited as formerly. When the energy flagged in late July, Alex began inviting his pals and brother Nick. Nick turned out to be a surefire keeper, and perhaps for the first time it appears we've got the young blood (Luke, Stephen, Alex, Nick) that could keep our Friday nights alive when time catches up with the old guys. Sadly, it was also the first year without Ron LeSarge.

Always the temptation to pass over the sadness and the loss, but they are interwoven with our Friday night journey reminding us to reflect upon our blessings. One of the blessings was the perfect mid September weather on tournament day. More often than not, it's chilly in the first game. I remember tournaments up in Kleinburg when the ball would come in from the outfield soaking wet, a boon to a spit ball pitcher, but not to a clean living guy like me. On this day, the morning grass was dry and the perfect weather continued right through to The Barbecue.

As we were gathering on Frank's and Susan's deck, Sandy arrived with two kegs of draft. Last year it was one, which means that while he loved us last year, he loves us twice as much now. As we were chatting on the deck amidst the pretzels and the Lowenbrau, he captured our attention and talked of what he'd seen and felt at the park. Sandy cannot be effectively translated into any other languages but Sandeese or Sandanian, but his words were something to the effect that we approach the game with mix of affection and competition to the game the likes of which in his many years of baseball he's never encountered. If he'd seen us back in the early days, I think he'd have liked us then too. Still there's been an evolution over the years. We're less inclined to take things personally or get on each others' cases.

Somewhere very early along the way, we started going to the pub. I remember Friday nights back in the eighties when I felt betrayed by my defense or hadn't pitched well. There was a feeling that shaking hands would be like saying thanks for the beating. When I got home, I replayed my discontent long into the empty night. There was something healing about the pizza, the beer, the conversation. Reminders that we don't play to exercise our attraction to misery. Somewhere else along the way The Barbecue came into being. Among other things, it softens the sadness of the season's end. I remember getting ready to drive back to the city after one of our barbecues, and Frank and Fred crying because the season was over. No wonder that it was Fred who first got us together that cold February evening in 1987 to remind us that spring would come once again and that baseball would arrive along with it. As for the morning of September 18, 2011, everybody showed up happy as heck to be to there and wired to win The Pig.

GAME ONE. Team Two versus Team Three. We scored four in the top of the first and they scored four in the bottom. We scored four in the top of the second and they scored four in the bottom. And so it went till the fifth when John L and his guys held us scoreless, leaving us the task of protecting a two run lead. I reached back to see what I had left. More than I thought. But that didn't stop them from getting runners on base. It was looking like another big inning till Gavin and Alex combined on a nifty play to get the lead runner at third. Definitely a momentum changer, but not out of danger. The winning run came to the plate with two out and runners on second and third. With the count three and one I got a break from the ump on a pitch up and away. Three and two. The place no pitcher ever wants to be with the game on the line. You can't think ball four, you've gotta think strike. Don't remember what I was thinking. Maybe nothing. And maybe that's why I got the K.

GAME TWO. Team One versus Team Three. This was anyone's game. Early on, the Team Three had the momentum only to have it broken in two potential big innings by double plays. It was four-three going into the fifth and had squeaker scripted all over it. Chatz pulled his iffy hamstring in the fourth. He was headed for third and pulled up about fifteen feet from the bag. It looked bad enough that I wondered if he'd be able to keep moving, but he shifted into willpower mode. He ended up scoring, but his guys would have been better off trading the run for a healthy hamstring because it was a different team without him.

GAME THREE: Team Two versus Team One. Three big innings in a row got us behind early. We settled down in the fourth and fifth, but Warren was hitting his spots and Eric was performing heroics at first. In the bottom of the fifth, we were not only looking at a drubbing but found ourselves one out away from the wrong end of a shutout. Lorne had led off the inning with a walk, but the walk was followed by two quick outs. I was the next hitter. I'd been taking first pitch strikes all day and told myself in the on deck circle that if the first one came down the pipe, I'd be hacking. I lined it into shallow left centre to keep the inning alive. Luke came through in the clutch and Lorne scored from second to break the goose egg. I was ready to stop at third but Sluggo was coaching third and - as you have probably guessed - waved me home. Our bats were finally in gear and we ran the rally to six. I could see Warren, having lost the shutout, in prayer mode. The answer to the prayer came in the form of a pop up to Warren himself. Can't remember a guy looking to so happy about having to take home The Pig. He's played with such skill and passion these past three years that it was fitting his guys should come out on top. Nonetheless, we don't give anything away. If you want The Pig, you gotta earn The Pig. Warren and his guys did just that.

Friday, Oct 28/11: ***:*** *Can't get game six of the World Series out of my mind. Texas one strike away from winning it all. Feliz is throwing in the high nineties. Napoli tells him the one thing he can't do is throw Freese something he can drive to the opposite field. The pitch isn't perfect, but it's on the inside half and Freese still manages to drive it against the right field wall. In the bottom of the tenth, Feldman tries to get Lance Berkman to bite inside and low. Berkman sniffs at the pitch with utter disdain. Despite that and despite the pressure, Feldman is pitching well enough to get the count to two strikes. One strike away once again. We get a close up of Berkman. He's totally focused. I want a routine out, but what I'm seeing tells me he is going to hit the ball hard. All I can hope for is that he hits it at somebody. He doesn't. St Louis steals Game 6 and rides the momentum to win Game 7. Texas becomes the only team to be one strike away from winning the World Series twice in the same game.*

I've had to keep reminding myself that the purpose of the game is not to satisfy my idea of who ought to win. The game takes place on the field with highly skilled and motivated athletes. Even so, I very much wanted to see Roy Halliday pitch in the World Series. The wish died with the 1-0 loss to his buddy Chris Carpenter in the NCLS. Remember the eighth? Men on second and third and one out. He threw three sliders down and in that made the same Lance Berkman who broke the Texas Rangers' hearts look like a chump. For my money, the best bit of pitching in the entire post season. Chris and Roy are best pals. They go fishing in the off season. They probably talk about that game now and then. Maybe Chris is happy about having the bragging rights, but I'm betting he knows it's more important that he and his pal created something beautiful.

(The news of Roy's death had me thinking, 'Did I hear that right?' It was so unexpected, so unlikely, so unwanted. I'm thinking now of his wife, Brandy. She didn't gloss over the tough stuff when she spoke at the tribute at the Rogers Centre. He had his demons and sometimes they get the best of us. Something about Brandy that told you she loved him for who he was, Roy the person. A more difficult and heartfelt story than the intensity harnessed in the service of excellence that got him into the Hall.)

Ron LeSarge and Mike Marino

Ted Bradan and Nelles Van Loon

Warren Quinn

Sluggo aka Doug Densmore

Craig Donovan

Craig and Sandy Douglas

Frank Trotz

Frank and his daughter Anna

Fred Breitner

Craig Donovan with son Luke

Fred with son Stephen and Luke Donovan

Fred hitting a home run.

Lorne Mitchell

Lorne in his long ball prime

Steve Chadwick aka Chatz

"Don't hit the Ball to Chatz"

Nelles

Nelles and Frank

Mark Riddle

Fred

John St James

John in full flight.

11

Freedom Ninety-Nine, Charlie Brown, Who's on First

May 4/12: Warren told me he has tendonitis in his pitching arm and the doc has told him there's no way he should pitch. Warren said, 'No way I'm not.' He started for the other guys and pitched two perfect innings. When it was over, we'd played five innings of scoreless baseball. I'd always hoped that somewhere along the line we'd have a 1-0 game, but 0-0 is even better. I'm just sorry I wasn't one of the pitchers. For the archives, the guys who pitched so well were (along with Warren) Craig, John Larocque and Luke. From my vantage point in left field, I was wishing George Gamester were with us once again to write us up for *The Toronto Star* so the whole world could marvel at the achievement. At Amicos, the light from the big front window mingled with the beer and pizza to give a lingering resonance to the talk.

May 18/12: On the way to the park I got offered a seat twice. Once on the St Clair street car by a woman in her fifties. I told her I didn't have far to go, but she insisted. Also on the subway by a young woman all aglow with kindness. I told her I was on my way to play baseball. She said, 'That's awesome,' and wished me a good game. It felt like a blessing and as I climbed the stairs to catch the Exhibition Car, I was pretty sure we were in for some good baseball.

It's ten-zip after two. In the dugout, I tell Frank, 'I've got nothing.' But they didn't score again till the top of the seventh. In the meantime, we climbed back into it and it was 10-9 when we took the field for the top of the seventh. I came to bat with one out and the tying run (in the form of John St J) on third and the winning run on second (in the form of Alex) hoping to be a difference maker, but I hit a routine grounder to Fred at third and hustled my butt down to first to avoid being doubled up.

The young woman on the subway would have been impressed by my wheels, but no doubt more impressed by Mark's tape measure shot. I saw the swing from where I was in left field, but couldn't pick up the ball. I didn't figure out where it was till I saw John St J running after it as it crossed the reeds behind the warning path. When he finally picked it up he was just a few yards from Lake Shore Blvd. At Amico's, Mark said he probably could have run around the bases twice. Which calls to mind that he'd stumbled fielding a ground ball at short earlier in the game and was slow getting up leading Fred to speculate as to how far he'd have hit it if he had knees. Lorne still has knees, but the hip is another story. The years are catching up with him and freedom ninety-nine is on the horizon.

(Lorne and Colleen had been talking with their financial advisor in the mid nineties and the question arose as to when Lorne might retire. The advisor suggested ninety-nine, meaning the year, but what Lorne heard was his age. 'Freedom ninety-nine' still oscillates between doom and euphoria with a resonance that lingers on.)

May 25/12: Come six o'clock, there were nineteen of us followed by three more after we'd got started. Mike, along with two new guys: Jon Brooks and Richard Veldhoen. (Not to be confused with Richard Cox, or Richard Quinlan of Richard and Dorothy.) Sadly, the game did not do justice to the weather. As Frank and I walked off the field at the end of the third, he said, 'That was painful.' I'd watched six (maybe more) sure outs being played into men on base and was in no mood to disagree. The subject matter certainly lent itself to satire, but I usually lean towards comedy. In the comic view of life, we transcend tragedy. Satire allows us to savour the notion of our superiority to incompetence and folly, but at a price. George Meredith puts the dilemma beautifully:

> If you see the faults of those you love and your heart
> is chilled, you are falling into the grasp of satire.

The ump's heart was not chilled. As we were shaking hands, I saw him off to the side and told him what a good job he'd done. He smiled a mile wide and said, 'What you guys did out there tonight, that was entertainment.'

P.S. The George Meredith quote is taken from his 'Essay on Comedy'. I was checking to see it I'd got it word perfect. Didn't find it. But found this which strikes the same note:

> To love comedy, you must know the real world, and to
> know men and women well enough not to expect too
> much of them, though you may still hope for good.

I liked comedy from as far back as I can remember. 'Winnie The Pooh', my favourite from the early years. And the cartoons: 'Bugs Bunny', 'The Near Sighted Mr Magoo', Wylie Coyote in 'The Roadrunner'. And the full length movies: Abbott and Costello. Laurel and Hardy, Charlie Chaplin, Martin and Lewis, the road movies with Bob Hope and Bing Crosby. It never entered my mind that any of this might have anything to do with my study of English Literature. This changed in my third year at U of T when R.A. Foakes gave a lecture on Ben Jonson raising the question as to why there was so much attention given to tragedy and so little to comedy. When I managed to squeak into grad school, I did my PhD thesis on Henry Fielding. I'd made a beginning, but I had a job and there was no need to continue. One summer which I sensed was slipping away unnoticed, I dug out what I'd written, a collection of reasonably sound observations, but with nothing to draw them into a unified whole.

The eureka moment came when I realized Fielding is best understood not simply as a moralist, but as a comic writer. Satirical as well, but in 'Tom Jones' his major work, the tone is predominantly comic. At the Upton Inn with the love of his life moments away, he is falling in lust with an older woman. He will lose the woman he loves when she discovers his infidelity and it serves him right. But that's not what we get. What we get is the lascivious supper. How can this be? Because he has a good heart? It's one of Fielding's major themes. Also because the scene catches the precarious relationship between the primitive and civilized without making judgements. Put Tom in a Jane Austen novel and he doesn't fare as well. Is Austen superior to Fielding? I love them both.

I had the opportunity of teaching a course on comedy while at Ryerson and fell in love with 'Lucky Jim' (little respect from my colleagues there) and 'Catch 22'. But it was Charlie Chaplin who impressed the most. We think of the tramp character as fully formed from the start, but the undersized jacket, the baggy trousers, the bowler hat, the moustache, the cane came together one piece at a time. Even when the character was fully realized, Chaplin didn't know what was at the heart of the matter. In a reminiscence, he tells the story of how one day he dropped into the local theatre to check out audience reaction. The laughter is loud and long. He tells himself, 'You're really doing it Charlie, you've really got them.' All of a sudden the laughter dies. He had them and he let them get away. How could he have been so stupid? A moment later the laughter returns, but now it's quiet, more like a chuckle. The tramp is standing up to the bully, fists raised and we're suddenly afraid for him. He can't win. The bully is too strong. Better to walk away, but the bullies of the world must not be met with timidity. It's the laughter of the heart. From that point on, Chaplin knew where his genius lay.

A word also for Stephen Leacock. Is Mariposa the most loved town in Canadian fiction? Very likely. The last chapter in which Leacock takes us from a busy Toronto back in time to the town as it once was took me along with it. Jack Hodgins puts the matter beautifully: 'In some magical way we have all come from Mariposa.' Alice Munro takes the genre into darker territory in 'Royal Beatings.' The subject is what sociologists term the dysfunctional family and this family dysfunctions like clockwork. But there's something holding it together. Munro doesn't tell us what the something is, but it's there for us to see if we chose. If not the first time through, then the second or third. Denys Arcand's 'The Barbarian Invasions' is a comedy about death and dying. Is such a thing possible? I wouldn't have believed it if I hadn't seen it.

Sept 15/20: Serendipity strikes again. Chatz is following up his One Hundred Greatest Players series with 'Baseball's 60 Great Moments.' This morning's entry hit me between my serendipitous eyes.

60 Moments: No. 23, Charlie Brown finally wins the game

I was under the impression that Charlie always lost. The sequence I remember best has him on third representing the tying (winning?) run. He tries to steal home, but slides too soon and doesn't make it to home plate leading to the usual catcalls with Lucy leading the barrage. The last frame shows him lying on the third base line late at night, looking up at the dark sky asking 'Why?' Maybe not the most poignant 'why' in literature, but right up there with Job. It's wonderful he finally wins one. One is all he needs. And even if winning continues to avoid him, he wins in a more important sense. He's a good person. He always was and he always will be.

One more. Abbott and Costello. 'Who's on First?' It's not really about baseball. It's about the difficulty human beings have communicating with each other. Every attempt to answer what appears to be the simplest of questions is spun farther out of reach as each convolution leads to another. Interesting and appropriate that baseball provides the metaphor. It's there in everyday speech. People agree to touch base. A guy likes a girl, but can't get to first base with her. Success is defined as batting a thousand or hitting it out of the ball park. 'How life Imitates the World Series.' Thanks to Tom Boswell for that, but what about 'How the

Universe Imitates Baseball.' A diamond whose lines extend to infinity encompassing joy, heartbreak and all things imagined or real. If Charlie Brown can hit a walk off home run, anything is possible.

June 1/12: They said it would rain all day and that's what it did. Fred, Austin, Frank, George, Chatz, Lorne and I showed up at Amicos where Fred presented Lorne and George with their framed retirement certificates, complete with photos. Lorne looking dangerous at the plate and George at full speed on his bike while ordering ahead to Amicos.

June 8/12: I opened the fifth by throwing eight straight balls and decided it would be wise to hand the ball to Craig. Frank wouldn't let me. He came out to the mound, insisting we do it the way they do it in the bigs and took the ball out of my hand. The drama required me to be pissed off at not finishing what I'd started, but my tantrum lacked all sense of conviction.

At Amicos the sweetness of the June evening flowed through the open front window, as if to point out once again that we had been blessed not only by the Baseball Gods, but by Mother Nature as well.

P.S. Will be doing Tai Chi this weekend, so will have to miss.

July 13/12: Newbies Rob (friend of Alex) Richard Veldhoen and Jon Brooks (via John L), Billy (friend of Walter). It was hot again. Thirty-two with more humidity than last week. No question the play of the day was Nick's (Alex's bro) shoestring catch in centre. I forget who was a bat, but it must have been someone with clout because Nick was playing him deep and shading him to right. He ended up catching the ball in shallow left. Alex and I talked afterwards about how far he'd run to get there. Thirty or forty yards? Maybe more. He had to get low to finish the job and ended up with a skinned knee.

Moving now, from the sublime to the ridiculous, comes the story of the ground ball that got past Alex at third. With the runner rounding first, the ball came to Sandy playing rover. In his eagerness to nail the runner at second, he brought his arm forward with lightning intent. Unfortunately, the ball wasn't in it. Undaunted and doubly eager to nail the runner at third, he reached behind him, picked up the ball, and once again brought the arm forward with lightning intent. Once again the ball did not cooperate. They say things come in threes, but either the runner was too tired or Sandy was laughing too hard, and the pattern was not completed. It was tough on Sandy who said after that he'd never in all his life made two errors on the same play. When I suggested that he think of the two events as if they were a compound noun (i.e. singular, like salt and pepper) he refused to pretty it (them?) up and insisted on the plural.

There was huge gang at Amicos. Wonderful energy, but even without one of those maniacal DJ's who think their purpose in life is to blast everyone's ears off, it was loud. I ended up at the south end of the table with Mark and Billy (Walter's real estate agent friend). Lorne was just to my left, but he was turned north to what he seemed to believe was more interesting stuff, so for the most part, it was Mark, Billy and me. Billy at one point put forward the notion that everything is an art. There is the art of pitching, the art of hitting, the art of cooking, the art of washing dishes and so on. We got to talking about science and young Stephen who never quite took to school was right on top of it. He says the internet is a wonderful educational tool. Which reminded me that given my acid reflux issues, I should be learning more about which foods are acidic and which are alkaline. In the middle of my searches, I spotted a baseball joke. 'Alkaline"'is spelled the same as "Al Kaline" the great Detroit Tiger's outfielder. I didn't Google the '68 World Series - the one where Mickey Stanley moved in from centre field to play short to make a spot for Kaline in the outfield. I kept on going. Less cheese. More avocados.

P.S. There is something called the game. It has its own particular beauty but it isn't always fair. If you resent the unpredictable, if you get pissed off because it doesn't always go your way and is on occasion cruel, you never really enter into it and you never learn the all important lesson that it's a whole lot bigger than you are. We are part of a creation which has taken on a life of its own and if we are true to it we can find our own small place in it and only then can we begin to learn to truly love it. (Though it's possible that by the time we figure it out, we'll be too old to enjoy it.)

Charlie Parker, Austin, Mike Marino, John LeSarge, Mr Bean, Noah

July 20/12: The game continued at Amicos as Mark chortled over catching Lorne's best hit of the year. Somewhere between the beer and the salad, we got talking about computers and artificial intelligence. Given the rate at which computers are getting both faster and smaller, the question arose as to whether they will one day outstrip human intelligence. For example, some jazz scholar with monster computer smarts programs every Charlie Parker solo and Sonny Rollins solo in such a way that if one were to make a recording using a state of the art music sequencer, he could press a button, and come time for the sax solos, he'd push the Charlie button or the Sonny button. He could do the same with the rhythm section with (for example) Ray Brown and Ed Thigpen, but here's the real question: Can a computer have a eureka moment? Don't bet on it. Programming Haydn and Mozart doesn't get you Beethoven. Programming Scot Joplin and Jelly Roll Morton doesn't get you Louis Armstrong. Programming Louis and Dizzy doesn't get you Miles. And no program past, present or yet to come, will ever get you us.

Fri, July 27/12: My back was sore enough to make me wonder if it would be wise to pitch. I thought, 'Trust what you've learned from Tai Chi, and see what happens.' I did fifteen minutes of tor yus - one of the two movements on which the Tai Chi set is based - and my back loosened up. I told Frank I might get through four or five innings if I stayed relaxed. I ended up going all seven. Austin surprised the heck out of everyone with a bunt. It was perfectly placed, too far away from both Alex at third and Frank behind the plate. I was the only one who had a play and even though it landed on the base line, I was thinking there was no way Austin's seventy-six year old wheels could beat the throw. The sheer, reckless audacity of it! But 'audacity' doesn't really do the job, so here's some help from my thesaurus: 'impudence, impertinence, insolence, presumption, cheek, bad manners, effrontery, nerve, gall, defiance, temerity, chutzpah, sass.' I emailed Austin as to which one he preferred. He said he liked them all.

Somewhere early on, Frank caught his first pop up since his eye trouble. He flipped back the mask, looked up and found the ball and got an out I wasn't expecting. Marc Hershoran was a late arrival, went out to centre field and hauled in everything within fifty yards of him. Russ filled in at short when George had to leave in the sixth. You'd never guess he doesn't have knees. Mike M has found his batting stroke. Experience tells me he has no holes in his swing. Which reminds me of the game at Eglinton Park back in the eighties. I was pitching and John LeSarge was catching. Things started going off the rails in the sixth, and John came out to the mound and told me to get behind the plate. Mike came up with the game on the line and John, who was never one to ask for advice, came off the mound looking like man in deep trouble.

'How do we get this guy out?'

'You tell me.'

'He hits everything. Inside, outside, high, low. What am I supposed to throw him?'

'Your guess is as good as mine.'

I forget what John threw and I forgot if we got the out or not, but I do remember the feeling of utter helplessness knowing that there was no available strategy, no pitch, even if perfectly executed, which was likely to result in an out.

John was with us in the early years and joined us whenever he was back in town. Not a big guy – about five eight – but a gifted all around athlete. He hit long home runs, and played all nine positions.

In keeping with the pleasant weather, the front window was open at Amicos. The evening air floated across the table adding flavour to the food and beer. Sandy also joined us, a rare but welcome occurrence. Frank lamented the Jays hitting in the series against Oakland. I'd heard from Pat (Tabler) and Buck (Martinez) that the A's had the best ERA in the American League and ventured my well considered opinion that great pitching stops great hitting. Didn't get much support on that one. I'm pretty sure Casey Stengel once said that pitching is seventy-five percent of baseball. But maybe it was Yogi Berra, and maybe he said, 'Half of baseball is ninety percent pitching.' In any case, Fred came up with something I'm pretty sure Casey actually did say, 'Great pitching beats great hitting and vice versa.' Still, I can't forget the '69 Miracle Mets: Tom Seaver, Jerry Koosman, Bobby Gentry and a young Nolan Ryan. Or Lew Burdette in '57 and Mickey Lolich in '68. They both won three games in The World Series.

Somewhere along the way, John St J called our attention to the TV set above the window airing a replay of the Olympics opening ceremonies. There was the bit with the Queen parachuting down to the crowd and the sequence with Simon Rattle conducting the London Symphony with Mr Bean as guest pianist. When we'd arrived, there was a police car parked ahead of the Amicos Fiat 500. Two cops, a man and a woman smiled at us as we entered. It seems they'd been called to deal with a row in the apartment building across from Frank's and Susan's place. Later, we saw them come in, walk to the back and leave with a couple of pizzas. They smiled at us again as they went by. It was that kind of evening.

Aug 3, 2012: When I got home after the game at ten thirty, I felt like I'd been away far longer than a few hours and much farther away than Strachan and Lake Shore Boulevard. I'd travelled to a country called baseball where fair is always fair and the grass is always green and the beer always tastes better. Contrast that with how I feel sitting in my reclining chair at three in the afternoon with inertia coming down from the ceiling in slow steady waves. It's a tough act to imagine I'll be pitching three hours later. Around four, I pry myself out of the chair, put on my jock and my shin pads, work my way down to the basement to get my glove and mask, walk a block down Arlington to St Clair to catch the street car, from there the subway south to Bloor, then west to catch the subway to Bathurst, up the stairs to catch the Exhibition street car. It's slow going most of the way down Bathurst and slower still making the turn onto Front St.

As the street car approaches the Princess Gate, I look towards diamond three and I usually see one or two guys playing catch, but it's too far away to tell who they are. Sometimes I ride all the way to the Exhibition, but it's a bit of a walk down Strachan, and it's a bit easier to get off at Fort York Boulevard. Most of the time, I'm one of the early arrivals - along with Frank. Fred, Lorne and Chatz. It's not a convincing game scenario at this point. It's too laid back, too social. Between 5:30 and 6:00 the others arrive in ones and twos. Mark, Warren, Walter (with dogs). Someone starts putting in the bases (usually Fred, or Mike, or Craig when he's not in Maine). It's then I start believing there's really going to be baseball which supplies the incentive to pace off the forty-five feet between the plate and the mound and hammer down the pitcher's rubber.

At some point, I'll start warming up with Frank - but not before he's done his back exercises - and I'm thinking something along the lines of, 'Yes there's going to be a game, and yes I'm going to be pitching.' But often in late July and early August there's a question of numbers. I can see guys playing catch in groups of twos and a few chatting and one or two sitting and I'll hear someone say,

'We've got fifteen.'

'I only see fourteen.'

'George went to the can.'

'Here's Mike.'

'What about Luke?'

'He told me he'd be late.'

'What about his pal?'

'We haven't seen him since April.'

'Here's Russ.'

'How many is that?'

Somewhere just before six, I'll call out, 'Let's get it together.'

There's usually a lot of conversation too important to be interrupted and it's at this point I have been known to get cranky.

'Line up where you were last week.'

'Last week, I was in San Diego.'

'Go where you were the week before that.'

'I don't remember.'

Through all this a few guys are still talking.

'We're not here to chat about our holidays or our jobs or those near and dear to us. We're here to play baseball.'

My impatience is met with bemused tolerance, but we eventually end up with the same number on each side, but not always before the ump calls out, 'Play ball!'

This week, the ump was a new guy. He got my attention and said, 'Can I see the captains at home plate?' 'Captains?' Maybe I should have explained we don't use that word, but I figured he'd figure it out for himself. He turned out to be a take charge guy and kept the game moving.

Let me see. I think they scored a few in the first and we went down one, two, three. Warren was making his pitches, but Wayne got a key hit to drive in a couple and Frank lined a double into right centre to score a couple more and we had ourselves a ball game. Important because there are games which never achieve the status of gamehood. They meander through the vales of mediocrity and while it feels good to have made the trek to the ball park, the sense of achievement is missing. Warren loved the ump's big strike zone. I'd have liked it better if I could have taken advantage of it. The new kid Billy, the guy with the billowing shirt tails who doesn't look like a ball player, can hit. By this time our hot August afternoon had turned to a balmy August evening. As if God had created summer because of baseball.

Walter's pal, Billy, is a real estate agent. His cell phone sat on his belt and it was always on. The rest of the team would be on the bench and he'd be behind the screen talking to a potential buyer. On one occasion, the phone rang just as he was about to step up to the plate. I forget what happened. Maybe he missed his turn and the next guy in the order took his place. More than once it rang while he was in right field. He always answered. Although I don't remember it ringing while he was tracking a fly ball. Maybe he'd have picked up the phone with his right hand and caught the ball with his left. He eventually decided it wasn't fair to us to be on the phone with the game underway and asked to have his name taken off the list. Looking back, I wish we'd found a way to work it out. He saw what we were all about and knew it was good.

One of the things we're about is an aversion to the realities of rain. Yes, it's needed and life on earth would be impossible without it, but the timing is sometimes god-awful, holding us in hopeful anticipation till the last possible minute. Sometimes when it announces its intention and the writing is in the sky, our heads say no, but our hearts (in particular the hearts in the persons of Fred and Frank) say yes.

Aug 10, 2012: The Weather Network was predicting rain all week long. On Thursday the POP (probability of precipitation) had reached 90% and by Friday morning it was 100%, prompting the following email from Frank.

Hi: Susan said that she thought there would probably not be a game today, judging from the weather. I told Susan that the final decision of a rain day does not happen until 2:00 p.m. She read through the hourly forecast for today. It seems that each hour reads

'Thunderstorms.' But at 2:00 am tomorrow morning there is a break until 3:00 am. So we could get in a few innings there. Also, at 7 am it clears. So we could do a game at 7 am tomorrow morning, although there might be a problem with the ump. I still await the 2 pm decision. Everything is always a go until 2 pm. So, I wait…

All we got in the morning was a sprinkle followed by a note from Fred.

Greetings, In case there was any doubt, today's game is 'on'! We look forward to seeing you at the park before 6 PM.

Fred's optimism was quickly questioned.

Nick: Really?

Mark: Currently raining here at leslie/eglinton area.

Nelles: It's a little before 3. Just walked home in the rain. Soaked. Can't see that the field will be playable.

Fred: Hi again. When I sent the notice a few hours ago, it appeared to be clearing up. Some of you have replied, questioning my sanity. Sadly, I have just cancelled the umpire & have succumbed to the fact that there will be no game tonight. If some of you would like to meet at Amico's at about 6 PM, please reply ASAP & we'll see if we have a quorum.

No sooner had we thrown in the towel, the rain stopped and the sun came out causing another round of uncertainty. I got out of my chair, ready to suit up and board the St Clair car, but decided to check my email first.

Sandy: The field is not playable. Infield under water. Animals are lined up in 2's. Sorry for bad news.

John St J: Good thing you checked the field, Sandy. And I'm glad I checked my email at 4:45! I was ready to head down there. And by the way, I hope you took on at least two dogs…

Sandy: only had room for 2 leopards and to add insult to injury not only did they get into a fight over who got the back seat I got a ticket 'cuz they weren't wearing helmets!

Lorne, Fred and I gathered at Amico's.

Ted Williams, Josh Gibson, Heart of Darkness, George and Ira Gershwin, Yogi Berra

Fri Aug 17/12: I had a four pitch inning in the top of the first. The next three innings were five run affairs. Go figure. New kid, Richard Veldhoen, came into pitch for our guys in the top of the fifth. There were any number of plays which could have been made and weren't - including my butchering a routine fly ball. A tough start for Richard, but he's going to be a good one.

Some nice swings from their guys, in particular, the curve that stayed over the plate which Warren hit hard to drive in runs three, four and five in the bottom of the third. But the best was Sandy's long drive to right. I was on deck and I saw the pitch come in high and away. Before it was halfway to the plate, I saw him turn, keep the weight back and get the bat out with perfect timing. Hard to believe this was the same man who had tripped over his shoelace trying to find the bag an inning earlier. We commiserated about our miscues after the game and he said that ten minutes later they'd be gone. I asked him if he believed there was a time when I held on to that stuff all week. He believed it.

Amicos are on holiday. We ordered pizza and reclined on Frank's deck along with the salad and beer. By now it was dark and the conversation had a special ambience in the candlelight. Don't remember it all, but do recall Frank lamenting the Jays' lack of hitting and Walter raising the issue of who had the highest batting average ever. Both Fred and I remembered it was Roger's Hornsby - .424, back in the '30's. Walter wanted to know who was the last guy to hit .400 and once again both Fred and I remembered it was Ted Williams: 406 in 1941. Fred told the story about Ted batting .39999999, close enough to .400 to be official. The manager wanted Ted to sit out the last game of the season so as not to jeopardize the splendid achievement. Ted would have none of it and ended up going four for five.

Was he the greatest hitter ever? He hit 521 homers even though missing three years during WW II and nearly two more during the Korean war, after which he came back to hit .342 in 1956. His last at bat was a home run. I tried to remember if he came out of the dugout to tip his cap to the fans, was guessing he didn't, but wasn't sure. I consulted John Updike's account of Ted's last game in the *New Yorker.* The crowd 'thumped, wept and chanted,' but Ted hid in the dugout and stayed there.

It's been bugging me that I didn't know when Ted left the Red Sox to be a fighter pilot during the Korean war. It's a bit complicated. He left in the spring of 1952 after playing six games and returned in late summer 1953 and played 37 games (ending the season hitting .407). The following year, he hit .345 in 117 games. He played six more and his batting average in his last season was .316. Found out as I was surfing that his career OBP (.482) is the highest ever.

Question. Who has the highest single season OBP? (Hint: it might require an asterisk.)

Dec 17/20: The Negro Leagues have been reclassified as a major league and the players records between 1920-48 will now join Major League Baseball's books. Satchel Paige with his 48 major league wins will add at least 146 more. The big item concerns Josh Gibson who slugged an estimated 800 homers although it's not likely enough records are in place for him to pass Barry Bonds and his 762. Josh's .441 batting average would edge Hugh Duffy's .440 in 1894. (I wasn't aware of Duffy's stats. I guess Hornsby's .424 is from the so called modern era.)

Babe Ruth, Bob Feller and Dizzy Dean, Joe Dimaggio among others, who played against black players in Exhibition games made a point of announcing how good they were. The long overdue justice of Jackie Robinson becoming a Brooklyn Dodger in 1947 covers over the sadness of the demise of the Negro Leagues. Black Baseball fans focused on Jackie and Negro League attendance plummeted. Many players who were good enough, but needed to be twice as good, didn't make it to the majors. Where did they go? And the ones who just missed. Like Dave Barnhill, who was with the Minneapolis Millers when Monte Irvin and Willie Mays got called up to the Giants in 1951. Leo Durocher wanted to call up Barnhill in 1950, but the Millers made it to the playoffs and needed him in Minneapolis. Barnhill was thirty-four at the time. That was his last shot at the bigs.

Aug 24/12: Anyone who said anything said this was our best game of the year. What else is there to say? Beauty resists description, but I'll do my best. Each team scored a run in the first and it stayed 1-1 till an erratic fifth after which it rediscovered its balance which was tipped in our favour by a single run in the bottom of the sixth. I remember thinking - as I often do - what I'd end up writing about it, and getting angry with myself for the thought, knowing that the game is now and now is where we live. Was I going to live this beautiful thing that had unfolded somewhat unexpectedly before us, or let it slip away? God knows I was looking for a way out after the messy fifth. Back on the bench I was a couple of seconds away from saying I was ready to hand the ball to John or Richard. Mark told me I was still pitching well. I wasn't so sure, but I saw Warren getting stronger and I felt I owed it to the game to give it a shot.

I don't remember much about the top of the sixth except that they didn't score and I didn't have to throw many pitches. All the same, I wasn't looking forward to the to the top of the seventh - the dreaded open inning - where fear and bad bounces conspire to convert achievement to disaster. Before I had a chance to let the monkey mind do bad things, three pitches led to two pop ups. Looking back, I can see Mike coming to the plate and I can see Mark giving me the target up and in and I can see ball four sailing high and away. I'm pretty sure I've tensed up somehow, but I'm not sure what to do about it. (I could have tried breathing, but that thought was nowhere on the horizon.) Nick was up next. I have no idea what he did, but whatever it was led to Mike getting himself too far off the bag at third. Mark threw a strike to Fred who applied the tag and raised his glove in triumph. Unfortunately, the ball wasn't in it. So it was back to the mound with the tying run on third and the winning run on second. The next batter popped up to Austin at second.

It wasn't till a few minutes later that I realized how tired I was, but it was a good tired. All spent, not frazzled and rueful. It might have been even better if I'd remembered a sentence from Eckhart Tolle's 'A New Earth': 'The present moment is the field upon which life happens.' We play not just to determine a winner but to become one with the game. Warren said this one reminded him of why he loves baseball. He was on deck when our guys got the third out and yeah, he really wanted to be at the plate with the game on the line, but it was good all the same. I said he'd pitched as well as I did. I remember, in particular, the pitch he threw to Richard to get the third out in the bottom of the sixth. A change up perfectly set up by the fast stuff that came before it.

But it was all of us. Both teams. I see Frank holding on to a foul tip to get the third strike. I see Chatz (just back from holiday) scampering from right to left to snare a ground ball with his momentum making the throw to first of its own accord. I see Fred moving to his right, glove stretching across his body and throwing darts to first. I see Nick - actually I don't. What I see is the ball going on a line to deep centre and Richard catching up with it. But, yes it was Nick who hit it. And his big bro, Alex driving a two strike rise ball way, way back into deep left field. I see Mark absolutely crush the ball to Nick playing way, way back in centre. It didn't get any more than ten feet off the ground. I see Walter's hat-off catch of a pop up - the right hand reaching bringing the cap down as the left hand rose to meet the ball.

There's a responsibility that goes along with knowing we can still create a game like that. I keep harkening back to a late May, early June stretch of games around the turn of the century all decided by one run. I'm pretty sure it was on one of those evenings that Ted,

Frank, John St J and a few others gathered beside our cars in the lingering daylight on the parking lot of the Pizza Hut and looked out at the lush greenery behind Black Creek Drive with a sense of disbelief that the summer, like all summers before it, would come to an end.

Aug 31/12: Somewhere among the balls and strikes and fly balls, Sandy hit for the cycle. I remember the home run to deep right on a pitch up and away. It was all hands and arms. Chatz saw it too and we both wondered how he could generate that much power without getting the hips into it. And I remember the single through the left side of the infield. He almost never hits there, his strength is to the opposite field. As for the double and the triple, all I seem to recall is a lot of running. Oh yes, I see him pulling up on third, a bit short of breath, so that was the triple. But I don't remember the double. Nonetheless, the cycle it was.

Apart from that, the game is blurry except for Alex at the plate and Mark wanting the two strike pitch up and in and it going in low and Alex hammering it past third a few inches foul, and Mark calling it again and this time getting it right and Alex popping up. (He told me later it was a great pitch, but between the lines he was saying, 'I'll get you next time.') Oh yes, there was Walter's two out line drive with men on second and third. And Jesse's upper cut fly ball to centre which made me dizzy to look at, but giving Marc H plenty of time to camp under. And Mark R throwing a rope to second and catching Warren trying to steal. And Warren's homer as his guys were narrowing the gap in the bottom of the seventh.

Things were lively at Amico's. At my end of the table, George, Frank and I talked about Samuel Beckett, meditation, James Joyce and Aldous Huxley. Good fun, but my big band, 'The Hurricanes', had a gig Saturday evening. A last minute turn of events had left us without a bass player and it was up to me to find one. The gig was an Italian wedding. The couple had come to hear us at rehearsal earlier in the year and decided we were what they wanted. A big band without a bass player is like swimming without using your legs and I didn't want to leave the wonderful young couple with a lame duck band. The pay was $85.00 each plus food. Little did we expect that food meant having two tables set aside for us and the same $150 per plate five course dinner served to the guests. The only downside was the DJ who seemed intent on destroying our ears. As for the young couple, I hope they liked the swinging arrangement of George and Ira Gershwin's 'Love Is Here to Stay', and I hope it's prophetic.

Sept 7/12: September baseball. The tournament just a couple of weeks away and the crisper weather giving birth to the wish for crisper baseball. A close game for five innings. Nice bit of hitting by Mark after I'd got him to swing and miss up and in. Frank called it again and Mark creamed it past third. Sandy went back to make a juggling catch of a two out Texas Leaguer at second. Chatz scampered behind me to make a spectacular grab of a hot grounder I'd managed to get my glove on and threw on the run to get the out at first. Walter made another of his hat- off catches at second, this one a bit more intricate than the one a couple of weeks ago. Warren pitched well. I've got so used to it that it's easy to forget he was a first baseman when I played with him back in the '80's in the Toronto Arts Softball League. This is his second baseball life in which, after his encounter with colon cancer, he has been reborn as a pitcher.

Towards the end of the talk at Amicos the subject came up of the shooting in Montreal in the aftermath of Quebec election. Me at the end, Frank to my left and Fred beside him and Mark on the other side of the table, though I think it started with just the three of us. I don't quite know who raised the question of whether this was the act of someone beyond the pale, or something that anyone might be capable of under certain circumstances. The answer started out as, 'of course not', but refused to stay there. Mark, who lived in Quebec for thirty-seven years witnessing the powerful feelings stirred up by the separation issue questioned our certainty. We stayed there for a while before realizing we had stumbled onto a much larger question. Frank, I think it was, brought up the subject of Michael Bryant driving his Saab convertible on a summer evening, his wife beside him, confronted by an enraged cyclist on the hood of his car. What would we have done? Walter told about taking his dogs down to the lake for a swim and a man screaming something about the dogs needing to be on a leash and proceeding to throw large rocks - i.e. rocks large enough to kill someone - at the dogs.

I wrote that last section in the wee small hours. Saul Bellow, I think it was, said you never need to revise anything you write at three in the morning. But after I went back to bed - or maybe it was when I woke up I thought about the great writers - how they take us on a journey we'd never willingly undertake, yet we end up glad to have travelled with them. Couldn't find my copy of *Heart of Darkness*, but was thinking also of Shakespeare, the great tragedies, what he knew of human nature.

Sept 14/12: I'd been looking forward to one last chance to pitch before the tournament and rain was nowhere in the picture till I checked in with The Weather Network while eating breakfast. There they were, those little icons with clouds and raindrops along with a ninety per cent probability of rain. The good news was the icons were only there from twelve to two, though it was still raining when I left Tai Chi at three. I had a nap and hoped for the best. When I looked out the window at four, the rain had stopped, but thought I'd better check my email.

> Tonight: 'Gentlemen, It is with great regret that I must announce a cancellation of today's game. I have just received a report from Sandy who is at the field. Apparently, Noah's ark has been located straddling second base at Diamond 3. When Sandy arrived, most of the animals had boarded. Therefore we will

> defer to Amico's to lick our wounds and partake in good cheer and fine beer at 6PM. Please drop Frank a line if you are planning to attend. Hope to see you at 6.
>
> Cheers, Fred."

I met Lorne waiting at Dundas West for the Roncesvalles car. Frank and Fred were waiting for us at Amicos. By now the sun had come out and we looked longingly out the window for the game that wasn't there. But conversation, too, is a sport. It doesn't get you much cardio, but it gets the digestive juices flowing so they can take on the gluten and that's no easy task. Your stomach will tell you that it loves good conversation, that it's the high point of the day, that if here's anything the world needs more of, it's good conversation. Though I have to add it occurred to me while I was trying to remember what was said that we are prone to wandering into hobby horse territory, as Fred pretty much admitted as he launched into yet another Yogi Berra tribute. But any subject that is both profoundly simple and richly complex can never wear itself out, although I have to say I was plenty annoyed when Fred trotted out the one where Yogi tells a reporter, 'There's no way I said all the things I said.' It sat on the table like stale bread till Fred upped the ante. 'When you think about it, it's wonderful. It's both a negation and an affirmation.'

It got me thinking that we'd stumbled onto the essence of the matter, which would be no small achievement. Even the most accomplished literary critics can't do better than 'oxymoron.' I submitted the oxymoron question to the net and got some examples: 'alone together', 'bittersweet', 'cheerful pessimist', 'deafening silence,' 'civil war', to which I'll add another: 'friendly fire'. Good stuff, but lacking Yogi's eloquent, mind bending simplicity, begging the question of whether or not we had been rewarded for the loss of our game with an astounding literary insight that might be worthy - at the very least - of an article in *The New Yorker*. Consider 'When you see a fork in the road, take it.' One the one hand, "You can't be in two different places at the same time.' On the other,' Just keep going.' A negation and an affirmation. It's a no brainer when you really think about it.

Sept 21/12: Two fellows showed up with a permit for diamond three. Frank was adamant, dare I say defiant, in defending our territory. It was too close to the apes at the water hole for comfort. He drove home to get our permit, found it, found also that it had expired last week. When he got back the other guys had graciously conceded and moved to diamond two. Before strapping on his catcher's gear, Frank walked over and apologized.

Tournament Sept 23, 2012

The summer always seems to unfold in the same predictable yet surprising manner. May is fine, because it's early and we're just getting back into the swing of things and it serves as a prelude to June. But the next thing you know it's 'Goodbye June,' and not much later it's 'Goodbye July' and the next thing you know it's, "What the heck happened to August?' Someone, usually John St J, sends an email to the effect that it's time for Fred, Frank, John St J, Lorne and I to gather at my place to make up the teams. We always make a pleasant night of it and over the years it's become one of our rituals.

Game One: Team 2 (my guys) versus Team 3 (John's guys). In the top of the first, we got the lead off hitter, but a pop up lost in the sun and a misplayed fly ball led to a five run inning. We got a five of our own in the bottom of the inning and it was back to square one. I was hoping to put the mercy rule inning behind me. No such luck. I never really settled into my feet all day. Still made enough good pitches to keep us in the game, but the other guys hit some pretty decent risers and they hit them hard. Especially Mike D, Sandy's invitee. We'd been warned up front that the guy was a good hitter, but I wasn't quite prepared for the reality. The first time up he took a low and away pitch to deep right for a home run. Second time up, I went low and in and he took that to right for another homer. The two long balls settled me down somewhat. Something about the challenge of pitching to a hitter who's that good. I threw him some mean shit after that. He hit that too, but not quite so far. He also made some great plays at the rover position.

Game Two: Team 2 (my guys) versus Team 1 (Warren's guys). It was deja vu all over again and we were deep in a hole in the bottom of the third when Craig's bunt attempt rolled into foul territory. I wish he'd bunted in the bottom of the first when he hit a monster shot to left. Batting ahead of him Eric, Warren, Alex and Wayne also hit the ball way, way back. Don't remember as many hard hit balls against me in one inning since Bindertwine in the nineties when the other guys hit four homers. Once again, not four homers in one game, four homers in one inning. Funny thing is, behind 13-1 in the bottom of the fifth we rallied to win that game. On this occasion, we were not so fortunate. We rallied for three in the fourth, but in the fifth with three more across the plate and our rally caps on, a double play ended it.

(There's a story that goes along with the four homers. John St James and I were helping Dave Bolland move not long after that year's tournament and we got talking baseball with one of the other guys. I mentioned the four home runs and he told a joke which goes as follows: A pitcher gives up a couple of long balls in a horrendous inning and he comes back to the bench ready to jump off a bridge. One of his buddies sidles up to him and says, 'Don't take it so hard. I can name at least four parks those balls would never have got out of.' There's a pregnant pause as the pitcher lifts his eyes looking for the light at the end of the tunnel… 'Banff, Algonquin, Yellowstone…')

Game Three: Team 1 (Warren's guys) versus Team 3 (John's guys). This was a sweet one with some of the best defense I'd seen in a long time. Looking at the score sheet, I see Warren's team scored one run in the top of the first. But I also see a star beside the fifth place hitter and a note at the top of the page: '9 - 5 double play.' Someone (was it Alex or Wayne?) hit a long drive way back in left. Justin made a great catch and threw a rope to Mark at third to nail the runner who left the bag too soon. It was a major momentum changer and snuffed out what had all the markings of a big inning. John's team rode the feeling and put up a four to take the lead. I had the feeling that Warren's guys would eventually get the upper hand. But the great defense kept coming. In the top of the second, Richard went way back in centre to take a home run away from Marc H. In the top of the third, Walter moved to his right to snare a hot grounder, planted, turned and threw a strike to Peter at first to get the out. I knew the play wasn't a miracle, but rather the outcome of a pile of hard work and determination (along with relentless coaching from his dogs) but it felt like it nonetheless.

Even though Sandy has been with us only four or five seasons, it's already become a tradition for him to remind us how wonderful we are. I suppose we already know, but the reminder seems to make us feel even more wonderful and the conversations become more animated and convivial. Another tradition is my cutting the cake which gives me a chance to make some remarks. I don't remember all the faces, but was Frank just to my left, Richard and his girlfriend were on my right. Anna was about halfway down on Frank's side. I'd already told her what a fine job she'd done behind the plate, but it seemed a good idea to let everyone know. Remarkable in view of the fact she hasn't played much for five years or so. There was a lot of back and forth as we talked about the new guys. It was also a chance to tell Sandy that he too is wonderful, and to tell Warren how much his knowledge and good energy along with his pitching give our season an extra spark. But I was thinking mainly of Frank and Walter, the health issues and how bravely and successfully they've dealt with them. As Walter talked about the way he'd handled the grounder to his right, I could see the boy in him. (The boy is eleven or twelve, which means he'll keep getting better).

One thing I forgot was to thank Frank and Susan for their hospitality extended so graciously year after year. How far back am I talking about? Not sure, but I'm guessing the first Bindertwine barbecue happened in the early eighties. I also forgot to mention the dogs, Lucy and Katy, both of whom had to be put down this summer. Katy was well along in years but Lucy was only seven or eight, a real heartbreaker. They always had as much fun as any of us. But Joe, a rambunctious collie, and Anna's dog (forget her name but she's a sweetie) were on hand to add their wonderful dogginess to the evening. Come to think of it, there have always been dogs around on tournament day, the most prominent of which was Cheers in our Bindertwine days. Like Joe, she was a collie and something of a control freak. It was our custom back then to gather first thing in the morning at the house on Windrush Road which was just up the hill from the park. Cheers welcomed us with loud and determined enthusiasm while herding us into the kitchen.

Got this from Frank the day after the tournament.

> "Hi: A few weeks ago at Amico's, Sandy co-opted the conversation, and his words were an accolade to me for playing as I had that night, and for coming through what has been a pretty tough three years. I was very moved by his words, and felt very proud. I had meant to write a response to his words, but had not done so then. So, here it is.
>
> On the particular night when Sandy spoke about me, and asked me to pee in the empty beer jug to find out what I was taking, something truly wonderful did happen. It seemed that during that game I somehow burst out of three difficult years into what I can only describe as a feeling of huge energy and a feeling of being freed from a lot that was indeed holding

me back. Last summer and last Fall were the most difficult because my vision was so impaired by the state of my left eye, and I was in a state of constant pain. I caught the tournament games last summer with my left eye closed because this was the only way I could see clearly. The three years had been a series of operations, the first two being unsuccessful, and this last one the most difficult because of what it meant, losing my eye. However, when I was able to get up and get out of the house, my vision was so much better, and the pain was gone. So, my vision has continued to improve, and I have experiences like the one during the games yesterday when something new happens to my vision and things become even clearer.

So that's one part of what has been happening. But the other part, and this part I believe is so important for all of us. It's not just what has been happening with my eye and my vision, but also what has been happening with my body. The impaired vision threw off a lot of my physical capabilities - because if I looked too quickly to the side or up I'd get dizzy. And then at times I'd see almost double. But what I was doing along with all of this was a regime of exercise 5 - 6 days a week, probably 30 - 40 minutes a day, stretching, weights, aerobic stuff. I was doing some research into catcher's exercises which I've incorporated into my regime. But what is most important to me is a sense that as we grow older, if we want to continue an activity like baseball, we have to work harder with our bodies. Last summer, in addition to my eye problems, I developed tendonitis in my throwing arm, which made it almost impossible to throw. And I lost the mechanics of throwing. It's taken me to almost half way through this season to begin to feel like the mechanics were coming back and I could throw to second base again. To get there I worked with exercises for tendonitis, and with a suggestion in one of my Google searches that catcher's exercises had to be fast because of the kind of movement that catching entails. So I picked up the speed of what I was doing and have pretty well double the number of reps in each exercise and this feels great. I'm not saying that everyone needs to follow my regime, or increase the speed of their exercises. What I am trying to communicate is how important working out is - especially as we grow older. I just accept as a fact that if I want to continue to play baseball next year, that I will have to work harder with my body.

And here's my answer to Sandy. It's because I get such joy playing baseball with all of you.

So, onward into next year. Get to it.

Cheers and much love to all of you wonderful people."

Friday, Jan 27, 2013. Help! The numbers are out of control. January is almost behind us already. The upside is that spring training is just around the corner. Some of us made the annual trek up to Fred's to celebrate the approaching return of baseball. In lieu of the limo, six of us opted for a Dodge Caravan with Eric as chauffeur. I didn't really miss the Scotch and it was nice to see where we going. This years' entertainment was Game 6 of the '75 World Series - supplied by Jim St James, returned after many years in Winterpeg. I remembered heroics of Carbo and Fisk quite clearly and assumed everyone else did too. Was booed loudly on saying, 'Which inning does Pudge hit the home run?' What I didn't remember were the ins and outs of Carbo's at bat with the Sox three runs down in the bottom of the ninth. He was barely managing to stay alive and some of the swings looked more like lunges. A base on balls would have seemed a blessing, and then - long into the count - the ball was somehow sailing over the fence. Also forgot George Foster's throw in the bottom of the ninth, bases loaded no one out, which beat the runner to the plate, and Fisk's throw to second to get the lead runner an inning or two later, an Dwight Evan's catch in deep right to rob Foster of a home run and his throw to first to get the double play. Warren raised the question of whether it was a better game than last year's game six. Nineteen seventy-five is etched on my memory. Two thousand and twelve is somewhere in the clutter of the recent past. I had to pause a moment to remember who played who.

March 19, 2013: Can you believe this weather? High of 21. It was just as balmy last Wednesday when I got a call from Frank. We'd been talking about getting out early to throw the ball and see how my riser ball looked to a catcher with one eye. Went down to his place and from there a few blocks north to Sorauren Park. I'd been thinking I'd start off with ten foot tosses and move back a bit from there. He had other ideas, made me move to forty-five feet after two pitches. I had my doubts, but ball and glove met as if no other conclusion was possible. Strange that it seemed so ordinary after appearing too much to wish for.

12

Stephen Sondheim, Richard, Fred Merkle

Fri April 26/13: Fred had called Frank and asked him if he thought we'd be good to go on Friday. Given that they both would play till December, it was a no brainer. Come Thursday, there was an email advising us that Frank had advised Fred that it was going to be cold on Friday and it would make more sense to throw the ball around at Sorauren Park eight or so blocks north of Amicos. I was walking along High Park Avenue just after six when a van pulled up containing John St James. John said the others were headed to Amicos and that he'd seen the solitary figure of Sandy in the middle of Coronation Park. He'd wanted to give him a heads up, but the Lake Shore Blvd traffic had other ideas. At the pub it was George, Fred, Lorne, Craig, John and I making brilliant conversation, although no one could think of anything brilliant to say about Sandy. Come to think of it, had George also gone to Coronation, I could have called this entry, 'Sandy in the Park with George.'

May 17/13: In the bottom of the first, I nearly had that most wonderful of pitching moments: the three pitch inning. Warren was the third man up with strict orders from Mark R to take a pitch and I had to be content with four. Lorne was five for five with a walk, Marc H made a great catch of Mark R's long drive to deep centre, running full tilt towards Lake Shore Blvd. Richard pitched four strong innings.

We were down by seven in the last inning and squeezed out enough runs to tighten things up.

Richard is not a big guy, about five ten, a hundred and fifty pounds, but the only FNB batter to hit a ball off the washroom roof behind Diamond Two. His swing accelerates through the strike zone and arcs up then down. It starts in the feet and moves up through the legs and core transferring the power through the arms and hands. When he's in the outfield he runs down fly balls like a laser on wheels. He'd never pitched before FNB, but his motion is simple and efficient. He loves the challenge and is getting better every time out.

June 7/13: Our guys got behind early and behind soon became behinder. In the dreaded top of the seventh with the mercy rule no longer in effect, it looked as if the other team would be at bat till August.

P.S. Will be away doing Tai Chi Friday the 14th.

June 21/13: For anyone wondering why Alex hasn't appeared in the lineup, it's because he's a new dad. If the kid stays with it as long as Austin, he'll be playing till 2091. At Amico's Walter read out some umping decisions he found on the net. Josh Willingham doesn't touch second on Justin Morneau's grand slam. The other team appeals and Willingham is called out. Should the two runs that scored ahead of Willingham be counted? (A juicier question might involve what Morneau said to Willingham when the inning ended.) Another one in which Nick Swisher pushed the runner ahead of him towards second because the runner thought a fly ball had been caught and was hightailing it back to first. Turns out there's no rule saying you can't assist a fallen runner. If Kirk Gibson hadn't been able to make it all the way round the bases on the legendary one legged home run vs Dennis Eckersley in the '88 World Series, Tommy Lasorda would not have been penalized for carrying him over the plate.

All of which reminded me of the all time classic boner involving a fellow named Fred Merkle who is remembered only for one unfortunate event. It's 1908. The Cubs and the Giants are tied for the lead in the last game of the season. Merkle is on first and there are other runners ahead of him. The batter gets a hit, the winning run scores. The fans run onto the field. Fearful for his health, Merkle heads to the dugout without touching second. A Cub player notices and gets (what he claims to be) the game ball and tags Merkle while he's in the dugout (or maybe it was the shower). The ump calls him out. The game is resumed the next day. The Cubs win the pennant. It would be interesting to know whether or not the rules have been revised to cover a situation of that kind. How much time and_distance have to elapse between the mistake and the call. What if you cross the international date line?

Just checked out the story in Wikipedia. It was Evers of Tinker to Evers to Chance who made the play, but he didn't tag out Merkle, he just touched second to get the force, which takes some of the fun out of my account. But there was a question about whether the ball was the game ball because the Giants' Joe McGinty threw it into the stands. Cubs pitcher Rube Kroh, who wasn't in the game, retrieved the ball and threw it to Tinker who relayed it to Evers. (In one account, the fan who got the ball didn't want to give it up and Kroh had to tackle him and pry it out of his hand.) By rule when a fan or player not in the game touches the ball, it should be ruled dead. It was one of the New York papers who called it a bonehead play and the fans picked it up. But Merkle's team mates didn't blame him. It was the custom for base runners to head for the dugout when the fans rushed the field and the out call was almost never made. Why it was made in this case is hard to fathom.

Rain, Paul Molitor, Rain, Robin Roberts, Rain, Tug McGraw

July 5/13: **I** started checking The Weather Network's long range forecast on Saturday. The icons showing sun, rain and a lighting flash were lined up across the screen. As I write this last bit, it's Tuesday morning, after yesterday's deluge. I've got the GTA section of *The Star* in front of me with a picture of a couple wading across Lake Shore Blvd and cars driving though water halfway up their hubcaps. Beneath that, there's a photo of people being rescued from the GO train which got stuck in the waters near Pottery Rd and Bayview. In the lower left corner, there's a headline: 'This is likely the wettest moment in Toronto's history.' More than 90 millimetres of rain in two hours starting at 4:30 P.M. The wettest day ever was Oct 15, 1954, when Hurricane Hazel dropped 124.4 millimetres over the whole day.

It was the day of the flooded basements. Mine had less than an inch, but Heath and Danielle in the other half of the semi, had to redo the family room. Big bucks. Similar story for a lot of other people.

July 19/13: Three batters into the inning, Frank pointed towards the outfield. I turned and saw a huge cloud of dust coming straight for us. A couple of seconds later, the dust was on us along with the wind. Walter said later he thought the wind was going to blow him into the backstop. We got the equipment together asap. When I opened the door of the Yaris, I could feel the car being pulled forward. I looked over at Frank in the driver's seat, and he still had his knee pads and chest protector on. The rain came down in buckets moment later. As we pulled onto the road, I saw George heading home on his bike. I heard someone wishing him luck.

At Amicos the new owner stopped by. Turns out he's a long time ball player and admirer of Paul Molitor. We invited him to play FNB, but he doesn't get off work till four A.M. (Molitor was the best hitter I've ever seen with the game on the line. Was '93 with the Jays his only World Series ring? Think he retired after that.) Frank talked about his eye. How the brain thinks the missing eye is still there and how this somehow results in his having three dimensional vision. Austin was in the middle trying to figure out which end of the table was more interesting.

'Live in the moment, Austin.'

'I wanna live in both moments.'

And so it went into the evening which was now calm and clear.

(Saw a sign on my friend Paul Wiggins' deck Monday evening. 'BEER: Because your friends just aren't that interesting.' I hasten to add 'except for us,' but it's interesting how we get smarter as the evening goes on.)

I've been thinking about Warren's deep affection for the '82 Brewers and remembered my love affair with the Phillies which began when I was visiting my grandparents in Jarvis Ontario in 1950. Home was Madsen Red Lake Goldmines and we got *The Winnipeg Tribune*. I'd never noticed the baseball standings in the Trib, but for some reason they caught my attention in *The London Free Press* while visiting my grandparents in Jarvis, Ontario. I focused on the National League. There were three teams in contention that year: the Dodgers (the defending NL champs), the Cardinals and the Phillies. I think it was because I liked the sound of Philadelphia that I decided to cheer for the Phillies. (I didn't know it meant 'city of brotherly love'.)

The Phillies pulled into a healthy lead in August, but I have a vague memory of reading about their star lefty, Curt Simmons being drafted into the army. Another pitcher, Bill Miller, slipped on some slippery stairs and was out for the season. With the weakened pitching staff, they lost steam and the Dodgers were gaining ground. It came down to the last game of the season on Sunday, Oct 1. By then I was back home in Madsen. I remember hearing on the radio that Dick Sisler had hit a home run in the top of the tenth that won the game.

It was the Phillies versus the Yankees in the World Series. You never got major league games on Canadian radio stations in those days, except during the Series and it was only then I began to find out who was on the team. Andy Semnick catching, Eddie Waitkus at first, Mike Goliat at second, Granville (Granny) Hamner at short, Willie (Puddin' Head) Jones at third. In the outfield it was Del Ennis in left, Richie Ashburn in centre, and Dick Sisler in right. Twenty year old Robin Roberts was the ace of the pitching staff. The average age was twenty-six and they called them the Whiz Kids.

The games were played during the day while I was in school. I'm pretty sure the fourth game was on a Saturday, because I remember hearing all about Whitey Ford being the youngest pitcher to ever win a World Series game. It was five nothing in the top of the ninth when Gene Woodling dropped a fly ball and the Phillies scored two runs. I shouted for joy and prayed for more, but that was all we got. Which meant the Yankees had won in four straight. It was a tough pill for a ten year old to swallow. Part of what we knew about the games we learned from other kids. I remember Warren Peterson talking about Ken Heintzelman as if he were third rate, but he couldn't have been too bad because the record shows he pitched seven innings and only gave up two runs. In the second game, Robin Roberts pitched brilliantly, but lost 2-1 in ten innings. I learned later that it was Roberts who had pitched the final game against the Dodgers, his third start in five days.

The next summer when I was back in Jarvis. Several people in town had acquired TV sets. A family up the street invited my brother and me to see the Dodgers and the Phillies on a Saturday afternoon. I knew ahead of time Roberts would be pitching against the Dodger's ace Don Newcombe. It was all I thought about through the week, but come Saturday we got word the game had been rained out. That would have been the only time I'd ever have seen Roberts pitch. It's remarkable that he's more alive in my memory than many other ball players I've seen at the ball park or on TV. I can still see him rearing back and throwing his fastball which Ralph Kiner said jumped six to eight inches and was the toughest pitch he'd ever seen.

(Kiner hit fifty-four home runs in 1949. *Sport* magazine got a lot of mileage speculating about his chances of bettering Babe Ruth's sixty.) I followed him all through his career. He was a perennial twenty game winner, and had a brief stint in the American league with the Orioles after he was supposed to be washed up. There was something eternally youthful about him. He wasn't supposed to grow old and lose his fastball. He was my link to immorality. He died in May, 2010 at the age of 83. He pitched 305 complete games.

After he was traded to the Orioles, I kept cheering for the Phillies. In 1964, they were six and a half games ahead in early September when somebody got the bright idea they should go with a three man rotation. They lost some atrocious number of games in a row and ended up losing the pennant. (The newsies named it 'The Phold'). They had another great team in the late 70's led by Steve Carlton and Mike Schmidt. They won the NL East in '76, '77, and '78, but lost to the Reds (twice) and the Dodgers in the NLCS. It looked as if they had the Dodgers number in '78 but they played the final game in the rain. Tommy John was pitching for the Dodgers. How do you stop a pitcher with a reputation of loading up the ball from throwing a spitter in a rain storm? In '79 it was all Expos and Pirates.

In 1980, the Phillies looked very much like a third place team, but the Pirates and the Expos kept saying, 'After you, Alphonse' and the Phillies caught fire (led by Larry Bowa at short). I wasn't about to be lured into disappointment once again, and kept my hopes in check. I remember a game in late September against the Expos. It was a close one and the Expos were threatening in the ninth. Tug McGraw came in to pitch. I took one look at his slider and knew I'd never seen one that disappeared from the strike zone so fast and so far. (Dave Stieb's is the only one I've seen to match it.) I thought, 'That pitch is unhittable'. From then on, I knew they had a chance.

They went on to win the World Series against the Royals. In game six, McGraw came in to relieve Steve Carlton in the bottom of the ninth. Philadelphia fans have always been fanatical to the extreme and there was a row of riot police with their attack dogs all around the field. Tug was somewhat spooked by the dogs but he thought to himself, 'There's no way I'm gonna be a dog out here.'

I was watching the game at Joe Leonard's place with a bunch of Royals fans. Joe was the only one who understood how much I wanted my guys to finish what had started with the Whiz Kids back in 1950. After the others left, he and I had an extra beer or maybe it was a scotch. On the way home, I felt peace and joy but mostly relief.

The Open Inning, William Shakespeare, Bobby Thomson, Tom Verducci, Pleasantville

Aug 9/13: When I walked to the mound to start the top of the seventh the ump came out to ask if it was an open inning. 'Yes, but if they go ahead by ten runs, then it's over, and since we're up by ten that would mean twenty runs, and by then I'll probably have committed suicide.'

'I'll keep an eye on you.'

Good thing he said that. We got the first two outs in good time, but the last one took forever. In the meantime the other guys had been joking about needing a touchdown and a field goal. By the time they were just two runs behind, they weren't joking anymore, they were walking up to the plate with destiny in their eyes and no sign of mercy for an aging pitcher. The low point had come several batters earlier when I'd gone three and oh to Lorne, fought back with two slow strikes, opted to go for something faster and watched the ball sail into the backstop. So there we were, two runs up, two men on base and Alex at the plate. All I was thinking was, 'Don't walk him.' I threw him the fattest pitch he'd ever seen. He hit it far, far, far into deep left where I saw George getting himself into position to make the catch. Chatz said later that it took a gymnast's agility to make the final stretch and get the glove into position. I'm sure he was right, but it happened so far away, it was hard to see.

At Amicos, someone mentioned the Ex. It starts this coming Friday (the 16th). It makes finding a parking spot more difficult, but as Sandy pointed out, the more difficult thing is that another season is approaching another end. There are lots of ways to say it, and I've taken many stabs at capturing the feeling, some more effective than others. Words are both referential (their purpose is to identify realities beyond themselves) and intrinsic (they have a life of their own). E.g. Tom Cheek's call on Joe Carter's walk off home run that won the '93 World Series. 'Touch 'em all Joe, you'll never hit a bigger home run in your life.' Lots of ways to write about Joe hitting the ball over the fence in fair territory. Some of the words would lie lifeless on the page and would infect the event with the same quality. 'It Never Entered my Mind' is a song about taking a loved one for granted and then finding her gone. 'You have what I lack myself / Now I even have to scratch my back myself.' (Kudos to Lorenz Hart.) And this from 'Life is Just a Bowl of Cherries': 'The sweet things in life to you were just loaned / So how can you lose what you never owned.' Good writing is alive. Shakespeare's lover is temperate. Not just for a day. Forever.

Here's the whole thing.

> Shall I compare thee to a summer's day?
> Thou art more lovely and more temperate:
> Rough winds do shake the darling buds of May,
> And summer's lease hath all too short a date;
> Sometime too hot the eye of heaven shines,
> And often is his gold complexion dimm'd;
> And every fair from fair sometime declines,
> By chance or nature's changing course untrimm'd;
> But thy eternal summer shall not fade,
> Nor lose possession of that fair thou ow'st;
> Nor shall death brag thou wander'st in his shade,
> When in eternal lines to time thou grow'st:

So long as men can breathe or eyes can see,
So long lives this, and this gives life to thee.

'Thy eternal summer shall not fade.' But there's a catch: 'Each mark against the chaos must be made well.' If not, it gathers with billions of others that clutter and obscure.

Aug 16/13: A perfect day for baseball, but the first day of the Ex. I was thinking about Frank as I got ready to go down to the park and could see him looking for a parking space with a car full of equipment and having to lug it a couple of hundred yards. There's a big and heavy black bag, and a big (also heavy) red bag, and a bag for the bats and one for the catcher's equipment and one for the bases. A lot for one guy, but he hauls the stuff from the legendary space under the fabled front porch of 84 Wilson Park Rd and loads it into the Yaris every Friday. Put some of that down to the fact he's a potter and has been lugging around fifty pound bags of clay most of his life. (You can see his work at Clay Design, on the corner of Harbord and Brunswick.) Turned out he'd got there early and found a spot just a few spaces east of the diamond. John L also found a spot along with Wayne. Fred elected to park up on King and ride his bike the rest of the way. Sandy, as usual, arrived by scooter. Chatz came in from Guildwood village via the Go Train. His nephew (Marc H) came by bike along with Richard some time later. I was going to take a cab but the Bathurst bus came as I was about to cross the street and I saved myself twenty-five bucks. I met Bill D on the Exhibition car and we were there by five thirty. The ump didn't have quite as good a go of it and arrived five seconds before game time.

A lot of runs at the start, but things tightened up in the third and it was still close after five. We put up a crooked number in the open inning, but they rallied to make it close. I'd gone out to play right field in the bottom of the sixth and came back in to finish up. Warren made a point of saying that I'd got the win and the save which reminded me I'd read something in *Sport* about a manager whose team was playing the Red Sox in the 40's or 50's. He pulled the right handed pitcher and brought in a lefty to face Ted Williams. He put the pitcher on third where Williams almost never hit and brought the righty back from third to pitch to the next batter. Which means that if his team were ahead by less than four runs, a generous scorer could have given the pitcher both the win and the save and he'd have shared the moment of glory with yours truly.

As we were driving back to 84 Wilson Park, Frank wondered aloud if the Jays were mathematically out of it. I wondered why even bother to ask, but he brought it up again at Amico's. We got talking about how many games they'd have to win to get into the post season which reminded me of the 1951 New York Giants who were thirteen and a half games behind the Dodgers on August 10th and went on to win the pennant. I'd read somewhere that the Dodgers didn't play badly down the stretch, which got me thinking about the Giants won - lost record during that time. When in doubt, go to Wikipedia: 'After a slow start, the Giants went 50 - 12 over their last 62 games.' Has any team ever put together a string to equal that? The race ended on the final day of the season with Bobby Thomson's walk off home run, 'The Shot Heard Round the World.' Right underneath that entry was another which read, 'Was the '51 Giants' comeback a miracle, or did they simply steal the pennant?' 'Every hitter knew what was coming,' said Al Gettel, 'Made a big difference.' Hank Greenberg once said he was the best hitter in baseball when he knew what pitch was coming. That one courtesy of Sandy who'd brought along his book of memorable baseball quotes. The one we liked best came from Stan Musial. 'I never had any trouble with the spitter, I just hit the dry side.' If the Jays start stealing signs and hitting the dry side, who knows? By now the evening had wound to its end. Over but not really. The game and the camaraderie had given us some part of the answer to the meaning of life's fleeting moments.

Aug 24/13: It was Susan's birthday and Frank hurried home at game's end. We loaded the equipment into Mike's Civic and Lorne's Matrix. (Any other night for the last eighteen years, it would have been his much loved Subaru Outback.) I could have caught a ride with Mike, but that would have meant three in the back. I elected to follow the equipment along the lane to Lorne. I could see two guys walking beside him and decided he wouldn't have room. I headed back towards Mike but he'd already gone. Just as I'd decided to head up to Strachan to hail a cab, feeling forgotten and abandoned, Mark showed up. Mike had asked Lorne where I was and they'd figured out what had happened. 'Amazing grace, how sweet the sound / That saved a wretch like me.'

At Amico's amidst the beer and pizza we talked - among other things - about video assist for umps. Lorne made the argument that since baseball more than any other sport is a metaphor for life, human error should be part of the mix. It was good stuff except for the fact there'd been a fatal accident just a few yards down the street. The police were there when we'd arrived. The body was lying on the pavement under an orange sheet. I'd like to say that because these accounts are about baseball, and baseball, as Lorne pointed out, is so closely linked to our perceptions of life that they can embrace all things. The words may exist, but I have little idea what they are and so will turn to Tom Verducci and his piece in *Sports Illustrated*, Dec 6, 2004, 'At the End of the Curse, a Blessing.' An sagacious reader might already have guessed from the title and the date, that it's about the 2004 Red Sox. However, the facts of the matter - i.e. beating the Yankees in the ALCS after losing the first three games - are so miraculous in themselves that they can easily reduce any attempt to write about them to redundancy. What Verducci does is tell two stories in parallel. Both are developed around long time Red Sox Fans. One, a young man whose wife is about to give birth sometime during the World Series and another fan in his eighties who's terminally ill and clings to life just long enough to hang in for the final game. Life, death, baseball.

Scary Moment

Sept 6/13: 'Some of you may not be aware that Richard was hit by a line drive while pitching in the 5th inning last night. I've appended this message with John LaRocque's report. I will send news along as it becomes available. In the meantime, we all wish Richard a speedy recovery.

Fred'

'Richard was released from St. Jo's last night at about 11 p.m. There is a fracture, so he'll be back in today for an MRI. He was pretty tired out, and in some pain, but his spirits were good! Steve and I were there, and ironically Ian was also there as his girlfriend was quite ill with a flue bug. Four fnb members in total at emerg at once.

I'll keep you posted. john (Larocque)'

'So sorry to hear this news. It's dangerous on the pitching mound! My wife doesn't care if I won or lost, just that I'm not maimed when I get home on Friday night. Give Richard my best to whoever sees him. It took courage [for me] to get back out there after being hit two Fridays ago.

Warren'

Stephen Breitner received a text message from Richard a while ago and the news is good. Although he has sustained a fracture of the cheekbone, the MRI he had today indicates that he will heal well. It's just going to take time; not sure how much time at this stage, but at least we are certain that there should not be any long term issues.

I have received a number of responses to my earlier email and will pass along best wishes to Richard from all. For those not present last evening, I can tell you that we stopped playing immediately and our discussion for much of the rest of the evening centered around protecting our pitchers. Two weeks ago, Warren narrowly averted disaster on a similar play, so what we are seeing is really powerful hits up the middle, where reaction time can be impossibly short. Nelles has wisely worn a protective mask for a number of seasons and we need to make this practice mandatory.

John LaRocque has said that he has a mask and will bring it next week. Craig had earlier posted a request for input regarding equipment and I will call him regarding this issue.

Get well soon, Richard. Our thoughts are with you.

Fred

Good to hear about Richard. All the best buddy.

I'm wondering if those new bats have anything to do with it. The ball seems to really jump off them. There's been HR's from guys who don't normally hit them

> and more screaming line drives. I don't think any of this is coincidental.
>
> I'm for retiring them immediately. Warren
>
> Hello fellow FNB'ers. I am writing this in response to the outpouring of support I have received from guys in the league. I thank you all for the emails and get wells you have been sending me and it just goes to show how much of a family the league is. I would like to give a huge thank you to Steven for driving me to the St. Joseph's hospital and waiting there for three hours while I was being examined by doctors and also to John L. who showed up to the hospital as well. To shed a little light on my injury, I was hit on the right cheek and suffered a small fracture on the cheek bone. It missed my nose and eye so there were no complications or any surgery required. After the MRI the doctor told me it would take a month to be completely recovered and back to normal as an injury like this can only be healed by time on its own. I did not suffer a concussion and I feel very lucky considering how bad things could have been. Again I would like to thank everyone for the support and hope to see you all on the field in the near future.
>
> Richard.

I was aware of a sadness afterwards, knowing that such things are possible in the game we love. Maybe some of the sadness was there because of the fear they might cause us to withdraw from life. I was reminded of one of the great underrated movies, *Pleasantville.* It's about a sitcom of the same name where life is pretty much the way it was in *Father Knows Best.* It starts out in black and white and as it opens to the rich complexity of the human condition, it gradually changes from black and white to colour, suggesting that life is both dangerous and beautiful as opposed to Pleasantville which is merely pleasant. I'm all too fond of pleasant, so it was a tough pill to swallow, but I still recall sections of that movie as clearly as the photo of Richard's shiner.

Tournament Sept 22, 2013

Every season has its own personality. This one will likely be remembered for the rain. We worried that the pattern might prevail for The Tournament. It rained hard on Saturday, but Sunday's forecast called for sun and cloud. John L, Richard and I got to the park shortly after nine to find Craig, who'd been there since eight, along with Lorne. There'd been water in the batter's box, which they had pretty much cleared out, but there was another large patch behind short and smaller patch in near third base, all of which we took care of before start time. Thanks to both, though they were unable to do much about the temperature - a chilly high of 13 with a wind and not much sun.

In Game One, it was Team One versus Team Two. We went down one, two, three in the top of the first, and didn't hit a well the rest of the way, but we kept it close thanks to two double plays. Marc H's near-to-impossible shoestring catch where we doubled up the runner on first, and Eric's bases loaded grab of a hot grounder where he stepped on first and threw home to get the runner trying to score from third. We tied it in the top of the fifth. A pretty piece of hitting from Fred who dumped an outside pitch into left to keep the rally going. Marc Hershoran's long drive to centre tied it up. It would have been a home run except for Richard's perfect throw to the plate. Mark Riddle was the first guy up in the bottom of the fifth and I was thinking, 'Don't catch too much of the plate.' Frank set up just off the outside corner. I thought it was a good pitch, but Mark drove it far into the gap in left centre. I still see him rounding third on his wobbly knees running faster than he had all season.

The team that loses the first game always plays the second game. Two pops ups behind second and miserable little piece of shit which dropped in front of short led to a five run first. In the second inning I hit a piece of shit of my own behind second, but was happy to take it. It was 9-6 in the top of the fifth and we knew we had to hold them to have a chance - which we did thanks in part to Eric's somewhat amazing catch of Billy's pop foul pop behind first. I saw the ball go up and Eric turn to go after it. It appeared certain he wasn't going to get his body in position, but at the last second he managed to spin just enough to get his glove on it. It was a big momentum changer and we came out loaded for bear in the bottom of the fifth. With two out and two on base, Ken came to the plate with Marc H on deck. Marc was our hot hitter and I was looking forward to seeing him come up representing the winning run. Ken hit a rope and our hearts soared, but straight to Chatz at short and that was all she wrote. None of us took it badly, knowing we'd played well and helped create two sweet games.

Game three looked like a runaway for team two with John L's guys up by ten in the bottom of the fourth. The first two games had been close and I wanted this one to follow suit. I was thinking it was too much too ask, but John St J had other thoughts.

> I knew we were in trouble when Warren slammed down his glove for the second time. His frustration was palpable. ('It's those two-strike hits I hate. I was mad at myself,' he said later.) Then he channeled that frustration, like no one else can, into a focused, bulldog determination to win the damn game no matter what. And so he got himself to 3rd in the bottom of the 5th and, fittingly, trotted home, arms raised, on Lorne's shot to the gap that ended a terrific

> contest between two well-matched teams. Though Warren will want to share credit for the win equally with his plucky come-from-behinders, they wouldn't have done it without him.

Got this from Warren.

> "I appreciate John's words. There are two reasons I get so …ahem…pumped up when I'm pitching. First is my respect for the league and the players in our league. I always want to give my best for my teammates and give my best out of respect for the other team. Second is the fact that if I didn't, I would be batted around like a piñata and be giving up 5 runs every inning. Don't want that to happen.
>
> As far as winning the tournament, Team 3 was excited at the end because it IS a big deal. It matters because it's so damn hard to win two games on the biggest day of the year. And when you win close games it takes big contributions from every single player or it's not going to happen. Everyone on Team 3 made an important defensive play, got a key hit, took an extra base or showed enough class and patience to take a walk and keep the line moving. Congratulations to every player on all the teams last Sunday for a great day of baseball.

Lorne's thoughts.

> I was very aware of Warren's presence on third as Wayne popped out and I limped to bat with two out. I pulled a hamstring earlier in the game and had Eric run for me. I was having a problem picking up Richard's lefty low

> outside pitches and got to two strikes. I wasn't sure if we were going to go extra innings if it was a tie. Warren had pitched so hard that I thought an extra inning would be very tough for him while Richard was still fairly fresh. I noticed that the outfield was playing me shallow. The one thing I didn't want to do other than strike out was hit a pretty fly ball to right field. I was expecting another outside pitch so I adjusted my wrists and left leg. I got the pitch I wanted.
>
> I'm limping around today with a pulled, hopefully not torn, hamstring muscle. Small price to pay for a great day. As all the other humble heroes say 'it was a team effort. Amen."
>
> Lorne

Got this from Peter Roach a few hours later. (Peter played with us in the late seventies and early eighties before he moved to Stratford. He always comes back for The Tournament.)

> "I always enjoy the year end tournament and appreciate your invitation to join you. This year was a particularly good tournament. Sharp hitting (Lorne you don't pull right anymore. We should learn), good defence. The double play with the bases loaded stands out. Damn you Eric. And the third base scoop on a scorcher from me and the long throw to nab me at first. Who is that lady?. (Her name is Kristy.) The pitching was great. The knuckleball from Warren was a wonder to behold as I watched it float by and dive over the plate). Nelles pitched like a demon. I know I got a good hit off of him but that at bat had me sweating with curves and drops and the prospect

of an ignominious strikeout. Nelles told me he would get back at me for the three hits two years ago and he doesn't seem to forget. Maybe when I'm 80. Nothing better than close games well played win or lose. Nelles thanks for the song. I had tears in my eyes and so did Susan when I played it for her. See you all next year."

There was a quietly powerful feeling in Frank's and Susan's kitchen as the day of baseball settled into mind and body. Having you all there to hear my version of 'Take Me out to the Ball Game' was different from holding Warren's guys scoreless in the top of the fifth to give us a chance to win. Maybe I shouldn't say it was better, but my heart was out there for all to see and to have it welcomed so warmly is something I wont forget.

My take on 'Take Me Out to the Ball Game' was inspired by Larry Goldings' solo piano version which I first heard on 'Radio Deluxe', the program which originates high above Lexington Avenue in the living room of John Pizzarelli and his partner Jessica Molasky. Larry plays it slowly with the feeling of someone who loves the game. I took it even slower than Larry with just bass, uke and guitar. Second time through I added some narrative over the melody:

Grass, sky, sun and the feeling summer will never end. Well you know they say the ball game is never over till the last man is out. Theoretically speaking, if the game never ended, the players would never die and Lou Gehrig and Shoeless Joe would still be with us.

And it's root, root, root for the old guys,
If they don't win it's a shame.
It aint over till it's over
At the old ball game.

To top it all off, if anything could top the rest, Ken Pagel's daughter Julia (rising star journalist) was with us for the day putting together a story. She said she wasn't sure it would fly, but she thought it might be interesting to see what unfolded. I got an email from Frank saying we were going to be on CBC's Metro morning at 6:25 A.M. Unfortunately, I slept past the hour, but got a call from Judy Grant an old friend from U of T days, saying she and her husband had heard it. I got the podcast from Ken on Friday morning and sailed through the rest of the day with it resonating through my bones. It was still resonating at Amicos during our first off season gathering. As we were leaving, a woman who'd been sitting across from us asked us if we were the guys she'd heard on the radio. We said yes and verified the report that we had been playing for forty years. She said that was the same age she was.

P.S. Got an email from Michele Alderton who works at the Heritage Centre up in Red Lake where I grew up. She'd heard Julia's story on CBC Thunder Bay and said Ron Buckler would be happy to know I was still playing softball. Ron was one of the best pitchers in the country. When the district all star teams went to tournaments in Winnipeg, Minnesota, Regina and other places I don't recall, they rode Ron's arm to victory. One night, he was throwing a no hitter against Madsen and I broke it up with a line drive into the gap in the ninth inning. I was feeling pretty proud of myself when we shook hands. He said, 'I guess I shouldn't have thrown the change up.' I was thinking, 'Was that a change up?'

Jan 12/ 2014: Apart from the wonderful tournament, what I remember most about 2013 is how quickly it came and went. I remember something – from a poem or story – while I was studying Anglo Saxon at U of T about a bird flying in through a window and out through another, symbolic of the brevity of our life on earth: 'Swa haet naefre waere.' (As if it never were.) Apologies to John Leyerle, my Anglo Saxon prof, if I butchered the original.

13

Sluggo

Fri May 23/14: It was tied at two at the end of the third aided by some fine plays in the field by Sandy, Mark, Fred and Chatz. They put up a four in the top of the fourth. Our rally to make it close came to an end with a double play aided by someone (me) forgetting how many outs there were. With the earliness of the season, the rusty joints and the sadness of Doug's death, four innings felt like enough.

At Amicos, Fred, Frank, Lorne, John St J, Craig, Sandy, Mike M, Mark R, Chatz, Austin, and I talked about Doug aka Sluggo and his full tilt, rough and tumble ways under which lay a surprising sensitivity. For Sluggo, there were no stop signs on the base paths whether running or coaching. It was always full speed ahead. Football was his natural sport and he translated the dynamics of football into his version of FNB. It wasn't aggression so much as joy. He was outgoing and friendly, a gentle soul at heart even when rounding third or taking that mighty swing. I love the heartfelt simplicity of Warren's email:

'Can't fully accept that it happened. Sluggo wouldn't take no for an answer when it came to me playing on Friday nights. I finally gave in and thanked him profusely every time I saw him. Always thought Doug was a little larger than life and I was always somewhat in awe of his energy and enthusiasm. Wish I could be there tonight. Hope someone turns a single into a triple in Sluggo's honour.'

I had spoken to Warren a couple of times about FNB without much luck. When he told me it was Sluggo who'd got him to join us, I could see them meeting on the sidewalk. Clearly it happened more than once and Sluggo's perpetual enthusiasm prevailed over the stubborn thing in Warren that was resisting. Only Sluggo could have managed it. If he'd sold Warren a new roof in the process so much the better. He sold me a new kitchen, although come to think of it, it was more like he let me sell it to myself.

Thurs, May 29/14: Sluggo's funeral was 11 A.M. yesterday at the St John the Baptist Church on Woodbine. There were about twenty FNB people there, some from earlier days - Bob McKenzie, Tom Christopher, Donnie Crawford, Ray Kerr and Sluggo's brother-in-law, Rick Traugott. The priest was Phillip McKenna who was also the priest at Doug and Jane's wedding. His opening address hit all the tough, paradoxical notes. There were touching tributes from Jane, his daughter Katherine, his brother-in-law David, his sister Karen, his good friend Ken Ludlow, as well as a few words from me on his connection with Friday Night Baseball. Afterwards we gathered at the Toronto Balmy Beach Canoe Club, Sluggo's second home. The beer and good feelings flowed freely as he would have wished. Towards the end of the afternoon, I sat in a lounge chair and thought about Sluggo playing volley ball on the beach and raised my eyes to see Lake Ontario extending to the horizon and meeting the sky.

The Monkey Mind, The Universe, Peter Hajdasz, Falls

May 30/14: The ump called out, Play ball!' and the first two pitches sailed over the batter's head? I remembered that thing about 'beginner's mind'. Every time is the first time no matter how many times you've done it. There's also the 'monkey mind', the nonstop thinker that doesn't know when enough is enough. What you want to do is empty the mind, which is not lack or loss, rather the capacity to be in the moment, along with the importance of the eyes, which must be focused outward, the difference between looking and seeing. I had some success with that, although it didn't stop me from throwing a three and two riser into the dirt.

It was good having Gilles back, slim and fit after a year's work inhibiting the enemies of his heart. I saw signs of the return of the tantalizing curve - as seen in his strike out of the mighty Mark R. The best play of the night was Wayne's grab of Warren's vicious liner down the third base line. His head went down and his glove went up creating the illusion of a leap, but it was actually a duck of a most judicious nature, leaving one to wonder how his glove knew where the ball was.

P.S. Remember tuning into a segment of the Paraplegic Olympics and heard a voice saying, 'Don't look down at your feet, look up at the stars.' Guessed, I'm pretty sure correctly, that the voice was Stephen Hawking's and knew immediately this was wonderful stuff. Not the monkey mind, the mind free to travel to the furthest reaches of the universe.

June 13/14: Austin has decided to retire. He turns 80 next February. Met with him for lunch on Tuesday to talk about life and art. He said my blog uses baseball as a reference point for the universe. One day I will compress space and time into nine well played innings.

June 20/14: The summer solstice called for a beautiful game, but what beauty can be found in four mercy innings in a row? Can a day in June be all bad? John Larocque made a nice catch in centre and doubled up the runner at first. Peter (new guy) Hajdasz fielded a ball in left and threw a strike to third where Wayne caught the ball on one hop and put down the tag. Mark R caught three pop ups behind the plate. Watching him flip back the mask, track the ball and snare it securely, beauty once again. There was a fourth pop up in front of him which he kept insisting he should have caught. I had to keep reminding him the ball was half way down the first base line.

Pete Hajdasz, the new guy, lives in one of the condos overlooking the park and can see the diamond from his balcony. He said it was a great game and was thrilled to be playing something a notch up from slo pitch. We talked briefly about his work situation which more than usually stressful. He sees us as an oasis of sanity.

We were a loud and merry crew at Amicos. Checked in with Frank who has the okay from the doc to play on the twenty-seventh. With the eye and the fall, he has had a rough ride of it, but is happy about getting back behind the plate. Something beautiful about that also.

Forget whether or not I mentioned the fall down the basement stairs which left him unable to talk. A couple of weeks in the hospital and a lot of hard work with his speech therapist.

June 27/14: I had a fall of my own getting out of bed on Tuesday and bruised a rib. That plus the humidity plus the usual resistance had me moving tentatively in the direction of the park. At Amicos Mike Marino said it would be a good idea for us to stop getting older.

McCormick Park, Molson Indy, Richard's Gem, Muenori Kawasaki, Eric Hellman

July 4/14: At six, we'd been short of players when we noticed a couple of young guys at the next diamond. It turned out their team hadn't showed up and we asked them to join us. Their names are Gagan and Andre. They had a good time and we've added them to the subs list.

July 11/14: It was an exclusion day at Coronation Park. Frank contacted city hall and the woman he talked to gave us McCormick Park south of Dundas near Dufferin. The diamond is pretty, with a red brick dust infield and lots of green, but the alarm bells went off when I saw the sidewalk behind the short porch in centre field and the row of houses not far from first base. Worse than either, the playground behind home plate which brought back memories of the foul ball that came down inches away from a baby carriage at

Viewmount. We appointed a player from the batting team to patrol the playground and pray.

Martin visiting from Australia, his only baseball experience the day he played with us four years ago, made a shoestring catch of Fred's liner into shallow right. Ash, friend of Martin, who's played almost no baseball, had some nice moments based on sheer athleticism. Amanda (Ash's friend) did a wonderful job with the score book. Frank said her work was so remarkable that she owed it to herself to take on the role for keeps. At Amicos, Martin said the conversation about the pizza toppings sounded the same as it did the last time he was with us four years ago.

The same, but not exactly the same. Everything is a theme and variations; FNB is a theme and variations; Amicos is a theme and variations; our life on earth is a theme and variations; the universe is a theme and variations. What is the theme? 'Fools rush in where angels fear to tread.' Better to let it rest quietly among the pizza toppings.

July 18/14: It was the weekend of the Molson Indy. At five to six the noise from the Formula Ones was so loud you couldn't hear the ump or the third base coach or anyone else. At Amicos, Lorne talked about being the hero of last year's tournament. He thinks about it every day. I scolded him for tooting his own horn. He retreated into modesty, but he sounded better when he was tooting. We contemplated the year's high scores and Mark mentioned that he was telling Warren that fifteen years ago, it was more along the lines of 6-5, 8-4, 9-7. After which he lamented being walked twice on four straight pitches. I promised better things next time. He gave me my instructions: 'A pitch away at the thighs and tell me when it's coming.'

July 25/14: Whata whata whata game! It began with misplays and bloops, and although it tightened up after that, no one could have foreseen the unbelievable finish. Us had gone ahead by two in the top of the seventh and Them scored two to tie it. The winning run was on third, in the person of Fred, with one out when the batter squibbed a pitch towards third base about two thirds of the way down the line. From where I was at rover, I could see Fred heading for home, but it wasn't Fred who caught my eye so much as Richard moving off the mound towards the ball and I was thinking, 'Nice try, but no cigar.' I saw Frank setting up on the plate expecting the ball, and wondered why bother because Richard's momentum was taking him away from the plate. I thought maybe he was thinking about making one of those backhand flips you sometimes see on MLB highlight reels which middle infielders use to get the force at second, but I could see the ball sailing well out of Frank's reach. But the ball I saw was not the real ball which had been backhanded in a perfect arc into Frank's glove. I'd seen it and I'd seen the ump make the call, but the incredible thing that had led to these indisputable facts mere seconds earlier was so close to impossible that I literally could not believe my eyes.

Remember Devon White's catch in the '92 World Series? Amazing in and of itself, but after climbing the wall, he threw the ball back to the infield to double off Terry Pendleton. John Olerud threw to third to trap Deion Saunders between second and third. The ump, perhaps believing that the odds against what his eyes had witnessed were close to infinite, signaled safe. I still see Gruber stretched flat against the ground and the ball grazing Saunder's heel. It was a moment where truth and beauty merge to burn with a gem like flame.

The "gem like" reference is from the nineteenth century critic, Walter Pater. I first came across it as a grad student at U of T. I looked it up on the net and found the passage it's taken from:

> Not the fruit of experience, but experience itself is the end. A counted number of pulses only is given to us in a variegated, dramatic life. How may we see in them all that is to be seen in them by the finest senses. How shall we pass swiftly from point to point, and

> be present always where the greatest number of vital forces unite_in their purest energy. To burn always with this hard, gem like flame, to maintain this ecstasy is success in life.

If you Google 'Devon White' you'll see 'Devon White catch' and you'll get 78,300,000 results. So far there aren't any results for Richard and (or for Jack's magical effort in the 2004 tournament) and I thought it only right to enshrine it to the best of my means. In the meantime, I'll bet the house that John St J is thinking about Derek Jeter's play vs Oakland game 3 of the 2001 ALCS. The batter drives the ball into the right field corner. One camera shows the fielder making the throw and another camera shows the baserunner headed for third while one of the announcers says, 'They're sending Giambi!' You see the ball miss both cutoff men and you see Giambi coming towards home. You see the ball in the catcher's glove, but you don't know how it got there. It's only in the replay that you notice Jeter on the edge of the screen. He's moved all the way from short to be there. You could call it 'presence of mind', or 'being in the moment', but words don't catch its perfect completeness.

Saw it again on one of those 'Fifty Greatest' compilations. It was even better than I'd remembered. Jeter didn't have time to turn and make the throw to home. He caught ball in his bare hand and shoveled it underhand while turning.

Back to July 25, 2014 with the score tied, two out and a runner at third. My version doesn't do justice to the gem like moment and I asked Richard to add his impressions.

> "As I was walking out to the mound in the bottom of the seventh with a 2 run lead, there was only one thing I was feeling. In the past this would have been nerves and the fear of giving up runs, but tonight

it was confidence. I›d be lying if I told you the thought of last year's playoff game didn›t creep into my mind, then quickly extinguish as I knew I had a job to do. The last two innings we had shut the other guys down and I was finding the strike zone with my fastball. A solid defensive effort from our team gave me a calming focus on what was important, concentrating on the batter.

After getting ahead in the count, the first two batters reached base with tough grounders that skipped through our infield. I still had a calming sense of confidence and knew we were in fine shape to close the game out. I ignored the fact they had good speed at second and first as my focus was locked in on the next batter. Lorne walked up to the plate and someone on the opposing team's bench yelled out for an encore of last years marvelous playoff winning walk-off. Still focused, still confident but with none out, I knew it wouldn't be easy. Despite Frank and I trying to keep the ball on the edge of the plate and away from Lorne's bat, the thought popped into my mind that I could beat him with some heat. I guessed wrong and he made me pay once again as he drove in a run with a single and moved the runner into scoring position at third.

With none out, the sight of the game slipping away was staring me in the face. I told myself all we needed was that first one, just get that first out, get that first out and the rest will fall into place. The first one came with the next batter, but at a costly exchange. It was an infield single, the only play being at first allowing the runner on third to score. Tie game, runner at third, no force and the outfield in. The last two hours spent playing ball suddenly disappeared from memory and the walls closed in. Like glass in a vice, it felt like the game had slowly squeezed me to its uncomfortable moment of truth.

Still focused, and the batter in the box, I delivered a first pitch strike. Knowing the power the batter commanded, I reached back for something extra and ended up putting the next one in the dirt. I sent one at the inside corner and it was fouled off ~ one and two. My slider hadn't been working much, but I chose to go with it anyway. He swung and the sound of the bat making contact made my heart skip a beat. The ball squibbed off the end of the bat and came bouncing down the third base line fair. Without hesitation to see what side of the line it would end up on, I made a charge. Scooping up the ball halfway down the third base line facing the dugout the split decision whether to shovel the ball straight out of my glove for a quick release, or transfer it to my throwing hand and send a sidearm toss down to home for a little more accuracy wasn't made any easier knowing I had to do this all while on the run. I opted for the latter. Tumbling over the line I strained every muscle in my body to watch how this story would unfold.

Taking the moment in with an image that will never leave me and a testament as to why we play this game, the ball landed squarely in Frank's glove, his feet planted with assurance on home plate catching the runner before he crossed home. A wave of alleviation flowed over me as the pressures of the game loosened their grip. We didn't win, but there was a sense of vindication knowing we had stolen one away from the other guys.

Looking forward to the next day at the Diamond."

At the pub it was Mark R, Fred, Frank, Lorne and I. Fred who said Warren told him he was demoting himself to Triple A for sending him home, but we all agreed that he'd made the right call since the odds of Richard's making the play were somewhere between miniscule and impossible. I don't remember what else we talked about, except that it seemed important at the time and I was hoping Amico's had abandoned its entertainment policy so we could do more of it. In the meantime, I'd noticed an attractive young woman talking to someone about the sound system. She turned out to be Katy Morely and she quickly won us over and got us to sing along to 'Helpless' and 'A Sentimental Journey'. We really got into it and she said, 'Great singing guys.'

Fri Aug 1/14: The last thing on my mind when I left the house at 4:15 was rain. I could see Frank emptying a bag of balls on the mound as I crossed Lake Shore Boulevard, but it wasn't till I got all the way across the diamond that I looked back and saw a solid bank of dark clouds to the north. Frank had been talking to Ken who told him it was raining hard in Orangeville. Steve Shapiro who had a huge part in getting us organized back in the late '70's and early '80's was down from Ottawa and planning to join us. He saw the same sky we did and figured there wouldn't be a game.

We'd have packed it in, but the sky to the west was lighter and there was a chance the bad stuff would miss us and we decided on scrub. Two batters later Fred hit a liner straight at me. There was a loud clunk as it hit the bottom of my mask. I was thinking I should be scared, but I was still standing and nothing hurt. Fred said he'd hit it hard, so it's likely I absorbed a good bit of the force with my glove. Next time up, he leaned way out over the plate and pulled an outside pitch weakly down the first base line. He was thinking anywhere but back at the pitcher. I didn't protest. We did well to keep the ball moving for an hour or so, but it was a mere shadow of last week's game, one of those nights when I wonder if we play because the beer tastes better.

At Amicos, we got talking about catchers. Who was the best of all time? Johnny Bench, Yogi, Carlton (Pudge) Fisk? I was thinking Fisk, then remembered the other Pudge, Pudge Rodriguez. We figured Fisk was a lock to be have caught the most games since a lot of good hitting catchers end up playing other positions. Bench moved to third and Yogi played a fair bit of left field. Marc H consulted his phone. Pudge R played one more game than Pudge Fisk who played one more game than Bob Boone.

We continued with some Jays Talk. It's hard to leave Muenori Kawasaki out of the discussion which reminded me of David Ortiz arriving safely at third and picking him up with a big bear hug. That's got to be a one and only. Later, Big Pappy said he and Kawasaki had been out to dinner and Kawasaki had kept him laughing the whole time. It's what we try to do at Amicos - if we don't achieve laughter we do manage to at least entertain each other. Have we ever come out on the losing end over beer and pizza? Not that I remember, though it's hard to beat the days at Giorgio's back in the eighties with the big table and the widow looking out on Dupont Street and all-time favourite waitress, Yvonne.

Muenori Kawasaki is the Japanese journeyman called up from Buffalo for a long cup of coffee. His fielding skills were good, not great, and his hitting was not up to the major league level, but he played with unbridled joy. Every catch every throw, every at bat a thing to be treasured.

Walter Goes Four for Four, Katy Morely

Aug 8/14: Another perfect day for baseball, but come ten to six there are just thirteen of us. I'm warming up with Frank and spot Warren who's supposed to be on the DL. 'What about doctor's orders?'

'I got a second opinion from my neighbor.'

We line up at six to see what we can put together and I see Chatz coming from behind the chain link fence at first (aka the cornfield) with two guys (Zak and Rob) who were playing catch on diamond two. We're up by five in the top of the seventh, not a huge lead in our game. Mike Marino starts the inning with an off field hit. The next batter hits a sharp ground ball to Bill D's right at second. He makes a backhand snare, turns, and throws a strike to first in one motion. Zak is up next and lines a bullet to Eric at first. That ball is moving folks. That ball is a Boob Boom Geoffrion slap shot. No matter. Eric does the splits and gets his glove hand out to make the save. The next guy hits one to Bill, who picks it clean and throws another strike to first.

As I walk to the infield to shake hands I see Mike coming down the line. He's already talking, laughing before he gets to me and he can hardly restrain himself. Something about what he heard me say to the outfielders and what he did as a reaction. I don't know what he's talking about and I wonder what made him so damn happy. It isn't till later, on the way to Amico's with Fred, that I remember I'd told the guys playing left and center to shift to the right because Mike always pulls the ball. He hit a lazy fly down near the foul line which I could have caught if I hadn't shifted so far towards center. He'd done exactly what he wanted to do. It was a great piece of hitting and that's another reason why we play this game. There's the good stuff and the not so good stuff, and now and then there's one of those gem like things that makes the game special.

Walter had one of those games three weeks ago. He told me about it at Amicos as we were heading out the door. He went four for four and I hadn't mentioned it in my blog and damn it, he wanted to read about it. Sometimes, probably more often than I think, I miss something memorable.

The Ex is upon us, starts next week. I was sure we were going to escape for one more week. Turns out Labor Day falls on Sept 1 this year.

Aug 15/14: Come game time, enough players had emerged from the cornfield to get started. It went along pretty well for three innings, but I had the worst inning of my career in the top of the fourth. There's always a sadness when you don't play well which is different from the disappointment of losing.

Every pitcher who has ever played this game has had the feeling he couldn't throw a strike if his life depended on it. I see major leaguers, relief pitchers with miniscule ERA's, fighting themselves and the ball and the batter and the ump and the catcher and the pitching coach and the crowd, fighting the events and decisions leading to this moment, fighting the game itself, the dirt, the grass, the sky, fighting the universe and everything in it and walking in the winning run. I'm inclined to rant at such displays of incompetence and have to remind myself I know the feeling all too well.

It was a long game and when we got to Amico's Katy Morley was setting up in front of the big window that looks out on Queen Street. There was a guy with a guitar setting up with her and I was thinking I liked her better alone, but the guitar guy turned out to be something special. I could tell the minute he started warming up that he had a beautiful touch - as if he couldn't play a wrong note if he tried. The musical highlight of the evening was a version of 'Blue Bayou' in which we were Katy's backup singers (just fifteen feet from stardom.) My seafood pasta arrived just before the other guys got their pizza which helped atone for the lateness of last week's pork chops. We got talking about Woodstock and heard that Walter had been there and had climbed six fences and got up on stage (carrying a jug of wine) pretending to be an electrician. At some point Katy said it was wonderful to see friends having a good time together and Lorne couldn't resist telling her I'd conked him on the head.

On the way home with Fred, I wondered if my pitching career has come to an end, but he was more interested in sharing his love of music than quieting my pitching woes and dialed up Mahler's tenth symphony. I've never heard so rich a mixture of dread and beauty. The big bang, too awful and immeasurable to imagine, and along with it the wonder of our life on earth and the seeming impossibility of so glorious a thing as baseball emerging from the chaos.

FNB vs Couch

Aug 22/14: It's a chore, at this late stage, getting ready for the game. Every day is a journey, but Fridays are more so. I assist Ray Bakey with his Tai Chi Health Recovery class from 12:30 to 2:00, though it's always longer than that because I like to eat my lunch while people are arriving and I don't like to rush away. Normally, come four in the afternoon, I'm ready to wind down, have a glass of wine and think about supper. Four o'clock on Friday, it's time to start moving. I'm a slow starter and even something as simple as putting on my jock and shin pads and changing my shoes is an act of will.

The St Clair street car has got to win the prize for contrariness. Every time I get to the corner, I see one I've just missed, or there's one on its way and its light is green and my light is red and I can't get to the platform in time, or there's no car in sight. It gets better when I'm in my seat and I can start my *Toronto Star* crossword. I can fill in a few squares on the way to the St Clair West subway. From there I go south and take the Bloor subway to Bathurst. Most days I can get a seat on the Exhibition car and it's a nice challenge to see if I can finish the crossword before I get to the park, though all that's somewhat misleading because this Friday the Ex is on and I take a taxi. But it doesn't matter if it's a taxi or a street car. Like being on a train, once you're on it, you're going where it's going. The question is, are you just going along for the ride or do you really wanna be there.

Sometimes I'm the first one there and it means I have time to relax. More often, I'll see Frank and Lorne unloading the equipment and Fred getting ready to put in the bases. Funny how the game starts to sneak up on me. Just saying hello to Frank is a start. Lately, I've taken_on the responsibility of putting in the pitcher's rubber. Pacing off the forty-five feet_and lining it up with second and home plate. At some point I do some Tai Chi, but there's still a resistance. Pushing against some something that's in the way that you're not sure you can get rid of, but you've done it before, so maybe you can do it again.

By now, Eric and Mike and George and Mark R are emerging from the corn stalks and there'll be eight or so of us playing catch and it's time to see if Frank has finished his pre-game exercises and warm me up. Funny how the flip side of resisting is wanting to rush it and get it over with. Rushing wont get you there. It's a false arrival, a presence without substance. The game will not open for you if you don't get to the door with a willing mind. It will come crashing down on you before you know it's there. Sometimes it comes crashing down on you anyway.

First innings. Where pitchers find their rhythm or don't. Seems to me I've had a lot of mercy rule beginnings this year. This time around, I felt pretty good. I hit most of my spots - not as many as Mark R (catching for me in Frank's absence) wanted but most. Just one hard hit ball and a lot of stuff that dropped in or found the holes and it was another five run first. It's not as bad if you're feeling good. What I like about Mark Buerhle. Doesn't matter if they hit him or not, his demeanor never changes. (I'm more like Dave Steib, which wouldn't be so bad if I had his slider.) The five run first felt better after we put up a five of our own. The five came against Warren whose five innings were mysterious in the sense that he had two five run innings and three no run innings and said afterwards that he'd felt about the same in all of them. Somewhere in the midst of the unpredictability, he snared Fred's line drive, reaching across his body it looked like he'd stretched halfway to first. Everyone called out, 'Highlight reel.'

My memory of the sixth is fuzzy, but I remember the score was tied when we took the field in the top of the seventh. I was playing rover, aware that it was an open inning and the mercy rule wouldn't be in effect. You can start the inning with the game still tight and have the roof fall in with nothing to protect you from the debris - which looked about to happen with one out and a runner on second and a tough hitter at the plate. The hitter hit a ground ball to Hugh who threw to Eric at first to get the out. Meanwhile the runner had run through the stop sign and tried to score all the way from second. Eric saw it and threw him out at the plate. It was then I realized how far I'd travelled since dragging myself into the shower at seven thirty this morning. The game had me. There was no escaping it. I was in it win or lose. In the bottom of the seventh, the batting order was Mark R, me and Hugh. Mark hit the ball hard, but there was an outfielder there to catch it. Last time up I'd swing at an inside pitch and popped out to Chatz at short. I'd been talking with Marc H about being patient at the plate. In the midst of my advice I found myself admitting how hard it is to lay off John L's stuff when it drifts just out of the strike zone. It's got a big sign on it that says, 'Hit me', and you feel like a dope you when hit some silly little piece of crap. This time I laid off the first one. The second was low and I somehow got down far enough to hit it hard, close to Stephen at third, but too hot to handle.

I'm on first base in the bottom of the seventh representing the winning run, feeling as if I'm being powered by some extra-terrestrial force. Mike M's got a blown rotator cuff that's never fully healed. I know what throwing with a blown rotator cuff feels like. It hurts and the ball has no force. I run on the first pitch and see George move towards second. Mike has somehow coaxed a big throw from the blown shoulder. I get my foot on second just before the tag, but it's close and I'm not sure if the ump saw it. There's a lot of chatter and I'm not sure where it's coming from, our bench or the guys on the other team. I stay where I am. No one tells me to leave. The voices are clearer now and no one can believe I've stolen second.

Hugh is up next and singles sharply through the infield. I'm ready to make the turn at third, but John St J gives me the stop sign. Danny is next. He lines the ball to Luke in centre. There's always an instinct that tells you to run on a fly ball, but it's a dumb thing to leave the bag before you see whether the ball is caught. If it falls in, you're going to score anyway. If you don't tag up, you have to go back to the bag and that's often the difference between being safe or out. I've seen major leaguers make that mistake, but not me. I tag up and see Luke move into position to make the catch. He makes a great throw, but the extraterrestrial force gets me across the plate just ahead of it and it's a walk off one run victory.

The game was still in my bones as we headed back to Amicos. I told the guys how I'd been feeling in the morning and how it's always an effort these days and how amazed I was to be standing on first base knowing all that mattered was the game. Fred said my steal was thing of beauty and not to be modest about it in my blog. As you may have noticed, I wasn't.

John Updike, Babe Ruth, Philadelphia Soul

I've received a couple of emails, simply but elegantly written, from Dave Bolland about his golf game. In one of them he wrote, 'Writing is fun isn't it?' I had fun writing this week's bit. It was a lot like what I wrote about getting ready for the game, tough at the beginning, but when it got going it was like it was writing itself. I like to read in my yard. I don't have the much to be wished for back yard, but I do have a front yard, with three large spreading yew trees providing privacy from the sidewalk. I like to pretend that instead of the street there's water - maybe just a river or a creek. I've got a lawn chair and a tiny flagstone patio and a little picnic table and I like to go out there just before supper with a book and a glass of vermouth.

At Amicos I sometimes talk with George about what he's reading. (Always more than I am.) He loaned me *A Confederacy of Dunces* which I didn't really get into, but it got me telling him about John Updike. When I was in third year at U of T, my modern novels prof, John Carroll, enthused about two books we all ought to read over the summer: *Catch 22* and *Rabbit, Run*. I read them both and still love them both, but there's something about *Rabbit, Run* that's stayed with me all this time and I'm still not sure what it is, and will probably never be sure, but telling George about it got me thinking I'd like to go back to it. Which I did, only to understand it's a whole different book when you're seventy-five than it was at twenty-two. Still wonderful, but Rabbit is a big kid and so was I was and still am, but now I can see it. Updike wrote a sequel some ten years later, *Rabbit Redux*. I read that too, though many years ago.

I learned Updike wrote a Rabbit novel every ten years, four in all, and eventually combined them into one long novel called *Rabbit Angstrom*. (He also wrote a novella, *Rabbit Remembered*, after Rabbit's death.) I didn't remember a whole lot about *Rabbit Redux*, and decided to reread it. All the way through, I kept hearing myself say, 'Holy shit!' at the sheer mastery of the writing, even though at times, I found it somewhat dense. In the course of the novel Rabbit's wife, Janice, has an affair; he gets involved with a black Viet Nam vet and a runaway eighteen year old girl; his sister, Mim, who's a Las Vegas hooker comes home to be with the mother who's suffering from Parkinson's and he finds out Mim's life, which he expected would be a mess, is more together than his. In the meantime, Janice who was a mouse in *Rabbit, Run*, has been fucking her brains out with this terrific guy and she's loved every minute, but she knows it's over and she wants to come back and there's a scene where she and Rabbit are discussing what to do.

There's been a fire at the house - probably set by some Nam vet who didn't like the idea of the black guy and the white girl living in Rabbit's house. He was okay with fighting shoulder to shoulder with blacks in the jungle, 'but the rules are different here.' With no house to go back to, Harry (Rabbit's real name is Harry) and Janice end up going to a motel and it's funny because they're married and he feels guilty because he figures the motel owner thinks they're shacking up and he doesn't want to upset him. Janice tells him, 'People screw, Harry, it's where babies come from. When are you going to grow up?'

Do they make love? He would like to and she would like to, but guilt and desire are difficult bedmates and they fall asleep. I turned the page and I saw, *Rabbit Is Rich* in bold print which is the title of the next novel and I realized that *Rabbit Redux* was over. I thought (once again), 'Holy shit! What a beautiful novel.' Not pretty. Beautiful.

As you may know Updike died a few years ago. He was 76. Just a bit more than a year older than I am as of this writing. Not that I'm in a big hurry to join him, but I wanted him to know how much I loved the book. I thought about what state he might be in and decided that when you die, you somehow stay connected to the moments you lived most intensely and for Updike, though I know little of his personal life, those moments would likely be when he was writing. I figured there would be a kind of glow about it and that when someone says 'Holy shit, what a beautiful piece of writing', the glow wouldn't get brighter, it would get warmer. Because, sure, who doesn't want fame? But what he did, he did out of love and I'm doing what I love, sitting in my back yard on my flagstone patio with a glass of vermouth on a perfect late summer afternoon and it's here and now and it's what I felt when I was writing about our game, and it's not exactly wrong to do something because you know it will get you attention, but it's best to do it out of love because you're just being yourself. And that, too, is a journey.

Aug 29/14: Warren had a three pop fly first inning. I had a release point which had disappeared along with the parking spots. I enjoyed the third inning though. The other guys were subbing a second basemen and made all three outs. Sandy, back from the DL, made some slick plays at first and hit a ball right at Marc H in deep centre, but the thing about it was the effortlessness. So often hitters muscle it. Take the easy swing, hit the ball on the sweet spot and it's like you've discovered the secret of life. Reminds me of the year Joe Carter came out of spring training with an ankle (or maybe it was a wrist) injury. Remember how he used to pull the low inside pitch a hundred and twenty miles an hour three feet foul? That spring all those balls were fair and I wondered if the injury forced him to be more relaxed.

Late in the game, I was in centre with Richard's other pal, Wilmer, next to me in right. There was a fly ball that looked like it had a chance to drop in behind him, I called out, 'Go back!' and he got there in time to get his glove on it. It was the third out and he was standing there with the ball looking puzzled because he didn't know who to throw it to. He's brand new at this game, but catching on fast. John St James drove a pitch into the gap in left center. He scored soon after and came back to the bench with a worried look. I told him about it and he said, 'Worried! It was the best hit I got all year.' I think it happened before Richard and crew arrived and the worried look was due to the absence of a third base coach - which at seven a side, is usually the same guy who's keeping score.

Richard moved backwards and to his left to snare a ground ball and turned to make the throw to first. These days if I ever did something like that, I'd write a book about it, not just the mere nine pages I coaxed out of last week's steal of second. On the other hand, how old is he? Twenty-five? Maybe Lorne and I and anyone else over seventy should get a medal (what would we name it?) for keeping Richard (and Danny and Wilmer and Luke and Stephen) on their toes. Anyone over sixty should get honorable mention.

There was no sign of Katy Morley when we got to Amicos. It was the same guy as last week who's big into Philadelphia Soul. Before he arrived, Chatz reminded us he will be doing a yoga workshop in Cape Cod for the next two Fridays, but promised to be back for the tournament. Frank and Fred spoke affectionately of their dogs and Lorne mentioned the Babe Ruth Brother Matthias connection which is of special interest to him because like Lorne, Brother Matthias's roots are in Cape Breton. We were just getting nicely into it when Philadelphia Soul launched into concert mode. He was in Massey Hall and we were in the tenth row with fifteen hundred other people. It's hard to tell a good story in a sound storm.

While sitting in my yard with my vermouth and my book the next evening, I thought about the conversation with Lorne. I was reading *Rabbit Is Rich*, inspired by the quality of the writing and thinking it was foolish to try to rise to that level, but I figured, what the hey, I am not John Updike, nor was meant to be, but there's a kind of free floating narrative I've been dabbling with and who knows where it could lead. I sat down at the computer for ten minutes or so and typed faster than I can.

I'm sitting in a nice little Italian restaurant with my baseball pals, and Lorne who's from Cape Breton, mentions the piece in the Sydney newspaper about Babe Ruth and Brother Matthias. There's a guy singing and playing the guitar in front of the window that looks out on Queen Street. He's about ten feet from where I'm sitting. He's got a great voice and he plays well and knows a lot of songs I don't, which is okay, I might like something I've never heard before. The thing is, he's on full mic and amp and it's as if he's in an arena playing in front of fifteen thousand people and I understand. He's a talent and he wants to be heard, deserves to be heard, but please God, not now, not here, not us. I'm trying to talk to Lorne about Babe. How they made two movies about him and they were okay but neither of them hit the mark like *The Lou Gehrig Story* or *Shoeless Joe* and I've often wondered why not. Maybe because tragic stories touch us in a way heroic ones don't.

Babe was a figure of mythical proportions. He changed the game, he hit fifty-nine home runs in 1921, when the most anyone had ever hit before that was twenty-nine and the guy who hit the twenty-nine was Babe. He hit sixty in 1927. He hit the fabled called shot in the 1932 World Series. The movie made a big deal out of the called shot, but the movie didn't get to the heart of the matter and I'm trying to tell Lorne the heart of matter for Babe was the relationship with Brother Matthias who Lorne tells me was six foot six and weighed two hundred fifty pounds. Babe was a tough kid, they said he was incorrigible, but he was no match for this guy. Brother M knew Babe was a natural hitter but thought it would serve him well to learn the art of pitching, the mental side, the need for control.

The first time I heard about Babe I was eight or nine, playing scrub on the mill tailings beside the club house before I was much good at baseball. I loved being out there with the big kids anyway. One night one of them hit one close to the water tower and Aileen Leonard said it was just like Babe Ruth. I'd never heard of him and when I got home, I asked my mother who he was. She said in the best way she could that he was someone special, but the writers in *Sport* magazine said Ty Cobb was a better player. It wasn't till I read Robert Creamer's biography many years later that I realized how good Babe was. His fifty-nine home runs in 1921 were accompanied by a batting average of .378 and an .846 slugging percentage. Creamer calls it the best year of any hitter in major league history. He was also the best left handed pitcher of his time. In 1916, he was 23-12 with an ERA of 1.75 and nine shutouts. He also had an insatiable appetite for beer, hot dogs, cars and women. Movies often make their subjects larger than life. Babe was already larger than life.

The thing about telling a story, is getting to the heart of it. In *Rabbit Is Rich* we see (once again) that Harry and Janice, are seriously flawed people, but Updike makes you love them and in doing so, has conferred a blessing upon the reader. Who among us is perfect? We struggle honorably, achieving occasional moments of magnificence, but most of the time we grind it out with our B game. Or worse. No doubt the guy in front of the window has had moments with the audience in the palm of his hands, Philadelphia soul people, who loved every minute and kept calling for more. On Friday August 29, 2014, he was at Amicos and no one was listening.

On the way home Fred and I picked up the Jays game. It was well past dark, June a distant memory, and the Jays were losing. On Saturday, the jets from the CNE air show thundered through the afternoon. The weather was warm, the summer we didn't have, perhaps a promise for a more of the same, perhaps telling me, as well, that it's too soon to give up on my curve ball, likely also stirring up in many of us the old dream of doing something special (magnificent might be too much to ask) in the tournament.

Field of Dreams, Stephen's Baseball Buzz, The Battle of the Bulge

Sept 5/14: I keep forgetting that *Field of Dreams* ends with the Kevin Costner character playing catch with his dad. When I was ten, I nearly died of a ruptured appendix. I remember looking out the hospital window in late February with everything cold and still. When I came home, dad and I went down the basement every night after supper and he taught me_how to pitch. There was something special about the arrival of spring that year, like being born into another world where I was still Nelles, but suddenly and amazingly no longer just Nelles. I was Nelles, the the pitcher.

There's still something of the same feeling the first time we get out on the field to start a new season. In September, there isn't the same raw promise, but our skills have been honed. Each of us bringing something of our own. The young guys, energy and enthusiasm, the old guys experience and longstanding devotion. With Mark it's the passion and the knowledge from all the years of Senior A ball in Quebec. Frank has the enthusiasm of the young guys along with thirty-five years behind the plate, a longer career than his dad. For Lorne, who's helping Frank lug the equipment these days, it's a lifelong love of the game, developed in the baseball rich tradition of Cape Breton where he played Little League and saw his name in the papers.

There was a lot of scoring and a fair share of shaky defense, but it was lovely the way the game went back and forth with the outcome in doubt to the end. And lovely too, the weather which had been depressingly hot and humid all day but cooled down just enough to have Frank, sitting beside me on the bench say, 'Perfect night for baseball,' not just once, but twice, then having to hurry as a bank of dark clouds edged closer. Fred and Mark R and I were just a few hundred yards alongLake Shore Blvd when the lightning began dancing across a black sky. The rain wasn't far behind. It was still raining when we got to Frank's place. We decided to go straight to Amico's and unload the equipment later.

Lorne and I picked up where we'd left off last week about his Cape Breton connection with Brother Matthias and Babe Ruth. I said maybe the real story was Lorne and The Babe. I was probably thinking about John Updike and how it feels when a writer keeps striking the words clean and true. Lorne mentioned he'd read *Rabbit, Run in* his twenties, along with Philip Roth, because he felt lost with no idea about what he wanted to do with his life. He thought writers of their stature could supply him with much needed guidance, only to discover that the protagonists were more fucked up than he was. Somewhere among the talk and the songs and the TV screen and the general restaurant babble I heard the words, 'To be human is to be fucked up.' The words were Lorne's and it was as if someone had rung a bell that no one had heard but me. I threw up the stop sign and said, 'Say it again, Lorne.' Maybe it's too rough and raw a way of putting it, so maybe you had to be there, but I like it better than 'To err is human.' However, it occurred to me later that it implies a corollary. 'If you're Cape Breton Presbyterian, you think you're fucked up even if you're not.'

Sept 12/14: Stephen came to bat with two out in the last inning and hit a double into the gap which drove in tying and winning runs. On the way back to Frank's place to unload the equipment, he said he had a baseball buzz and there'd been butterflies when he came to bat with the game on the line. He's learning quickly that if you enter the game and embrace it, it happens inside you. Hugh postponed the drive back to London and joined us at Amicos. He mentioned on the way while listening to the radio, he'd heard about the greatest game ever pitched. I thought he was going to say it was Harvey Haddix's twelve perfect innings May 26, 1959, which ended with Joe Adcock's home run in the 13th. It's still my bet for the greatest game ever pitched by one pitcher. The game Hugh was talking about was a sixteen inning pitching duel between Warren Spahn and Juan Marichal, July 2, 1963, which ended with a Willie Mays home run. Spahn was forty-two. He was 23-7 that year and 363-245 for his career which lasted twenty-one years. It would have been longer had he not spent three years in the army during WW II. He fought in the Battle of the Bulge, a brutal campaign with 89,000 American casualties and 19,000 deaths. He had three bullet wounds and would occasionally pull up his jersey to reveal the scars. He often said that the pressure of pitching a big league ball game was nothing compared to that: 'No one is shooting at me.'

14

Tournament
Sunday, Sept 21, 2014

This one almost didn't happen. The fact that it did is testament to whatever it is that keeps us going over forty years after our inception, for which reason it gets a chapter all to itself.

THE TARP

The Weather Network forecasts the weather a week in advance. There's a band of icons on the top of the screen: one showing the sun, one showing a cloud, one showing a cloud with raindrops and so on. The one you hate shows a cloud with raindrops and lightning. About half way down you see the temperature. At the bottom of the chart, you see "POP" which stands for "probability of precipitation". I stopped checking half way through the week because I kept seeing the sun icon, a high of 23 and a POP of next to nothing. I thought about the years - there were at least five of them - when hurricanes were moving up the Atlantic seaboard, and was happy to know there'd be no need to go into emergency mode with last second phone calls and emails Sunday morning. I was jolted out of my complacence by Craig's email sent 10:59 A.M. Saturday:

I'm attaching this note to Fred address list about tomorrow's tournament; this after playing some wonderful ball last night at Coronation 3. After the game, we gathered to talk about the tournament, and Frank made it clear that, this year, there is no other date/field available to us. It is more than likely that Coronation 2 will be drenched from overnight thunderstorms; and that Sunday itself will be nip 'n tuck with regards to scattered showers. However, I have a thought to stave off the disappointment of arriving at the park to an unplayable infield: Why not tarp it overnight as do the 'bigs' of MLB? I recently had my roof redone and, in the process had to purchase the largest blue tarp made as a temporary roof while the guys waited for dry weather. Though I could man-handle the tarp and spread out the tarp, myself, it would be much easier if a couple of guys could meet me down at Coronation later this afternoon 6 PM.

Saturday afternoon, I drove down to 84 Wilson Park to help Frank and Lorne make the hamburgers. We talked about what we'd do if we got rained out and decided that at the very least, we'd gather at Frank's and Susan's for the barbecue. I mentioned Craig's email and my intention to help with the tarp. There was another email from Craig when I got home.

Peter Hajdasz, who lives in a condo just across the street, just called me from Coronation Park reporting that the traffic was absolutely crazy down there. He was there in case Luke and I showed up at 6 PM and wanted an extra hand with the laying of the tarp. I will now drive down at 9:30 PM and rendezvous with Peter and a friend of his. They have offered to help with the tarp. Peter also told me that no one was playing on the diamond (at least not now, at 6:40 PM) and he was pretty confident that nobody else would be using the diamond later this evening.

Craig and Peter went to the park at nine and secured four tarps at home plate, the mound, second and third bases.

THE RAIN

The Weather Network had called for the rain to begin in the evening and continue through till morning. I got up at five thirty and found an email from Frank.

Hi: I walked my two dogs and it was not raining when we left. It was, strongly, on our return. Craig asks what we will do if rain continues. I think we will get to the park, see what happens, and play when we can. If we cannot play, then I say we start the BBQ here at 3:00. We have all the burgers made, all the hot dogs ready, and folks have said they will be bringing various kinds of salads. So: onward and upward whatever happens. A lot of beer here to drink.

It was still coming down at nine. Not a downpour, but steady along with a solid bank of cloud to the west. I'd thought about joining Frank at the house, but figured I'd be more comfortable at home. If the weather changed, I'd take a taxi to the park. A couple of minutes later, the doorbell rang. It was John Larocque. I thought about telling him he was on a fool's errand, but got in the car instead. As we drove west along St Clair, the solid band of cloud was still there, looking stubborn and immoveable. It looked just as stubborn when we turned south on Lansdowne, but about halfway to Queen street, we saw clouds breaking up south of us. When we got the house, Fred was there along with Anna who'd driven down from Huntsville. Frank sent out another email:

> Hi: It›s 9:40. Sandy has called from the park to say it's OK. We are heading out to the park now. So, please come if you can.

I don't remember what I saw first when I got to the park. The water or Wayne and Sandy trying to get rid of it. Come to think of it, it was the blue tarp, but it was a lot smaller than I'd imagined. I guess it was smaller than Craig had imagined too, but big enough to cover the area around home plate. Along with the smaller tarps on the mound and at second and third, it was a step in the right direction. More important, it symbolized our determination to make whatever we could of the day. That, too, is what Wayne and Sandy were thinking, Sandy with a big bristled push broom moving the water away from first, and Wayne with a shovel making a drainage ditch behind second. I'd brought along a small pail to bail with and went after the pool behind third. I wasn't sure it was making a difference, but it seemed important to keep going.

Meanwhile, a few others had shown up, among them Chatz, who was uncharacteristically pessimistic.

> Early Sunday morning listening to the rain, tournament day checking the forecast many times. There is no way we are going to play. What to do now? What the **** am I going to do? Prepare, make the salad and sandwiches. Down to the ballpark to check it out. Got to be with the guys. Miserable, sad, irritated as I am driving with Heidi on the way to the park. Drop off Heidi at her exercise class. I arrive. Craig had laid the tarp with help of Pete the evening before. See Sandy and Wayne digging and making trenches to clear the infield, the rain pouring down. These guys are nuts!! Nelles arrives and I say, there is no way we are playing if the clouds remain. The outfield will not dry unless the sun shines.

THE SUN

It happened so suddenly. There was grey and then there was blue. We didn't even have time to wonder if we'd been witness to a miracle. Chatz had left to drop the car off to Heidi, but had given me his cell phone number just in case.

> I get the message from Nelles on my cell that something is happening, the guys are showing up. I arrive and there are 20 guys assembled and ready to go! Wow!"

THE GAMES

Game One: It was somewhere near 10:30 when Chatz got back to the park. He hadn't been there to see the guys arrive. I was there and I didn't see them either. They'd walked out of the cornstalks when I wasn't looking. Sandy saw them. Maybe he knew all along. Twenty was enough for two full teams plus a rover. Forget scrub, there was going to be a game. If more guys appeared, we could play two. Even in the midst of a miracle, three seemed to much to ask for. Fred had other ideas:

'How many guys are here from Team One? How many from Team Two? How many from Team Three?'

It was like the rain had never happened. The feeling, I mean. Knowing that in ten minutes I'd be pitching in the tournament and wanting very badly to do well. Not enjoying the pressure, but riding with the excitement. Nothing I do requires as much sustained effort and concentration and punishes the failure to execute so persistently. At the barbecue, Warren told me he was almost hoping it would keep raining - that thing about expectations and the fear of failure. It's like that in the eight other positions when your team is in desperate need of an out and you're not keen about seeing the ball coming your way, but for a pitcher the pressure is relentless.

That having been said, I felt good warming up. I had a one two three first inning - a hot ground ball to Fred at third, Richard's running catch of a shallow fly ball and another good play I've forgotten. We got the first two outs in the top of the second, but John St James got a hit prompting Sandy to come over and say I didn't have to worry anymore about the no hitter. A couple of batters later, a run scored which meant I didn't have to worry about the shutout either. Two hitters later, the bases were loaded. At times such as that, my mind makes a bee line to the worst case scenario. I did my best to slow down the bees and let my defense get the third out. It came on a ground ball to second that new guy Rob had to stick out a leg to stop.

On the other side, John Larocque also had a one, two, three first inning. A tough luck mercy rule second put us up by five, but John kept his composure and we didn't do a lot after that. On his good days, and he has a lot of those, he puts the ball where he wants to. When I came to bat, I was aware of not feeling comfortable. Nothing he threw me was in my wheelhouse. If I was going to put the ball in play, I'd have to adjust my swing and, more important, not go for the stuff that was coming in just out of the strike zone. We took the field in the top of the fifth up by five. Chatz put down a near perfect bunt and Mark H hit a pop up in front of me that I couldn't get to. Two on, nobody out. Somewhere among thoughts of an open inning disaster, it occurred to me that the game happens one pitch at a time. What Leo Mazzone said about Greg Maddux. 'He makes pitches.' I didn't make all my pitches, but I made enough, and the defense did the rest. Chatz and Mark scored, but we got the last out on a ground ball to new guy Hugh at short. I turned to see him get down, look the ball into his glove and make a perfect throw to Sandy at first.

Somebody must have provided the offence for our guys, but it wasn't me. I remember Sandy hitting the ball hard to right field, and I'm guessing Richard, Stephen and Sandy got key hits. On the other side, I have a clear memory of John St James who's been on a tear since early August, pulling an outside pitch into left. I was trying hard, very hard, to keep the ball away from Mark R., but watched in horror as a would-be outside pitch went right down the middle. He was putting on his catcher's gear between innings and I told him he'd never see another pitch like that from me as long as I live. He came up later in the game. Same damn thing.

After all the thoughts about the perils of being a pitcher, I feel honor bound to add that pitching well is deeply satisfying. There were times this summer when I thought my mound career was coming to an end, most notably the fourth inning on August fifteenth, when I couldn't throw a strike. It made pitching well in the tournament a bit sweeter than usual, one strikeout in particular, a three and two rise ball on the inside corner to get a tough hitter. I was surprised, but realized later it was a helluva a pitch. I thought about it on Monday, Tuesday, Wednesday, Thursday. Today is Friday and I'm still thinking about it.

Game Two: Gilles had looked good on Friday. Warming up with Frank and me, he had better stuff than I did. He had a one two, three, first inning in Game Two and it looked as if we were going to see a pitcher's duel. When he came back to pitch the second, he'd lost his release point. He battled to get it back, but it was one of those days where you try too hard and think too much. I was keeping score, hoping his team would make a game of it. There was a ray of hope, though it was more like a lightning bolt, when a pitch exploded off a bat and sailed fifty feet behind the left fielder. I was thinking, "Who the hell hit that?" I saw a guy in a white jersey running down the first base line and it took a moment to realize the guy was Wayne. I'd seen him pull the ball hard, usually against me, but this one was in another category. As if it came from some unseen place Wayne had contacted in a rare and magical moment, one of those things that turns you into a mystic. Wayne might also have been wondering where it came from as he rounded third and twisted his knee. He had to sit out the rest of the game, but what a way to go. John Larocque came back to pitch when Gilles bowed out, and quieted the big bats, but Warren was pitching well for the other guys and his defense was solid and they were looking like the team to beat.

Game Three: With the uncertainty around the weather, we were a few players short and did more than the usual amount of substituting. It's something I hate overseeing on Tournament day when my focus needs to be on the game not administration. I agreed at the beginning of game three Chatz could play along side Fred on the left side of their infield, something I swore I would never let happen to my team again as long as I live, but I knew they had to be strong at shortstop. Somewhere along the way I realized they also had Mark H in left along with Luke in right, Zak in left and Craig at rover. All in all, it was one heck of a team. On the other hand, we had the Richard factor. He's pitching better each time out and was on an end of season home run tear. We were solid all through the order and I knew Warren had his work cut out for him.

By now the sun was positioned over the backstop which was tough on the outfielders. Peter H had moved to centre field, Danny was left, Ken in right and I was playing rover. Peter had to run in and get low to make a catch. He was just behind me and I heard him say, 'I didn't see that ball.' He made it look easy, but it was a great catch. There was an SUV on the lane and the sun was bouncing off the windshield. I saw a ball shallow fly ball drifting over second there was an awful moment when I didn't know where it was. I'm still not sure how it ended up in my glove.

It was the second inning, I think, when they got their mercy rule five. Come the top of the fifth, I was surprised to learn the score was just 9-5. It was the opening inning and anything was possible. Richard walked and scored on Hugh's single. They got the next guy, but Stephen hit the ball hard and I was thinking the rally was on. It would have kept going if not for a great play to get Hugh trying to take third. Somewhere in all that Eric, playing first, ran half way to home to catch a pop up. He's been nursing a bone bruise and has been using a pinch runner. I called out my concern for his health and advised him to take it easy. He thanked me for my good intentions and continued in his heedless ways.

It was wonderful to be out there, and it's fun to be writing about it, but there's a lot of good stuff I don't remember and so asked Warren to jog my memory.

> I felt I pitched well both games but it was team 2's defense that stands out to me. Hard hit grounders gathered up neatly by all the infielders. Stephen not flinching as he streaked across the field to snag a liner in traffic. Luke fighting the sun, the wind and the

> ball to make a spectacular over the shoulder catch. Luke's perfect throw to Chatz who made a perfect throw to Fred to make a crucial second out in the final game. All the big two out hits we got in both games to keep the inning alive and extend our lead. Anna's tough catch – acting like she had been playing all year - on a popup that snuffed out yet another rally. Eric calming me down when he realized I was starting to get hyper.
>
> I don't tend to remember the good pitches I make but I do remember the ones that get hit hard. I hung a knuckleball to Richard that as I recall bounced off the roof of the washroom in right field. Until I see video evidence to the contrary that's how I'll remember it. I've hung knuckle-balls all season long. It still takes a great hitter to square it up like that.
>
> I remember the sound of the line drive Stephen hit head high just to my left. It had a menacing hissing sound that I never want to hear again. I remember Wayne and Mark making great swings and hitting rockets on what I considered to be very good pitches.
>
> I remember during the tournament feeling a fraternal pride in how well Nelles, John and Richard pitched and feeling Gilles' pain at not being able to find the proper release point – a lonely place every pitcher has visited more than once.

There was also a key double play that was a big momentum changer. I asked Fred to provide the details.

> I believe it was in the 3rd inning, with nobody out and runners at first and second. It was a 5-6-3 play (Chatz to me to Eric) that was pivotal, as it erased 2 runners and effectively ended what could have been a strong rally. Although I am not sure who the batter was, my enduring memory is Warren pumping his fist as the batter was called out at first (by less than half a step).

Other Stuff: One of the difference makers in Game Three was new guy Zak who got two big hits to right. Lorne was disappointed with his day at the plate, but his swing looked good from where I was. Could be it's his eyes, or maybe just being too tough on himself. (There's a rumor about his being Babe Ruth's nephew, so maybe the expectations are getting to him.) When he finally hit one on the screws, it went straight into an outfielders glove. Sandy wasn't saying much but he looked stiff and sore. He said something about having missed one tournament (because of his back) and not wanting to miss another..

There was a big pile of bricks behind the dugout. Craig and Peter had used them to hold down the tarp. It was a lot of carrying for just two guys. At the end of the day, some of us helped him carry them back to the car. Craig congratulated me for carrying two loads. It was the least I could do after his efforts the night before. Walter showed up with one of his dogs. He figures his leg will stay in the cast another six weeks. It will be a happy day when he can walk the dogs again. Some players from another league showed up at about 11:30. Someone loaned them the big push brooms so they could get rid of the water on Diamond 3. All the same, I was surprised at what the sun can do. The field was completely dry by noon.

Bill D had a fall while riding his bike, and was too sore to join us. Mike Marino had an important family obligation. I was hoping to see Austin. Maybe the rain scared him off, but he was there for the barbecue with Marilyn. Marilyn likes my blog (some episodes less the others). Austin has written a memoir which has given him much satisfaction and is now content just being. Is that the same as serenity? Serenity is what my long time Ryerson colleague, John Cook, said was his primary retirement goal. I mentioned that to Austin, but forgot to add that John bikes several times a week with a group of friends.

THE BARBECUE

I'd been thinking I this section should be titled 'The Celebration', but the whole day is a celebration. Thanks to Frank and Susan, the barbecue has taken on a meaning all its own going back to the tournaments at Bindertwine Park and the house on Windrush Road and the backyard as big as the eye could see. We were there from the early eighties until the move to 84 Wilson Park Rd. It's wonderful the way the Wilson Park kitchen opened onto the deck and the barbecues are as congenial as ever - there's an intimacy about the deck - but the Windrush days remain a large and special part of our history. We'd been at Wilson Park for a few years when Frank wrote about attending Pierre Berton's funeral and being asked to drive Lister Sinclair back to the city. I'd never thought of us in the light of *Peter Pan,* but the audience's willingness to suspend their disbelief to save Tinker Bell has a good deal to do with men becoming boys again. Along with the counterpoint of the play's heartrending conclusion wherein Peter tells Wendy he has some magic powder that will allow her to fly away with him and she says, 'I'm sorry. I got old, I couldn't help it.' No wonder Frank nearly drove off the road, suddenly confronted with subtle, potent mixture of truth and beauty which lies at the heart of great art.

The mixture was with us on this day as well. All summer long, Gilles had been working on his painting of Doug, sending us progress reports along the way and ending up doing not one painting but five, wanting passionately, desperately to find the means to capture

Doug aka Sluggo, the guy who rounded third with an impulsive joy that was impervious to stop signs. Gilles' efforts put me in mind, once again, of the Walter Pater passage from my blog of August twenty-fifth.

> To burn always with this hard, gem like flame, to maintain this ecstasy is success in life.

For the artist the task is twofold: not only to live in the moment, but to live in the moment of creation as well. And for all of us on this day, the challenge was to be present for Gilles, and present as well for Doug's wife, Jane. We knew it was going to be a tough day for her and hoped it would be rewarding, possibly cathartic. There were a lot of us in the kitchen, including Jane's sisters, Helen and Ginny and her daughter, Katharine, who had come to give much needed support, but my memory, as the painting is unveiled, sees Gilles and Jane. Gilles offering his heart and soul, overcome with emotion for a moment, but finding his voice, talking with charm and humour, and offering not only the painting but a smaller, self supporting bookshelf version, with replicas of all five paintings, and on the other side two photos, one of Doug and one of Jane on their wedding day. And Jane coming to the front of the room, saying she was not a speech maker and finding the right words anyway. Said she never had a date on Friday night because Sluggo was with us and could never understand why it was so darn important to him, but over the years had begun to understand and never more so than today.

I don't know what Walter Pater would have to say about the beer and burgers, or the change in the weather and the talk and the deck, but it's my belief that the gemlike flame burns more softly in the midst of festivity. The greatest number of vital forces in their purest energy is a tough order. The feeling in Frank and Susan's kitchen was warmer, more comfortable. Frank cooks with ardor and flair, but a kitchen without a woman to tell us how wonderful we are is not the same. Susan has been there all these years, opening the door, happy to see us, enjoying our camaraderie. No welcome sign needed, it's there in her smile, in her eyes.

We got the news on Monday that Gilles had a stroke last week. The good news is that there's been no brain damage or loss of movement. Nicole is keeping us posted on his recovery which is going well. This along with news Peter Roach has been diagnosed with melanoma. Somewhere in all of this is Frank's lost eye and as if that weren't enough, the fall last December. In both cases, many of us wondered if we'd ever see him behind the plate again. He put on the shin guards and the chest protector and the mask this spring and the spring before that and in the space of a few pitches he was Frank the catcher again, and it was easy to forget what a rough road he'd travelled.

Frank, Fred, John St James, Chatz, Mike, Wayne, Lorne and I got together at Amicos last Friday for our first off season meeting. We talked about the civic election and the MLB playoffs with the usual enthusiasm, but drifted inevitably to the tournament and it was clear the day was still with us. Wayne talked about digging the drainage ditch with the rain coming down. Forget whether he said he thought he was crazy, but it wouldn't surprise me. There was some other good talk which would get lost in translation, but I'm guessing that everyone who showed up that Sunday thought there was a good chance they were making a futile gesture. Here's Lorne's take:

> Like everyone else I'm disappointed to wake up to the sound of rain pounding down. I'm confused. What are we going to do. I was to pick up Frank and the equipment at 8:30 am. Frank called about 7:30 to discuss the situation. Not looking good at all. Depressing. We can't decide on anything more than to wait and see. Confusion. Frank calls again at 8:00 am. Still no decision. Raining like hell. No hope. We'd have to be crazy to go the ball field. More depressed.

> More confused. I go back to bed, not able to face the day. Can't sleep. At 8:30, Frank calls again. Fred's at his place. We're going. Come and get the equipment. Still crazy after all these years. I'm a seventy-four year old kid. Too late to change. What the hell, I'll go. Loading the equipment at Frank's, still raining, we see a break in the clouds. Off we go. What a sight as we approach the field to see Sandy, Wayne, Craig and other crazies clearing the field. I didn't play as well as I hoped, but what a day.

Heard someone on the CBC put forward the thesis that because of the internet, History will no longer frame itself around the lives of famous persons. Historians now have the world wide web and social media at their disposal. For the purposes of History, if you're not on the net, you don't exist. One day this account of our miraculous day will hit the net and go viral, so apologies to anyone whose endeavors didn't make the blog. I didn't list the names of the players in the normal manner because there was more than the usual amount of substitution. But here, for posterity, the players who took part in that most remarkable of days.

Frank, Ken, Sandy, Hugh, Stephen, Richard, Peter H, Rob Baral, Warren, Anna, Eric, George, Fred, Luke, Craig, Zak, John Larocque, Mark, Lorne, Danny, Chatz, Wayne, Mark H, Gilles, John St J, Nelles.

15

Bill Davidovitz

The fall that kept Bill from joining us in the miracle tournament was likely related to his struggle with Alzheimer's. The diagnosis had come some years earlier, before the rest of us were aware of it and while he was still doing good things at short. He was a solid performer at that demanding position for over forty years, a pesky hitter who hit the ball where it was pitched. His love of the game goes back a long way. I remember him talking about not having many other kids to play with. He would play catch all day with the schoolhouse wall, the backyard wall, any wall available, pretending he was Peewee Reese or Phil Rizzuto. I don't know if there were injuries back then, a scraped knee or bleeding elbow from a ball too zealously pursued, no doubt followed by adamant words of caution from his mother. But I do remember a broken leg in the eighties and a serious wrist injury in the nineties and perhaps another after that - serious enough to dampen the passion of a lesser celebrant, but Bill always came back the next spring. This time round, as it became clear it wouldn't be wise for him to continue, he'd say as much, then forget.

There is always the temptation to make sense out of what resists any pretense to meaning which I will forgo.

16

Nolan Ryan, Richard's Dad, Serena Williams, Taoist Tai Chi

Fri May 1/15: This winter it was hard to believe in spring. One day after another when we thought for sure we'd seen the end of minus twenty, only to have it show up again a day or two later. This February, more than usual, I needed to know that the pitchers and catchers had showed up for spring training. Part of me didn't think it would happen, that this was the year when winter had dealt baseball a fatal blow and spring along with it. I kept checking the papers and the games were being played and the familiar names, Batista, Encarnacion and Reyes were mixed with new ones, Martin, Donaldson, Norris, Castro. All the same, March was its usual stubborn self and the snow sat on the front yard grass like it owned the place. Is it harder believing when you're seventy-five? Is it a rebirth or just more of the same dull round? Taking my swings and missing the easiest of batting practice pitches, I was inclined to think it was the latter.

At Amico's we got talking about food and the goodness of quinoa and Fiesta Farms, the super market health food store, and steered to the Blue Jays and their unpredictable young pitchers. How did we get to Nolan Ryan? Maybe because we'd been talking about Mark Beurhle and his longevity. Ryan still threw in the high nineties when he was forty-two. He never became a finesse guy. Just the high hard one and the curve ball. I tossed out the idea of his being the embodiment of the tragic hero - the man who cannot settle for half and is compelled to test his powers beyond their limits. I have a clear memory of him walking off the field after giving up a grand slam homer. Was it the last pitch he ever threw? I think it was in Seattle, and the applause for the fallen warrior continued long after the cheer for the home town heroics.

It's such a storied game, baseball. There was a piece in *The Star* a few days ago about Babe Ruth's first major league home run, one hundred years ago, while he was pitching for the Red Sox. My favourite Jays story? How about Devo's catch and the triple play that should have been? My favourite FNB story? How about Gilles breaking a finger in game one of one of the Bindertwine Tournaments and returning from the hospital to be the winning pitcher in the final game? But enough of looking backward (for the moment). The past lives inside us but does not burn with a gem like flame. The flame burns in the here and now. Baseball is back and calls upon our belief once again.

Fri June 19/15, McCormick Park. With the cold damp weather in May and two rainouts in June, this felt like our first real game of the season. Jean Marc hit a two strike pitch over the fence to straight away centre. He hit another one the next at bat. He's the definitive ringer. The player who comes out of nowhere and whoever gets him wins. (Not exactly nowhere. Sandy called him because he knew we'd be short of bodies.) I struck out Fred with a change up during a long at bat in the fourth. He said he was waiting to see what I'd write about it.

It was a long game, but we were not inclined to stop given that we'd had so few innings to date. Hunter sat patiently behind the bench the whole time. When it was over, I saw him shaking and wondered if he'd got chilly. It wasn't the temperature, it was the frisbee which he knew Walter had put in hiding. When the time came, he showed why he'd be a cinch for frisbee gold in the All Dog Olympics.

Katy Morley was back at Amicos and we marveled once again at her way with a song and an audience and left her a hefty tip.

Fri June 26/15: After being rained out on June 5 and June 12, we were back at McCormick Park. There was a guy lodged behind the backstop who cheered whenever Richard threw a strike. I felt like going back there and telling him I was pitching against a guy fifty years younger than me. Turned out the guy was Richard's dad, so I guess he was allowed. There was no strike out of Fred this time round. I threw him another three and two change up and he hammered it a few feet foul before lining a base hit to right centre. John St James was back after getting his throwing hand in the way of a fly ball a couple of weeks ago. He dinged me for a two out gapper that put the icing on a mercy inning. He looked a tiny bit embarrassed about how happy he was to inflict the damage. At the end of four, we'd given up seven. Not too bad in our game, but we couldn't get anything going against Richard. Inspired by the presence of his dad, I guess. He added to his laurels with a homer that cleared the centre field fence and just missed a black VW Jetta.

Upstairs at Amicos there was a buzz around the table and in a moment of enthusiasm (?) impatience (?) childish bad temper (?) I went off the rails. I got back on pretty quick, but it surprises me how wound up I get sometimes get, but it's better than boredom. Although it's tough when the beer arrives just as you're ready to spring something wonderful.

Fri July 3/15: I had some anxious moments after talking to John Larocque about his conversation with a lawyer who used to live near McCormick Park. The lawyer's view is that McCormick is an all purpose field. The liability issues are more troubling than with a designated ball diamond. In the meantime, Eric had been cycling along side Coronation park and seen a group of people playing ball.

He emailed Frank who contacted City Hall and was told Coronation was ready for play. The infield is now red clay, a superior surface, firm but with some give.

Fri July 10/15: I started the day mindful that I'd be pitching at six and wanted to be present to the task. I arrived at the park with a touch of spring in my legs. When I warmed up, I was hitting my spots. Come game time, the first two pitches I threw went into the dirt. It was illuminating to read about Serena Williams sixth Wimbledon title. Five double faults in the first set. She said afterwards that there's a song she sings to herself. 'If I stop singing it, I usually start losing, then I go back to singing.' Pointing to her head. 'It's crazy up there. You don't want to be up there.'

Fri July 17/15: It had been raining off and on all day and was still raining at three when Fred elected to cancel the ump. Fred, Frank, Lorne and I met at Amicos and Sandy dropped by to share a glass. Somewhere along the way it seemed necessary to explain that I'd be missing on the 24th, that I'd be at The International Centre for a week of Tai Chi. For some of you this will be more significant than for others, but it so happens that the centre is the former Therafields farm. I was up there about twenty-five weekends a year and always felt better for it. Someone asked me to compare the two and I found myself saying they were both about self discovery. Later in the week it came to me that FNB has been also.

I arrived at the International Centre at five and hadn't been there more than ten minutes when I had a conversation with someone who'd experienced many of the anxiety issues I'd dealt with after my car accident in 1995. After supper we went upstairs to the practice hall where I talked with a young man from Columbus Ohio who'd been diagnosed with MS in 2011. His doctors had told him that the nerve connections between his brain and the muscles in his legs were deteriorating, but he'd learned from one of our senior instructors who is also a medical doctor that it's still possible to restore a connection between the brain and the legs through the stretching of the muscles and the tendons. The work he was able to do had given him hope.

A full day begins with chanting in the temple at 7:30. Breakfast is from 8 to 9 followed by clean up and dishwashing. The morning session goes from 10 to 12:30. Lunch is at 1. The afternoon session goes from 2:30 to 5:30. Supper is at 6. The evening session goes from 8 to 10. It's a full day, especially when you consider that we help with food preparation and dishwashing and cleaning, but there are half hour breaks in the sessions and a fair bit of explaining and demonstrating. Someone up from the city on the third day asked me how I was feeling and found the words for me. 'Sore, tired and happy.'

All of us had issues of one kind or another, some more serious than others, but the International Centre is a joyful place. I was asked to be part of a musical hour Monday evening and we put together (after ten minutes of rehearsal) 'The Health Recovery Anything Can Happen Band.' Ted from France, Simone from Switzerland, John from New Zealand, Blaise from Quebec, Nelles from Toronto.

In my absence, The Douglas (aka Sandy) captured the game with understated eloquence.

Fri July31/15: The day dawned with the sun smiling on those awaiting the appointed hour. Fourteen souls eager to engage in the weekly mind over achy joints and the rising fastball like wraiths filtered onto the red clay of the appointed diamond. What followed can be summed up in a paraphrase of Skip, the venerable coach of the Durham Bulls - the pitchers threw the ball, the batters hit the ball and for the most part, the fielders caught the ball. While the score mattered, the outcome didn't. As always, camaraderie and the love of the game prevailed.

As the dust settled and the accoutrements of the game were stuffed away - like the peal of Big Ben the question rang out - who's going to Amico's? Suds were poured and quaffed, salad / pizza /

special plates were ordered and devoured. Probably some more suds in there someplace and then it was hugs and cheers all around and an another beautiful Friday night went into the history books.

As my bestest friend has taught me to say - until the next 'play ball' is called - keep your chins up and faces to the sunshine.

Fri Aug 14/15: The Weather Network was calling for showers in the afternoon and evening, but Fred didn't cancel the ump. His faith was rewarded with a perfect day for baseball. Hugh drove from London to be with us once again. He mentioned he was with some people excited about the Jays Yankees game who were heading to the Wheat Sheaf Tavern. He was thinking, 'While you're watching, I'll be playing.'

Hugh is in his sixties, can handle hot ground balls to third or short and make the throw to first. Hits for power. Sweet, effortless swing. Can't think of anyone who lives as far away who's made the commute to be with us every week. Not a fierce competitor. A higher form of energy. Pure love of the game.

Fri Aug 21/15: Second week of the Ex. Traffic issues derailed the ump. The catcher's tough job was made tougher by having to call balls and strikes. Anna called a three and two strike on her dad which was up around his eyes. At Amicos, we learned that Eric will be moving back to Vancouver in November. He's been a wonder to watch, belying the ravages of time, getting better every year. He didn't echo Douglas MacArthur 's 'I shall return,' but hope springs eternal.

Tournament Friday Sept 20, 2015

Last year's tournament was a miracle. This year's unfolded naturally, blessed with perfect baseball weather.

Game 1: TEAM ONE vs TEAM TWO. We gave up five runs in the top of the first, but scored four in our half and the game tightened up the rest of the way. We were in trouble in the third or maybe it was the fourth. Stephen fielded a hard ground ball, stepped on third to get the force and threw home to cut down the runner trying to score. Frank had to get low to take the throw, ended up stretched out on the ground, but held on for the double play. In the bottom of the fourth, Pete's throw from deep centre beat Luke to the plate. We were up by one when I went out to pitch the top of the fifth - the dreaded open inning. I committed the sin of walking the lead off hitter, but we limited the damage to one.

I'm on the bench watching Lorne get set to lead off the inning and thinking a tie wouldn't be such a bad way to end it. I see him at the plate, and I know he's not the hitter he once was, on top of which he came to the park feeling weak from dealing with a nasty virus. Warren is throwing hard, making his pitches. There's some chatter, but it's a bit on the polite side. Then I see, we all see, the ball sailing to deep right field. In the days when he ran the hundred yards in ten flat, it would have been a walk off homer. Still, the winning run is on second with nobody out. The feeling on the bench is different now. The chatter is louder and there's more intention in our bats. Warren digs deep and gets two tough outs. Gagan comes up with Lorne on third. He fights off some good pitches and hits a two out, two strike pitch over second to score the winning run. It was the closest of close games. The kind Ted Bradan used to say it didn't matter which side you were on.

Game 2: TEAM TWO vs TEAM THREE. I kept thinking TEAM TWO would put together a big inning every time they came to bat, but whenever they got something going, the ball was hit right at some one. Between innings, I heard John L and Anna talking about pitch placement. Not sure exactly what was said, but they were definitely on the same page. Along with Warren's almost shutout a couple of years back, it was one of the most effective pitching performances in recent tournament history. I could have said "dominating", but "effective" is more in keeping with John's way of getting it done.

Game 3: TEAM ONE vs TEAM THREE: Not sure who was on base when Richard came to bat and hit a ball that landed twenty or thirty feet behind the narrow path behind the outfield and bounced onto the porch of the public washroom. When we came into bat in the top of the fifth, we were up by a run. Warren was keeping score and said, 'You guys need some insurance.' What I remember next is Lorne coming to the plate, with one out, nothing across, and Richard in the hole. Lorne hits a triple which scores a run, but if we're talking insurance, that's still not comfortable. Richard gets his shot and hits another homer. We've got our insurance. Good thing because Hugh's drive to deep left would have cleared the bases had not Luke been perfectly positioned. I was watching intently from the rover position and saw him flinch then recover to make the catch. I think he lost it in the sun for a moment. Kristy was next. She hadn't played much all year, but she'd hit the ball hard the last couple of times. There was a big bopper on deck and I was trying to send good thoughts to Richard on the mound. 'Don't overthrow,' 'Stay relaxed,' 'Let the body do the thinking.' He threw a perfect pitch on the outside corner to end it.

It was nice to win The Pig, but humbling to know how easily each game could have gone either way. No doubt some key moments have got lost even in this relatively short passage of time. Some appear ordinary at the moment, but set the stage for bigger things. Like Derek Bell's two out walk in the ninth inning in the second game of the '92 World Series. Derek was in Cito's dog house for his hot dog ways, a rookie whose enthusiasm was often unbridled, who would not have understood that discretion is the greater part of valor, but coaxed a walk off Geoff Reardon that set up Ed Sprague's game winning two run homer. In ninety-three the same Ed Sprague had a woeful World Series at the plate. In Game Six, with the Jays down by a run, he came to bat in the bottom of the eighth, and worked the count for a walk which guaranteed that the number nine hitter would not lead off the bottom of the ninth. Ricky Henderson got on base, Paul Molitor got a hit, bringing Joe Carter to the plate. His home run wont be forgotten, but it all got started with Sprague's base on balls.

It was a pleasant surprise to see Martin Peike and Stephania and their daughter at this year's tournament. Martin was my first therapist. I wasn't an easy task, but we hung in there, and after a year, we got to a better place. I reminded him of the Nobleton tournament. What does it mean when you strike out your therapist? That you've aced your therapy? I suggested as much and he informed me they were going to construct a monument in my honour to commemorate the occasion. I surmised he would be the principal donor.

It's wonderful to have a history and a joy to revisit it, but not as easy to capture the feeling of the day. The games lend themselves to story telling more readily. There are big plays and turning points, specifics which support the illusion of relived moments. The feeling on Frank's and Susan's deck is more elusive. Perhaps it begins with the house, a front door that opens and welcomes you. There are always dogs. In Bindertwine days it was Cheers and Belle, these days it's Joe and Sasha. But it's mostly Frank and Susan, happy to have us there.

I am on intimate terms with Frank's burgers. I go to 84 Wilson Park on Saturday afternoon to dig into the big bowl of ground beef and shape the patties. The beef comes from a neighbourhood butcher and is of the highest quality. Crushed garlic, chopped onions, freshly ground black pepper, a touch of sea salt, a dollop of dijon mustard. Almost forgot the eggs, necessary because they help hold the mix together, but which make the mixture somewhat squishy. I don't like squishy, but no matter, we dig our hands in and make the patties. Frank is a chef on a roll, preparing a feast for his friends. He's also an organizer. Who will bring salads, who will bring beer, who will bring wine? No one else is thinking about these things. We're busy packing the equipment, eager to get to Amico's and that first glass of

Amsterdam Blond. Frank knows better. We plan for the necessities of life, but also for celebration.

The talk has a resonance you don't get every day. It's enveloped by the table and chairs and the trees whose branches overhang the backyard deck. I see Jack the ump, and Jack Alvo, and Susan and Peter here once again from Stratford. Richard is here, looking a bit shy after his shining achievements on the field. John Larocque, who doesn't always stay very long, seems more relaxed, readier to take it all in. Eric calls for our attention. He tells us he's not sure if we appreciate this wonderful thing we have created. That he's played with other groups and nowhere has he found the mix of friendship and competition he's found with us. Later, newcomer Hugh, tells us he's played with a countless number of teams and he has never found a group in which the love of the game runs as deep.

And of course there's the cake with the miniature fielders and batter, the candles in the shape of a diamond, green icing to suggest the grass, with the anniversary number along the top. It comes from The Harbord Bakery. Susan says it's been so many years that they remember us when she places the order. I'm always called to cut the cake and say a few words. I'm a good performer and I enjoy the attention, but this time around I think about what Eric has just said. I can't say it any better and give the floor to Frank. He's so darn happy to have us there. He thanks Susan for her support and she tells us how much she enjoys the day. Stephen, who had not yet arrived on this earth when we started, tells us about watching us as he grew up and how much he has learned about the game (I think he also said about life) since he joined us. Anna tells us about watching us over the years, not just on the field, but how we support each other in tough times.

While we were playing ball and feasting, Sue Breitner and Mary Beth Wheeler were with John St J's wife, Sandra, who has been dealing with M.S. for many years. They meet in the afternoon and have supper together. This year, Fred arrived at the park with two sets of keys and realized one set of keys was Sue's. How was she going to get from Richmond Hill to John and Sandra's condo without a car? Fred was due to play in Game One and the thought of having to miss it must have been deeply distressing. Craig agreed to deliver the missing keys. The extent of his generosity didn't dawn on me till I talked with him about it later, how anxious he felt about not making it back in time to take the field in Game Two. There was the usual traffic jam at Steeles and the Parkway on the way back. Maybe he was fantasizing about the Batmobile (am I right in thinking it can fly) or maybe a Sherman tank, as he waited for the traffic to thin out. Perhaps Craig was aware that as much as he loves the game, no one loves it more than Fred.

I don't think I'd be playing at my age if not for the friendships, but it's the game that brings us together on summer Friday evenings. Lorne often talks about moving to new town when he was eleven or twelve, feeling lost, being invited to join a team, discovering he could hit the ball a ton, and the favourite memory of his youth and the bold print in the local paper that came along with it. He's had memorable days with us too. His walk off hit to win the tournament a couple of years ago. If that had been the last of his great days at the plate, it would have been enough. Nothing could have prepared him or the rest of us for what he did on Sunday.

> I don't recall all the details about my at bats but I think a little background would help put the day in perspective. I can remember five hits, two singles, one double and two triples (back to back). There may have been another single but I can't recall. As you know I was under the weather with a cold, sinus headache, very weak, low energy etc. I agonized over whether I would be able to play or not, but decided on Sunday morning after a decent night's sleep and talking with Colleen that regardless of how I felt

the prospect of staying home on a beautiful day and missing an event that has meant so much to me over the years and sharing the experience with my friends was totally depressing. I had a cold, not the black plague so, if necessary, I thought, I could get a substitute runner or a sub player if I found I wasn't up to it. At the beginning of game one I felt better than I expected. On my first at bat any thought of getting a sub disappeared. In the first game I looped a single into shallow centre field and a hard hit single between first and second. On the third at bat, bottom of the 5th, with the game tied, I felt, WOW! this is exciting. Can't recall how many outs there were. Warren was pitching well with his usual determination. Right field didn't look too inviting with the rover and centre fielder pulled over. Left field looked very inviting. I adjusted my feet to cut down on pulling the ball to right and hoped for an outside pitch. I can't recall what the pitch count was. Might have been the first pitch. A nice clean double. Richard did the rest. We win game one.

With time to rest between the first and third game I was excited to play again. I felt good about my fielding and don't recall making any errors. After I hit the first triple I couldn't believe how fast I was running. Again, not only was left field wide open but the fielders were playing me quite shallow. It was an open invitation to slug away. My memory can't separate the two triples, but I recall that I had two strikes in the second and fouled off a few pitches. As always John was pitching well, mixing up his pitches, always around the plate. Because I had pulled a

> hamstring in the 2013 tournament, I tried to modify my running over the last couple of years. I didn't always remember, but overall I slowed down and avoided an injury. This year I totally forgot to slow down. My instinct was just to run like hell until the third base coach told me to stop. I bet Sluggo would have sent me home. Fortunately my legs survived the workout. Two close hard fought games with all three teams battling hard. It doesn't get any better than that. We won but it could have gone either way. A wonderful tournament.

I could also have asked Richard to write something about his day. Two home runs and a commanding pitching performance in the final. But everybody on our team played well. Sometimes it happens that way.

Tuesday, Oct 20: If I'd had to choose between the Jays beating Kansas City or getting rid of Stephen Harper, I'd have gone for the latter in a heartbeat. All the same, it was gratifying to see the Jays hit like we know they can. Deeply satisfying as well to see Ryan Goins get the key hit after his struggles at the plate and his misreading of the pop fly in Game Two. It's harder as time goes on to get myself moving in the direction of the park, but it surprises me to keep discovering the game's power to enchant. I grew up in a mining town of six hundred people in Northwestern Ontario. We got the Winnipeg radio stations and there were no broadcasts of Major League games during the regular season. Not much newspaper coverage either. Despite the dearth of regular season news, the World Series was the talk of the town. The games were on radio when the men were at work and the kids were at school. I'd run home to see who'd won. My mother always made a point of listening so she could fill me in. Those were the years of the legendary Yankees Dodgers contests in the fifties. I could always tell from the expression on her face if the Dodgers had won or not. I remember best the day I came home to find out the Brooklyn pitcher had set a World Series record for strikeouts. She was excited on my behalf, but couldn't remember the pitcher's name. (The pitcher was Carl Erskine.)

It was my mother who gave me 'The Boys of Summer' while she was in the late stages of the cancer that would take her life. I was in the living room, more comfortable chatting with dad. I heard a voice say, 'If you want to talk to me, you're going to have to come in here.' She was an avid reader, and was going through the complete works of Charles Dickens for the third time. She'd got wi of Roger Kahn's book, read it and knew I'd like it. Gifts sometimes come when least expected.

Thurs, Oct 22: I liked Bruce Arthur's take in *The Star*: 'It's an exhilarating feeling flirting with disaster and coming out alive. It must be what tightrope walkers feel when they reach the other skyscraper.' Estrada kept doing it for seven innings. Not to forget the guy on the mound for K.C., Volquez, who pitched brilliantly. Two pitches made the difference: the three two pitch to Batista and the three two pitch to Encarnacion, either of which were close enough to be called strikes which set up Tulowitzki's bases clearing double. I was listening on the radio, in the process of moving from the studio to the kitchen to get supper going. My mind had wandered thinking about what to have with my rice and chicken. Jerry's partner, Joe, was telling a story and suddenly Mike Wilner was shouting something about a ball bouncing off the wall. (Rereading my commentary, I'm thinking, 'Where's the bat flip?' It happened in the previous series against Texas, Oct 14. Especially satisfying after the Jays had lost the first two at home and had to win both games in Texas to bring the series back to Toronto.)

11 A.M. Oct 24/15: The byline for Bruce Arthur's article is 'Amazing Jays A Fine Fall Gift.' When I saw it, much of the carping about what should have happened and didn't went out of my head.

Fri Oct 9/ 20. The thought came last night, one that's occurred to me many times. That it was the game that brought us together and kept us together for forty-three plus years. Although my sport is baseball, I'm often thrilled by hockey, soccer, football, tennis, golf, basketball. The grace, the skill, the courage, the beauty. And the power, not as assault, but as an expression of the universe. This would seem to rule out boxing, but Ali's knockout of George Foreman was a triumph of mind and spirit over brute force. Foreman had knocked out Ken Norton and Joe Frazier with ridiculous ease. Both those fighters had taken Ali to the limit. I remember walking up Church Street towards Maple Leaf Gardens and seeing the poster advertising tickets for the big screen. My first thought was that I didn't want to see him suffer the same fate as Norton and Frazier. My second thought was that I'd admired his skill, endurance and integrity for many years and owed it to myself to see him through to the end. Maple Leaf Gardens was sold out and I ended up seeing the fight with Jim Conlin in a theatre at the CNE.

The first six or seven rounds were like watching the school yard bully make mincemeat out of a scared kid who was just trying to get home alive. Jim didn't see much of the fight. He leaned forward with his hands over his eyes. I managed to keep watching the onslaught. The rope-a-dope strategy with Ali leaning against the ropes, protecting himself with his arms, allowing Foreman to punch at will seemed desperate, almost cowardly. Wikipedia gives a fairly detailed account of the events, noting that Foreman was tiring and becoming increasingly frustrated. In the seventh round, he landed a right to Ali's head with all the force he could muster. Ali wrestled him into a clinch and said, 'Is that all you've got George?' I'd been watching with my mind, not my eyes. The sight of Foreman flat on his back seemed to have come out of nowhere. It was the most miraculous event I've ever witnessed in all my years of following sport.

Many years later, I saw 'When we Were Kings,' the movie based on the fight and the lead up to it. The moment I remember most clearly is George Plimpton at ringside saying that the fear in Ali's eyes was palpable. To win the fight, to even have a chance of hanging around for a respectable number of rounds, he had to deal with that most dangerous of enemies. He was a mountain of a man in body, mind and spirit. Foreman, on the other hand, looked like a man ready to kill someone. He later developed a loveable public presence. I seem to remember him saying the fight was the best thing that ever happened to him.

17

Sandy's Hip, 'Nice Hit', FNB in Florida

Fri May 13/16: I got to the park at about 5:45. Sandy was standing beside third with three or four others having what sounded like a serious conversation. His hip had been wonky all last year and gave way during his Wednesday game. He'd talked to the physio people at Sunnybrook about the chances of it healing with exercise and they determined it was too far gone. He's due for hip replacement surgery, but plans to come every Friday to keep score and cheer us on. We played three innings with the catchers (Mike and Frank) calling balls and strikes. The five pitchers (John Larocque, Warren, Gilles, Richard and I) each threw one inning. It was snappy stuff for so early in the season and ended with Warren's walk off to deep left to make it 3-2. Along the way, I smacked a first pitch line drive over short and everyone said, 'Nice hit.' You never get over the good feeling that comes with that.

Fri May 20/16: At quarter past six we had thirteen, not quite enough for seven a side, but their guys sent us an extra sub. Who got the walk off hit? What sometimes happens when I don't get around to finishing the blog till Thursday. But I do remember Stephen's monster day at the plate (with girlfriend, Megan, looking on). A home run - or was it two - and a couple of doubles. Sandy gave an all star performance coaching third for both teams. He was there to greet me after I'd forgotten how many outs there were. Chatz and I chatted as we lined up to shake hands. He wants the game to be crisper. What he saw down in Florida.

Chatz, Mike and Walter drove down to Florida to play with two established Seniors Leagues earlier in the year. Some guilt on my part about not going with them, but I feel little urge to travel long distances anymore. Mike Marino wrote a piece on the adventure from which I steal at will.

"At 6:30 a.m. on the Thursday before March break I climb into the back seat of Walter's new Mercedes SUV. Steve sits up front and navigates. The border guard in Buffalo seems to have a chip on his shoulder. In addition to the standard questions, he asks us to name the park where the Toronto Blue Jays play in Florida. "We don't know, but it's in Dunedin. Is it Tropicana Field?" "Wrong. That's where the Marlins play." He shakes his head, but lets us through. On *Google* we see that the park is called Florida Auto Trader Stadium.

After a rainy Sunday night Steve and Walter and I walk into the Sid Lichter baseball complex in Dunedin at ten to eight on the Monday morning of March 14. Soon we see the regulars arriving, all by car. They are dressed in green or white T-shirts and black shorts, white socks and a variety of sneakers. Almost all have, slung over a shoulder, a baseball bag with a bat protruding from the zippered section at the bottom. They walk unhurriedly but with purpose. Though some have stooped backs and most have wrinkled faces, they are welcoming, smiling, introducing themselves. Their first names are printed on the front right side of their uniforms along with '3Score.' Later, I realize that score is the Old English term for twenty. You have to be at least sixty to play in this league."

The league plays slo pitch. Each player brings his own bat and gets five pitches to hit. The batter begins an at-bat with a count of one ball and one strike. A batter who hits a foul ball with two strikes is out. Walking is possible if three pitched balls hit the ground without hitting the plywood home plate. There's no bunting. A ball that hits the protective screen beside the pitcher is considered a foul ball. There are two women on the opposing team. 'One is tall, blonde, slender athletic.' Is she really 60 plus? The other is not as tall but more curvaceous, striking with auburn hair. Mike has to remind himself that getting to first base with her is (a) not going to happen (b) not the base he's here for. As they shake hands and high five 'Great Game, Great Game!' In spite of having fourteen players per team they'd played nine innings in less than two hours. Little wonder Chatz wants FNB to be crisper.

There's another group called Top of the World that plays Tuesday and Thursday mornings in nearby Safety Harbor. They don't wear uniforms. There's a three-run cap on each inning instead of five which keeps the game moving even faster than 3Score. Danny from Pittsburg hits a monster shot and two other players are home run threats whenever they come to bat. Easier because the park is scaled to Little League dimensions. Players are allowed only one home run per game. The next ones are ruled doubles.

Steve has been playing where he's asked. He finally gets his chance to move into the infield and (so it is said) a member of the batting team is heard to say, 'Don't hit the ball to Chatz.' Mike has trouble adjusting to slo pitch. He'd rather smack my best riser into the gap. Towards the end of the week he's adjusting his swing and getting his hits. A big moment for Walter playing outfield. He takes a few steps in, reaches down, and makes the catch. His team mates cheer. The league organizer suggests that he keep the ball as a memento.

Earlier in the week the guys bought three T-shirts and managed to get them embroidered with *FNB Spring Training 2016*. The letters FNB are embroidered in black. Spring Training 2016 is done in grey. Mike, Steve and Walter have reduced the six degrees of separation between 3Score and FNB to none.

It's tempting to make comparisons, but I'll forgo the exercise, except to say that FNB never aspired to become a league. We were the kids in the school yard. 'Bill D. go there,' 'Chatz go there,' 'Frank stay here,' 'Mike over there,' 'You need a centre fielder,' 'We don't have enough hitting,' 'How 'bout we give you Alex?' Not what you'd call orderly, but miraculous things often emerged from the chaos. There's a sadness about not being able to pass the torch to a younger group. There was a space of time when we thought it possible, but we were the product of a particular place and time.

The Queen Car, Cuba, Shostakovich, The Koch Brothers

It's a long way from Florida to Queen Street, but enough to say that after the May 16th game, I didn't get my usual music appreciation ride home with Fred. It's a long haul on the Queen car from Roncesvalles to University and I was passing the time singing to myself.

I was really into it when I noticed a voice on the car's P.A. A baseball announcer's voice. He sounded like Mel Allen who used to do the Yankees games back in the fifties. I was still deep in song, when I noticed people on the car were laughing. Maybe I'd figured out the voice belonged to the driver, but I must have wondered what the heck he had to say. Usually it's a sentence or two, 'This car will be going out of service at Ossington.' But this guy was doing paragraphs. He made the turns in and out of the King Street detour sound like going over Niagara in a barrel. When we got to University Avenue, he said it was the first subway stop. 'Amazing folks, simply amazing. You've never seen anything like it.'

If you can have fun driving the Queen street car, you can have fun anywhere.

Heard from Steve Shapiro the other day. Steve was one of the founders of FNB. He was a superb organizer and kept track of the attendance better than I ever did.

Hi Nelles: It's been a long time. I thought I would bring you up to date on our old table saw that Peter Dill, you and I bought so many years ago. Pat and I moved to a new and smaller house about a year and a half ago and I have been setting up a new shop ever since. In the process I purchased a new and more efficient table saw. So, what to do with 'Old Faithful' which was still functioning well. I was contacted by a man who, as a volunteer, turns baseball bats on his lathe for baseball players in Cuba including for members of the Cuban National Baseball team. He spoke to members of my Woodturning Club about helping to upgrade the skills and equipment for baseball bat turners in Cuba. So I, as well as other members of the club will become involved in some way. In the meantime, the Cuban National Baseball team will be playing a series of 3 games against the Ottawa Champions of the CanAm League in mid June. The woodworkers in Cuba need all of the tools they can get so I donated the saw to the cause. So after all of these years our old saw will end up in Cuba involved in the manufacturing of baseball bats.

Does Friday Night baseball continue?

Pat and I will contact you when we visit Toronto this coming August.

Best Wishes, Steve

(The next time you see the Cuban National team take pride in knowing there's an FNB connection every time a Cuban player gets a hit.)

Fri May 27/16: The temperature hovered around thirty degrees celsius on the sidewalks, but it was cool by the lake. Afterwards, I told Frank I hadn't pitched very well, hoping he would disagree. He didn't. We have a new waitress, don't know her name yet, but very nice. Some people downstairs had given her a rough time and I think it helped her to talk to us about it. The beer arrived quickly, salads soon after. Most opted for pizza, but Gilles ordered one of the specials. I ordered the chicken parmesan sandwich. George ordered nothing at all, having already done so by phone.

On the way home, Fred dialed up a piano concerto and asked me to guess the composer. There were a lot of strings at the beginning, slightly atonal.

'Sounds twentieth century.'

'Yes.'

I was thinking Benjamin Britten. I don't think he ever wrote a piano a concerto, so I'm glad I didn't jump the gun. Somewhere in the mix, I heard some chords that reminded me of Rachmaninoff.

'Sounds Russian.'

'That's right.'

It sounded too understated for Rachmaninoff, but I couldn't think of any other Russian it could be.

'Don't think it's Rachmaninoff.'

'Someone a fair bit later.'

The name popped into my mind without thinking.

'Shostakovich.'

Shostakovich is the creator of a musical universe larger than I will ever travel. More impressive still because he composed under Stalin's watch. The anger is there, along with the beauty, but the Kremlin bosses were too tone deaf to notice. I remember hearing a story – on the CBC I think – about a performance of a new work in St Petersburg during WWII while the city was under siege by the Nazis. There was no heat, people were starving, but the hall was full.

I mentioned the performance to Fred, wishing I'd remembered more of the details.

A visit to Wikipedia informs me that the composition was Shostakovich's Symphony No. 7. Most of the musicians were suffering from starvation. They frequently collapsed during rehearsals, and three died. The orchestra was able to play the symphony all the way through only once before the concert. The performance received an hour-long ovation. Many in the audience were in tears.

Fri June 10/16: It's easier to write about pitching badly than pitching well. This week, I pitched well. Mike told me later at Amico's that they were talking on the bench about what I'd say in my blog. It was bad enough watching it, they didn't want to have to read about it too. Mike led off the next inning with a sharp single to left centre and that was the end of the no hit bid. Mike didn't score, so it was four innings of shutout ball, surprising after my struggles in the previous two weeks. It might have had something to do with the book Frank gave after last week's game. It's called *Stillpower* and balances the theme of inner stillness vs willpower. It questions the idea that you can will yourself into a good performance vs the idea of playing freely. That thing about getting out of your own way. So simple, but so elusive.

At Amicos, we talked long and loud about Mohammed Ali, Gordie Howe, Mitch McConnell and the Republican extreme right. It gave me a chance to talk about Jane Mayer's *Dark Money*, a chilling account of how the Koch brothers made mindless ideology respectable. Buy your way into the *New York Times* and the universities. Establish charities with names like 'Americans for America' which lobby for decimating the regulations put in place to protect the ecosystem.

Fri June 24/16: There were smiles all around at the end, but just twelve of us at six. Warren suggested we play a more serious game of work ups with an ump, real pitching and catchers in full gear. We were pulling it together when the kids showed up - now numbering four with the addition of new guy Kevin - and all of a sudden the number was sixteen, enough to play full field. The question arose of how long we'd play. I thought, given the late start, five would be enough. My legs and stomach agreed, but Chatz, who'd play till midnight, pushed for six.

Just five of us around the table at Amicos. When I sat down, I reached for one of the two remaining glasses, meanwhile looking at Lorne across the table looking thirstier than any of us, but not reaching for anything. The thought crossed my mind that it was an exercise in patience with the goal of eventual abstinence. It came quickly to my attention the jug contained Steam Whistle, which is against Lorne's religion. Happily the Amsterdam Blond made its way up the stairs via Sarah, our charming and efficient waitress.

I'm surprised to find there are no entries for July or August. It comes back to me now that the numbers weren't there. There'd been departures, injuries and retirements. The youngsters bring good energy to the game, but there isn't the same level of commitment. Those of us who've around a while (some of us a forty years while) make it a priority which sometimes requires more than ordinary resolve and determination. No doubt there have been many such occasions, but two in particular come to mind.

Lorne's Drive from Kirkland Lake

"Among the countless great memories I have about Friday night baseball, one that stands out as an indication of my passion dates back to the late 1980s when we were playing at Ramsden Park. I was travelling a lot with my job at Magic Lantern Communications and always tried to schedule my time to be in Toronto on Fridays during the summer. I was working in Northern Ontario one week and had no choice about keeping an appointment in Kirkland Lake on Friday. I tried to plan the meeting so I could be at Ramsden for the 5:30 warm-up. Kirkland Lake is 600 km from Toronto, a 6 hour drive if all goes well. The meeting with the Northern District Library

System was crucial and turned out to be a large sale. The meeting dragged on as I kept looking at my watch, thinking about the game. I finally hit the road around noon. No stops on the way except perhaps a bathroom break. Pedal to the metal all the way. I arrived at the park, changed into my baseball gear and was ready to play just past 6 pm. The game was already underway. Milton McCrystal greeted me by telling me that I was too late, there were nine players a side, no room for me. I was about to explode but thought better of it since anyone who remembers Milton knows he was a gentle soul but built like a tank. Not someone to tangle with. My sense of disappointment was considerable but as the inning ended it all got sorted out and I played. I don't recall exactly but that may be the game where I hit a home run into the tennis court in right field."

Fred Flies in for the Game

"The summer of '82 was special in many ways. My first son arrived on the scene in late June, I was spending a lot of time abroad in my new role heading up the Canadian distribution of the incomparable Danish Bang & Olufsen line of audio products and I was a member of a group of passionate enthusiasts who played baseball every Friday night at Eglinton Park. Inasmuch as I loved my new job, I was faced with a schedule conflict. I was scheduled for a nine day business trip to Denmark, leaving on Wednesday July 7 and returning on Friday the 16th. Bad enough that I was going to be absent for the July 9th contest, I was determined to not miss July 16 as well. There's an old saying that's indispensable to anyone who has difficulty in organizing life's obligations and events. 'The things that you schedule first get done.' So with the July 16 game in mind, I packed my baseball jersey, cap, shoes and glove, stuffed them into the trunk of my trusty Volvo and headed off to the Park 'N Fly facility at the airport.

The return flight on the 16^{tth} was scheduled to touch down at 3:45 PM, so it would take a bit of luck to land on time, navigate through security and exit the parking garage. In planning my escape, I eliminated the need to wait for luggage by cramming my necessities into carry-on. The flight docked about ten minutes late and I practically leap frogged to the security kiosks to save as much time as possible. I was worried that the customs officer would be suspicious about my anxiety, but held my breath long enough to pass scrutiny, despite the beads of sweat across my brow.

I shuttled over to the car park, hopped into my Swedish sedan and headed to the exit turnstile as quickly as I could. It was an interminable wait, as each driver ahead of me seemed to enjoy passing the time of day with the attendant. Finally I was on the open road, heading over to Eglinton Park. I arrived at twenty to six, just enough time to dress and have a few warm-up tosses with my baseball buds.

It was an improbable evening of baseball. Perhaps a time shift of six hours relaxed my jet-lagged bod, or perhaps it was just plain luck, but I went 4 for 4 and made a handful of plays at the hot corner. After the game we went to Mother's Pizza on Eglinton for our customary celebration, remembering my teammates' suggestion that I should go to Denmark on a regular basis."

Fri Sept 16/16**:** Only twelve or so of us at six. I generated a game of work ups. It was moving along quite nicely when four late comers arrived. I was thinking the scrub had a nice flow, let's stay with it. I signaled my intent from my position in centre field. A couple of minutes later I saw a gathering near the mound. Next thing I knew we were being divided into teams. I just stood by and went where I was told. No input from me asked for or required. At Amicos, it was just Hugh, Frank, Fred, Walter and Marcus Farrugla, Frank's next door neighbour. We learned that Hugh was driving back to London to play in an all day tournament tomorrow. He'll be playing with us on Sunday. Guess you'd call that a good definition of a busy weekend. On the way home Fred dialed up Sibelius' Seventh Symphony. I sensed in myself a reluctance to surrender to life's endless possibilities.

Tournament 2016

Such a year we have never seen. Eric's departure, Mark busy with his renovation, Sandy's hip, Fred's knee, Lorne's hip, John St J's prostate, my battered shins. Add to that three games lost to the heat. Add to that Chatz missing The Tournament for the first time ever. Doubts concerning numbers for the big day added angst and sadness to the mix. It reminds me of the year I lost my childhood excitement about Christmas. I sang the carols, thought about the presents, watched my mother make Christmas cake, but it wasn't the same. I didn't know William Wordsworth had covered this territory until cramming for the final exam on the Romantic poets in my third year at U of T. when I came across Harold Bloom's commentary on the Wordsworth Immortality Ode.

THERE was a time when meadow, grove, and stream,
The earth, and every common sight,
To me did seem
Apparell'd in celestial light,
The glory and the freshness of a dream.
It is not now as it hath been of yore;—
Turn wheresoe'er I may,
By night or day,
The things which I have seen I now can see no more.

What has a nineteenth century English poet got to do with baseball? For some of us the game still holds the visionary gleam, nowhere more intensely than in The Tournament. Would this be the year the gleam lost its glow? No one was more upset by the possibility of ending the season with a whimper than Frank. Now and then at Amico's, he talks about his technicolour dreams wherein we walk out of the cornfield - to borrow from Wordsworth once more – 'trailing clouds of glory.' It's not only the game, it's the barbecue, his party for his baseball pals, the best party of the year. I was thinking we'd work it out somehow. Fred had a plan in place involving two teams if necessary, but Frank was talking as if something precious had died. Fred and I took the cue and headed down to Wilson Park earlier in the month than intended. The month being bittersweet September, which as I write, has sadly left us. We talked about the weather and the Jays and some other stuff I don't remember, but when we were done Frank was smiling.

I went down to his house on Saturday afternoon to help him make the traditional hamburgers. On Sunday morning, I got my traditional ride to the park with John Larocque. It was beginning to feel a lot like The Tournament. More so when the names became faces. The pitchers warmed up, the infielders took ground balls, the outfielders shagged flies. Fred called us together, bats were tossed, the umps went to their stations and Team One and Team Two took the field.

I'm short on the specifics of Game One, but remember that Mark Hershoran, who stung the ball all day, had some big hits. Kristy kept dropping liners over short. Warren pitched well and our guys didn't get much going until the fifth. Too little too late, but there was some comfort in making the score somewhat respectable. We fared better in the second game. We were one up in the top of the fifth, the dreaded open inning, when the roof fell in. While John was toughing it out on the mound, I was in right field glad it wasn't me, this being the first Tournament in forty years when I haven't pitched. I missed not being at the centre of the action, but I didn't miss the pressure. It gave me the space to be more welcoming, especially to the new faces like Will's brother-in-law who's never played with us before and who hasn't played much ball since public school. During the warms ups he joked about the rust. It was fun to watch him get better as the day went on.

My absence from the mound came by way of two line drives off the shins earlier in the season. Both times I left the game and lay on my back, not knowing if I'd be able to walk when I got up, and decided it would be wise to step back from pitching. An embarrassing moment when Wayne and Janet from my Monday Tai Chi class were strolling through the park. I'd been telling them about playing baseball and that I was still pitching, and the only time they see me, I'm flat on my back.

In Game Three it was five all in the fifth, which brought back memories of what it takes to find the stillness required to deal with the pressure. Both Warren and Richard were facing the toughest part of the other team's lineup. Both got three quick outs. They made it look easy. It's never easy.

I thought of myself as being low key, not present in the usual way, but when the ump called a strike which landed six inches behind the plate, I said something to the effect that while I'm normally a mild mannered man, I feel obligated to inform him that the *^*#$* pitch landed six inches behind the plate. I felt somewhat embarrassed for myself, but when I step up to bat, I want to see the ball carry into the gap, 'apparell'd in celestial light.' I also had thoughts of taking the mound for an inning, and wowing the crowd with my stuff. Maybe mom and dad would notice this time round.

Now and then I recall the days when I was discovering baseball, none more memorable the bright Saturday afternoon in early spring the year I turned ten. We were playing on the patch of gravel in front of the school because the playground hadn't dried out yet. I'd never shown much talent for the game. A good day meant not being the last kid picked. When it came my turn to bat that day in the school yard, I was expecting the usual mediocrity, but first time up, I hit the ball hard. Same thing, second time. Same thing, third time. Melvin Calder came along. He asked how the game was going. Aileen Leonard said, 'We can't get Nelles out!' Whether or not the light of that April day was celestial is open to question, but as I write, with the light of an October afternoon, streaming softly through the window, I have a feeling, perhaps transitory but in this moment real, that the while the world may be too much with us, the unexpectedly wonderful is still possible. There are 'obstinate questionings' and 'blank misgivings', but Wordsworth would have us believe something deeper and stronger lies in waiting.

Hence in a season of calm weather
Though inland far we be,
Our souls have sight of that immortal sea
Which brought us hither,
Can in a moment travel thither,
And see the children sport upon the shore,
And hear the mighty waters rolling evermore.

While the rest of us were sporting, Lorne was in St Joseph's with his broken hip. (He broke the hip running to first faster than he had promised himself not to.) He's at St Hilda's senior care facility at Dufferin and Eglinton. I've been up to see him and he is bearing up well, happy to see me, fun to talk with. It's the nights that are the toughest. They feel interminable. It takes god only knows what sort of resolve to see the light at the end of the tunnel and with all due respect to Wordsworth, it's a good bet Lorne doesn't care whether it's celestial or not. I told him that I'd been having trouble getting something cooking for this year's Tournament piece and that I'd been trying to construct it around Wordsworth's poem. Lorne reads vastly, has a fine literary sensibility and I was pleased when he said he liked the idea.

Which brings to mind the story he's often told us - which I'll do my best to reconstruct. As I remember it, his family had moved from New Waterford to Sydney and he was feeling somewhat lost. I think there was something about a baseball glove in a store window along with visits to the ball park watching the bigger kids play. Probably dreams of greatness along with the feeling he wasn't meant for such wonders. One day, a friend of his mother's spotted him looking wistfully at the glove. The mother's friend turned out to be the coach of one of the local Little League teams. He said something along the lines of, 'Hey there Lefty, how'd you like to play some baseball?', and invited him to join the Shipyard Red Sox. Lorne became the speedy outfielder who could hit the long ball. He was no longer the lonely kid on the sidelines. He was Lefty.

But then was then and now is now. The bible tells us as much. 'When I was a child, I spake as a child, I felt as a child, I thought as a child: now that I am become a man, I have put away childish things.' Wordsworth puts a different spin on it.

> My heart leaps up when I behold
> A rainbow in the sky.
> So was it when my life began;
> So is it now I am a man;
> So be it when I shall grow old,
> Or let me die!
> The Child is father of the Man;
> And I could wish my days to be
> Bound to each by natural piety.

'The Child is father of the Man.' Something about the well intentioned notion that we must discard the yearning as we adjust to the demands of adult life. My heart still leaps when I hit the ball square and solid. Or when I make a running catch in the outfield. I don't like to think about the day I hang up my spikes, but I know the game will continue to enchant me. I choose to think that had Wordsworth lived in the appropriate place and time, he'd have been a baseball fan. His heart would have leapt when the Babe hit his sixtieth, he'd have cheered when Ernie Banks said, 'Let's play two,' and he would have understood why Lou Gehrig called himself the luckiest man alive.

P.S. I did my best to capture the day, but was short on details for Game Three. I asked Warren to give his account. Put him on a ball field and Warren still believes there's splendour in the grass. He gives himself to game in full awareness of its fickle ways.

"The things I remember are that Team 1 had a lot of players who hadn't played much all year. I was thinking that if we could get through the first game, then we would probably be a lot better in the second game. Sure enough in the first game we showed a lot of rust at the plate and in the field. I knew Kevin and Marc (who also only played a few times this year) would have to be the offensive cogs until the others had a few bats under their belt. It really started to come together in the 5th and last inning of the opener. Everyone looked comfortable at the plate. Kristy (who swung the bat well all game), Anna, Will, Craig, George and Cam) suddenly started hitting and taking walks and we had a monster inning. It's every pitcher's nightmare to have a bad open inning, especially in The Tournament, but if anyone can shrug it off and keep pitching well it's John.

So we felt really good going into the final. I knew it would be a close game but thought that our crew was finally rust free and ready to play. Pitching and defense make for good games and that defines the final. Wilmer played really well as a replacement player and Kevin, Marc and Kristy got enough key hits to give us a 5-3 lead heading into the fifth.

I really wanted a shut down inning but good hitters will get their hits and despite some good defensive plays - especially George, Craig and Marc fighting the sun - they managed to tie it up. Even though Richard was pitching great, I never imagined we wouldn't score the one run we needed to win it all. He stepped up however and despite getting runners on base, we couldn't score. I remember standing on deck with two outs and thinking succeed or fail, I really, really want to get to the plate, but it was not to be. As Tom Hanks said 'There's no TYING in baseball!' (or something close to that) but by the time we all got over to Frank's it felt somehow a fitting ending to a really good tournament."

George Wheeler, Marc Hershoran, Wayne Oake

Ray Kerr, Peter Roach, Doug Densmore

Sandy Douglas and Nelles

Umpires for one of the tournaments

Upper left Eric Hellman, Upper right Warren Quinn,
Lower left Mike Marino, Lower right Ray Kerr

Upper left Peter Roach, Upper right Stehpen Breitner, Lower left George Wheeler, Lower right Wayne Oake

Stephen Breitner

Eric Hellman making one of his sensational plays at first.

Ken Pagel

Ken's daughter Julia who put together the story that aired on the CBC's 'Morningside' the day after the 2013 tournament.

Stephen Breitner putting the tag on Peter Hajdasz.

Marc Hershoran

Don't hit the ball to Chatz one more time.

Luke Donovan

Nelles circa 2010. Iden Ford shot this and the players had it enlarged and framed and gave it to me at the dregs of winter meeting. Probably the best present I ever got. (The original was lost so the quality is less than optimal, but hopefully adequate.)

18

Jaclyn, Hugh's Bat, Roger Maris, Mickey Lolich, Bob Feller, Count Basie, Wilmer, Alexander Fleming

Fri May 12/17: I got off the street car at five forty-five, looked towards Coronation park, not a soul in sight. Thought maybe I'd see someone as I got closer. It was a good bit chiller by the lake, not the kind of weather for stretching out on the grass and taking in the sun. Waited till ten after, still no one. Thought about *Field of Dreams.* Maybe I'd lost the faith. Like Kevin Costner's brother in law. The players were there but I couldn't see them. Thought about writing a piece on that theme: Sluggo running through a stop sign at third, Joe hitting a miserable little pop up calling out 'Fuck the British', Craig making a circus catch, Austin's one and only home run, all of us playing catch with our dads. Then thought that if they were there, they'd be thinking the same thing I was. Too damn cold. Walked up Strachan to King, caught the King car, checked in at Amico's. No one. Checked out the shops on Queen St W. went back to Amicos and there they were. I'd missed Frank's email about McCormick Park. Cold or not, I wanted to catch at least one fly ball.

Fri May 19/17: Gilles had put down the bases, a good sign, except there were just three of us. Warren arrived shortly after which brought us to four. He observed that it was opening day, saying the words with a kind of reverence in keeping with his love of the game and its traditions. The all too ordinary raised to the magical by the yearnings of the Irish imagination. Sandy was next, followed by Richard and the three musketeers: Danny, Wilmer, Kevin. Then Stewart, Chatz, Marcus, Pete. (Stewart is a customer of Fred's home theatre enterprise. They got talking baseball and Fred invited him to join us.) Everyone got two at bats, and after an hour, maybe less, it was over. As we packed up the equipment, it came clear there was just one car headed to Amico's and that car was carrying Gilles, Frank and the equipment. I thought about walking up to King like last week, but it's a long trek so decided to go straight home, meaning no one would be going to beer and pizza. A sadness as I hailed a cab when I thought about Lorne expecting us and finding no one.

Fri June 2/17**:** We celebrated the beginning of June baseball with the best game in recent memory. There were so many good plays I can't begin to remember them all, but do remember both Jordain and Chatz stretched out on the ground flipping balls to the nearest base to get the out. Also Stephen looking steadier at third this year, fielding hot grounders and making strong accurate throws to first. And Danny racing towards second to nab my liner up the middle, stepping on the bag and turning a hit into a double play.

It was 2-0 till the fourth. Both our runs came on sac flies courtesy of Wayne. In the bigs they high five sac flies, bunts, anything that moves a base runner. Good stuff, but the best plays were off the field. Frank talking to Jordain and Jaclyn who were spotted playing catch before the game. Hugh convincing a reluctant Jaclyn to play after she said she just wanted to watch. (She made a nice catch at rover and had a go-ahead hit in the fifth.) We could easily have ended up with a tie, appropriate given the excellence on both sides, but new guy Curtis Smith hit a monster shot to cap a five run sixth inning. Which begs the question, 'Who is Curtis Smith?' He's renting Craig's and Frances's house. Craig and Curtis got talking baseball and he said he'd love to play.

Fri June 9/17: Richard was feeling ill and not up to pitching. Sandy figured he was good for a couple of innings and ended up going all seven. His guys had tough bottom of the sixth - two quick outs followed by five runs. Tough on a pitcher, but he took one for the game. All in all (to quote a phrase) he pitched his ass off. Gilles also went the full seven and had more movement in the late innings. Both guys will be feeling it on Saturday. Sandy said he was feeling it already. Iden joined us for the first time since the early eighties. He was rusty, but determined. Got a couple hits and wrestled three or four ground balls to first to get the outs. Before the game he expressed a wish for a spot in my report. All things considered, he did pretty well, but what is most writeworthy is that he talked about the game like a twelve year old. Ready and raring to go, if not quite sure where and how.

I saw Richard and the three musketeers lounging on the bleachers after the game, happy to have been on the field together. Baseball is good for friendships. I hope they find a way of playing the game when they're in their seventies. I would have said eighties but we're not (except for Austin) there.

Yet.

I thought Austin might continue to meet with us at Amicos now and then. Maybe he found our Indy 500 approach to conversation favoured speed over substance. I forget which off season Friday it was that Mike M sent him a special invitation to join us at Amicos. He gave us his news about life in the mid eighties. The news is good. Wish I could remember the details.

Fri July 7/17: It started with a sprinkle in the top of the second. A couple of batters later, the drizzle became cats and dogs. One and a third innings into our first game since June 16, it was over. Any doubts that we might have given up too quickly were erased by the ensuing downpour. It was still raining hard when we got to Amicos where we found out it was also raining on Alex Sanchez, courtesy of the Houston. Warren wanted to know how many intentional passes Mickey Mantle got in 1961. I guessed twenty-five, Hugh guessed thirty-five. The answer? Zero. Roger Maris was batting behind him. Hugh wanted the name of the Canadian who played fifteen years with the Astros. Warren guessed correctly that it was Terry Puhl from Melville Saskatchewan. Somewhere along the way Wayne talked of his affection for the Detroit Tigers which reminded me of the 1968 World Series, the year they beat the St Louis Cardinals and Bob Gibson. Mickey Lolich won three games for the Tigers. To the best of my knowledge Lew Burdette, who did the same for the Milwaukee Braves in 1957, is the only other pitcher to equal the feat. (Not so fast. Christy Mathewson won three games in the 1905 series. Stan Covelski won three series games for the Indians in 1920 and Bob Gibson won three for the Cardinals in 1967. Madison Bumgarner won two games and saved another in 2014, equally remarkable given how the game has changed.)

When the bill arrived there was some confusion about the total. Some eyes turned my way and I said I didn't have a head for numbers. Warren speculated that it depended on what kind of numbers and that I probably remembered Lolich's ERA. I didn't, but it gave me the opportunity to say I remembered why he won those three world series games. The story behind it so unusual as to sound apocryphal. Here it is in his own words.

> I got a boil on my penis a few days before the Series Started. The doctors loaded me up with antibiotics and that made me pretty groggy when I went out to pitch the first time. All my life I'd reared back and thrown as hard as I could and as a result I never really had good control. I'd been an all brawn pitcher. But that day I didn't have the brawn. I had to use my head. I had to pitch to the spots. I had to nick the corners. And I won. The next time I pitched I had my full

> strength and I was rearing back and throwing as hard as I could. Well, right away, in the first inning, I was behind [in the count] 3-0 when [Orlando] Cepeda hit a home run off me. After that inning, in the dugout, I said to myself, 'Hey, you did pretty good pitching to the corners. Why don't you go back to throwing that way.' I did and we won. When I went out to pitch the seventh game I had only two days' rest and was too arm weary to throw real hard, so again I used my head and pitched to spots. After I won, I realized I could be a control pitcher and I could pitch within myself. I didn't have to be throwing as hard as I could on every pitch. When I needed to, then I could rear back and throw aspirins.

Frank was amazed at our recall of ancient events and wondered aloud how such feats of memory were possible. The beginnings of my interest in the game go back to 1948. I was in Grade Four that year and I'd figured out that if you hung around with the big kids, you'd get pushed around sometimes, but you could learn things you didn't know before - like the day Vernon, Lloyd and Jackie arrived at the school yard talking about some wonderful event which had happened the day before in some far away place where somebody had done something wonderful and someone else had something even more wonderful. There was a feeling that the first somebody was better than the second somebody, but something had happened that shouldn't have. The thing that shouldn't have happened had something to do with second base. It seems the pitcher had thrown the ball to someone but someone had made a mistake.

I was full of questions I didn't know how to ask, but by the next day I'd learned the big kids had been talking about the first game of the World Series. The two teams were the Cleveland Indians and the Boston Braves and the first somebody was a pitcher named Warren

Spahn and the second somebody was a pitcher named Bob Feller. Someone had been tagged out but the umpire had called him safe. The Braves had won the game 1-0 because of the mistake. My dad said that Bob Feller had pitched a better game even though he lost.

I liked knowing who Bob Feller was, but no one knew as much about baseball as Mel White. He came in from Red Lake to cut hair every Wednesday and he could talk baseball for the whole time you were there. He'd say, 'The Yankees won the game, but Don Newcombe pitched just as well as Allie Reynolds.'

'I love Dimaggio, but it's Yogi Berra who gets the big hit when you need it. '

'Casey Stengel is ten years ahead of his time.'

I loved listening to him thought it would be a wonderful thing to know all about the Yankees and Joe Dimaggio and Yogi Berra even though I liked the Dodgers better.

Fri July 28/17: We were short a catcher and Wilmer volunteered to go behind the plate. From out in right field, in the fourth, or maybe it was the fifth, I saw him take off his mitt, take a few careful steps, put his mitt back on a get back into his crouch. A half inning or so later, Sandy said, 'When you write your blurb, you've gotta write about Wilmer. He's the star of the game.' From my perch in right field, it hadn't registered that he'd taken a foul tip to the gonads.

It's great to have a game, though I'm more and more aware of what has to happen beforehand. Someone has to pay the fee for the park, someone has to collect the money, someone has to arrange for an umpire someone has to bring the equipment to the park, someone has to put in the bases. This week, we can add Frank's wife, Susan, to the list. She drove the equipment to the park.

Fri Aug 11/17: The rain prevailed yet again. In lieu of baseball, Nelles, Frank, Fred and Lorne gathered for beer and pizza at Amicos. Early on, Fred mentioned that he'd heard Steven Hawking express a concern about artificial intelligence, i.e. that he was worried about what would happen if it learned to reroute itself so as to be able to think outside the box. Each of us can best answer in terms of our particular computer experience. Mine is based on the use of music software. I run a program called Logic which allows me to write arrangements for a seventeen piece big band which I can then play back through my speakers. I was feeling pretty pleased with myself till I tried lifting Count Basie's 'Corner Pocket.' I should have known better since I had learned over time that the notes on the page sound mechanical when played back exactly as written. I had juiced up my version with some variations in time and volume, but when I got around to listening to the original again, the variations were so many and so subtle that yes, a computer powerful enough could come close to reproducing them. If you A B'd the endlessly edited computer version with the original maybe you'd be hard pressed to tell the difference, but over time you'd be able to make the distinction. Fred said he hoped I was right.

We went on to talk about Einstein. When he was a student at university, one of the maxims of science was that energy and matter were different entities. How did he arrive at the conclusion that they were different emanations of the same essence, leading to E = mc squared? It had something to do with the nature of light. How did he get from light to his theory of relativity? I don't understand, but I'll venture the opinion that leaps of thought are not only beyond me but artificial intelligence also. Then again, if a computer could beat Bobby Fischer at chess, what do I know?

Flying the face of my ignorance, I'll persist nonetheless. Computer programs are designed to operate within a single frame of reference, in this case, the parameters of the game of chess. The eureka moment, integral to the act of creation occurs when two distinctly separate frames of reference interact in some unexpected and unpredictable way. In 1928, Dr Alexander Fleming returned to his lab in London after vacationing in Scotland to find an experiment that had apparently been spoiled by mold. He was about to throw it out, but something flashed through his mind beforehand - the recognition that the mold had killed the germs. In this case, the first frame of reference is the spoiled lab experiment. The second is that the mold has killed the germs. If Fleming remains focused on his disappointment about the experiment gone wrong, he throws the experiment into the waste bucket and it's goodbye penicillin. Instead there's a flash of awareness - and "flash" is the right word. I can see it leaping from one part of his brain to another.

The issue reminds me of the implications of Pavlov's experiments with his dog and the writings of B.F. Skinner, the founder of behaviourism which postulate a human brain seen as a receptacle which responds to whatever information is fed into it. Behaviourism is the ally of text book education. You take the course, you write the exam. Two marks per point and two marks for style. It is the enemy of the belief that education ought to teach students to think. Many students prefer the text book approach. Certainly, the ones who used to ask me, 'What are you looking for in this essay assignment, sir?' 'First, that you've read the book.' (Funny how many didn't think that was necessary.) 'Second, that you've spent some time thinking about what you've read. Third, that you've made a decent effort to express your thoughts clearly.' My heart always leapt when a student approached me and said, 'I'd like to improve my writing.' I could pass on what I'd learned from my own efforts, but it would come to nothing without the student's honest efforts.

Sometimes writing involves the best way of communicating an established truth, other times you're searching. You may have an idea about what you want to say, but you never really know till you get there. It's the process, the doing, the interaction between the known and the unknown, the tangible and the intangible. If you're lucky enough to get hooked on it, it's as good as it gets.

Fri Aug 18/17: Just ten of us, but Hugh saw the logic therein and suggested we play nine in the field with one batter. Frank donned the catcher's gear and went about his job with a happy sense of purpose. Warren bounced one off the fence. Hugh's relaxed, effortless swing kept sending the ball far and high. Mike M showed once again why he's the toughest out in FNB. Low, high, in, out, it didn't matter. He hit them all. Sandy and Warren helped things along by throwing lots of strikes. Standing on first after working my way round from right field, I took a moment to feel the sweetness of the August evening. One of those moments when you know there's no place else you'd rather be.

Fri Sept 8/17: Just twelve of us at five to six, but Hugh arrived on the hour. We kept the faith and started with seven on one side and six on the other. Kevin and Pete arrived shortly thereafter and to make a long story short, we had a game. Our first since July 28. The one before that was June 16. The kind of summer it's been.

Sun Sept 24/17 Tournament 2017

My clearest memory of the day is the tail end of game three. Warren sat beside me in one of the deck chairs, gathering himself to close out the game. His son, Gavin, came to the plate. The score was tied and he looked awkward on a couple of high and away pitches he shouldn't have swung at. The next thing I saw was the ball sailing deep, deep, deep down the left field line. I thought, 'Where the heck did that come from?' But there it was and along with it a two run lead going into the top of the fifth. I watch the game mainly from the pitcher's point of view and remembered all to vividly how it feels to pitch in the tournament and protect a lead late in the game. I knew Warren was feeling that mix of fear, determination and desire that comes with the territory. Don't remember much about the bottom of the inning other than Hugh's blast to deep centre which put Richard's guys ahead.

Later at the barbecue, I was talking with Peter Roach. I knew he'd had a serious health issue a couple of years ago, but didn't know how serious. Scary serious. I knew about the melanoma but didn't know it was stage four. I didn't know about the pancreatic cancer. The survival rates were 13% for the pancreatic, 4% for the melanoma - maybe the other way other way round - not sure it matters. His one out single started the game winning rally for Warren's guys in Game Three. It was the only hit he had all day. Was he thinking, 'The odds of my getting a hit aren't great, but better than the odds that I'd be here today.' There was another out after that it so I'm guessing that the rest came with two out. Apologies to the batters who set the stage for Warren's at bat. Clear memory of him leaning over the plate to take a low and away pitch in the hole between short and second to drive in the winning run. He sent out this email a week after the season ended.

I was the only one to show up at the diamond last Friday – hoping for a better turnout tonight!

> Seriously, what a great day and what a great tournament.
>
> Really missed being at the BBQ but the send off for José was tremendous – and Brandon caught a ball. Just a great day all round.
>
> Fred you might have got word through your Youth Employment Network but I was heartened to get the response below from Kevin.
>
> *(Kevin tore his hamstring on his way to first while pinch running for Lorne.)*
>
> Hey Warren: Thanks for the email. I went to hospital, got a scan done on the hamstring. I tore it in 2 places, but small enough that they are non-surgical. I just need to ice and not work the leg much until it heals.,

I already feel better, just some discomfort and the odd pain if I put pressure the wrong way. Limping around pretty good.

Sad I didn't get to play the rest but it's all good – heard from Danny it was a crazy ending. I enjoyed coming out too when I could this year – I was surprised I wasn't on your team for the tournament, I felt we played together all year this year and the one previous. Was a blast – see you on the diamond next go around. Cheers, Kevin

19

Hamstring Woes, Adam, Dennis Ekersley, Kirk Gibson

Fri May 11/18: Just for the record, we were there with bats, balls and gloves. There being Sorauren Park because of the exclusion date at Coronation. Weather on the chilly side. Just when I thought we'd had enough, we kept on. From tossing the ball, to infield practice, to hitting. Richard and Gilles pitched. We all got five hits.

Fri June 8/18: At six we were twelve hoping for two more to bring us to fourteen, play two fields and sub one player. Ended up with just thirteen, but Frank and Chatz agreed to (respectively) catch and play short for both teams. Which meant just six in the batting order for one side and five for the other. Guess our guys were the five because Warren was on third when his turn to hit came round. We sent out a pinch runner and Warren batted himself in. (A first?) In the top of the fifth, Stephen, subbing for our guys, made a running catch in centre for the second out. After which he stood at the plate and hit a bomb into the gap to drive in a run for his guys.

Fri June 15/18: I played outfield for the first time this year and was feeling pleased with myself after catching Mike M's sinking liner. One batter later I stepped into a hole chasing down Hugh's drive into the gap. Felt something grab in my right hamstring. Too sore to keep on playing. Sat out the rest, paying enough attention to cheer the good plays, but not enough to have much to write about. (I have a grade two hamstring tear. There's an ugly purple bruise down the inner thigh and top of the calf. Along with that, a sprained ankle.)

Fri July 27/18: My first time at the park since the hamstring issue. Just nine of us at six. Someone spotted a fellow watching from behind home plate. Asked him if he wanted to join us. He said he'd never played baseball. Sandy? Frank? said not to worry. That brought us to ten. It was decided to go with one batter and nine in the field. The ten included me standing in right field, moving only to retrieve anything hit my way. Peter H arrived after we got started followed by Wilmer. Some impressive hitting from Warren, Marc, Sandy, Mike, Fred and Adam - the new guy - who hit the second pitch he'd ever seen into right field. While playing first, he snared a hot liner - had to move his glove across his body, turn it thumb down. It was the thumb down bit that impressed me most. For a beginner the tendency is to move the glove across the body without the turn. Sandy took time to give him a few hitting instructions which he soaked up like a blotter. By the time we'd finished, he'd absorbed as much baseball as most beginners do in a couple of years.

While watching all this I was reminded - as were Frank and others - of the TV ad in which some kids are playing their usual pickup game. There's a dark skinned kid looking wistfully through the screen behind home plate. Someone says, 'Wanna play?' The kid says he's never played baseball. That's okay, except one kid is pissed because the new kid is going to be on his side. Next thing we see is the ball sailing high and deep. The new kid is greeted by a happy mob of teammates as he crosses home plate.

'I thought you said you never played baseball.'

'Cricket.'

An hour ago he was the loneliest kid in town, now he's the happiest. Adam isn't exactly a kid, I'd guess he's thirtyish, but there's a kid in all of us. When it was time to pack it in he was feeling mightily pleased with himself. We asked him if he was available

Friday nights. Turned out he's visiting from Montreal and is just visiting. His home is actually Lyon, France. Reminds me of how we met many players over the years, an invitation and a welcome.

(Little known fact: Ted Williams mother was born in El Paso Texas, though she wasn't able to document the fact. It's more likely she was born in Mexico. Williams was advised against disclosing his Mexican heritage for fear of prejudice. The more things change…)

Fri Aug 30/18: Thirteen guys were ready to brave the Ex and play baseball. Weather looking good, until four when the rain was thick and heavy. Saturday evening it's the Bosox vs the Rays and I'm in the booth with Dennis Ekersley and the other guy. Jays fans didn't like Dennis when he was closing for the A's, but he's a wonderful color guy, articulate, honest, knowledgeable, funny. He's heard about me from somewhere, tells everyone that Nelles pitched for the better part of fifty years and knows a few things about the game. What I know from watching David Price on this particular evening is that he's got his good stuff and a 5-0 lead in the third. Suddenly there's two on and nobody out and the camera closes in on him taking off his cap, wiping his forehead, taking a couple of deep breaths, reminding me there's nothing harder than being the winning pitcher in a major league game. It was tough enough in FNB. It must be that times a lot in the bigs. This I know. This any serious pitcher knows. Position players think they know. They don't.

Standing on second base in the tournament a couple of years ago, I saw Warren struggle like I have seldom seen him struggle. The bases are loaded, one out and he can't throw a strike. He's thinking, 'Please God, let me find the plate,' although I'm pretty sure the Irish don't address the Deity in such even tempered tones. It's just the first game and I'm thinking, 'Who else have they got, he's not going to make it through this game let alone the next.' He fights his way through the frustration, the agony all those things pitchers know so well. His team wins The Pig.

The year Gilles comes back from NB. Hasn't pitched for three months. Looks awful the Friday before the tournament. Spends Saturday in the gym and the sauna. Shows up Sunday, throws a lot of balls, maybe more balls than strikes. Steps off the mound, tells himself he didn't come back from NB to look like a bum, keeps coming up with the big pitch when he needs it. His team wins The Pig.

Enough about them. What about me? The last game I pitched in the tournament, age seventy-six. Five run mercy rule first. From then on it was digging deeper than I've ever had to, or ever wanted to. We win the game. Richard pitches the next game Somewhere along the way hits one against the wall of the public washroom. We win The Pig.

I rarely hear Hall of Famers like Eckersley say these things, although I've heard John Smoltz venture in that direction. Maybe some unspoken rule that the pressure goes with the territory and it's unmanly to talk about it, maybe why men who come back from wars don't often talk about what they went through. Dennis lived through one hundred and ninety-seven wins, and three hundred and ninety saves. Wonderful career but it's more fun in the broadcast booth.

'By the way Nelles, how come you never made it to the bigs?'

Okay, Dennis didn't ask me that. What actually happened is I fell asleep and missed my chance to talk about umpires who don't understand that if one millionth of the seam catches the extreme edge of the plate, it's a strike. After the game, we get talking about FNB and I ask him how he heard about us. 'Anybody who loves the game knows about you guys whether they know it or not.'

I tell him about The Tournament and The Barbecue and Jack's amazing dash across the infield to pat the bouncing ball into Lorne's glove and Craig's miracle over the shoulder catch and Rolando's no hitter and 'Don't hit the Ball to Chatz'. The talk moves back to Fenway and Mookie Betts and J.D. Martinez and the closer, Greg Kimbrell. Most of the present day closers are power pitchers and I get talking about how Dennis could move the pitch away from the batter half an inch at a time. Somewhere along the way, I ask him what was the first thing that came into his mind when he heard he'd been inducted into the Hall.

'The pitch to Robbie Alomar.'

'What was the second thing?'

'The one I threw to Kirk Gibson.'

(Dennis is an emotional guy. He was probably too teared up and happy to be thinking anything except how blessed he felt.)

Sun Sept 22, Tournament 2018

Picture a man getting out of a taxi on the northwest corner of Strachan and The Lake Shore at 9:40 A.M, Sunday Sept 30, 2018. You might hesitate to call him old, but you can tell from the way he maneuvers himself out of the cab he's seen his share of Septembers. As he walks along the bike path, you get a glimpse of the lake on his left and a boy playing catch with himself on the ball diamond to the right. Up ahead you see public restrooms and a large covered picnic patio. As he approaches the patio, you see there are two more ball diamonds, one a couple of hundred yards ahead, and one much closer where you see a scattered group of various ages playing catch on the outfield grass. The way in which they've come into view as he follows the curve of the bike path in the quiet of the September morning gives the impression of their appearing from out of nowhere.

It was a lot like that. From the north side of Lake Shore Boulevard, I hadn't seen any red hats or jerseys. As I walked along the bike path, I couldn't see past the Diamond One bleachers. I wondered for an awful moment or two if there had been a change of venue I'd somehow missed. A few steps later, I could see baseballs being tossed back and forth on the outfield grass. I'd left my glove at home, afraid I'd end up re-injuring my hamstring and was struck by something akin to remorse as I thought about it lying neglected in my basement.

I knew the day was going to be chilly and had toyed with the idea of dropping in later in the procedures as some sort of symbolic gesture. Another idea, the one I'd decided on, was to sit quietly on the sidelines making notes for my annual tournament piece. I'd brought a notebook and pen for exactly that purpose, but at this moment I wanted to play catch with my pals. I hadn't worn a baseball hat either, had even been thinking about a toque. The first player I talked to was Ken, happy to be with us again. Given that he lives on farmland north of Orangeville, you might say he actually did come out of the cornfield. My baseball pals were there all right, not as many as hoped for, but there was a sense nonetheless that something remarkable was about to unfold once again.

The season had been a long string of games that never happened. Enough players for a few games in May and June, from that point either nothing, or only enough for an extended practice. There was one high point among the latter. The evening we met Adam, on holiday from France and invited him to join us. There were some lively episodes after that, but no game. At Amicos we wondered if there'd be a resurgence the week after the Ex. It didn't happen. We'd been sure there'd be interest enough in The Tournament. Now even that was in question. But out of somewhere came a voice.

'If you hold it, they will come.'

Among those who came were fathers and sons. Fred and Stephen, Craig and Luke, Hugh and Ryan played catch with each other. Add to that father and daughter, Frank and Anna who'd have done the same were it not for Anna's being felled by bronchitis. Over the years there have been others: Sandy and Gavin, Chatz and Eric, Warren and Gavin, Tom Christopher and Danny, John LeSarge and Mike and Greg, Dave Bolland and Mark and Chris. As well as uncles and nephews, Chatz and Marc, Lorne and Paul.

But there I was, no glove, no baseball hat. Somewhere along the way a third plan had been forming. I would play half an inning without coming to bat. Become the unsung hero of my own novel.

The Moonlight Graham gambit probably wasn't necessary. It had already been foreordained that I would be asked to throw the first pitch. I wondered aloud about the absence of ESPN. Good thing they weren't there, the ball barely made it to the plate. Lorne and I were invited to captain the teams. Just two this year because the numbers were down.

The first (for real) pitch had not been thrown and already I was feeling the day, the game, our collective joy, drawing me out of indifference. The feeling was confirmed later with the arrival of John St James who sat beside me in the dugout. As we talked, other players came over delighted to see him once again. The affection was palpable. He told me his long ordeal in the hospital with an affliction that refused to name itself had left him feeling disconnected, and that coming to the park to be with us had changed things. I forget his exact words although I felt then, as I do now, their full intent. Something akin to being drawn out of an isolation we retreated into early in life, not necessarily a bad thing - it gave us comfort to know we had the wherewithal to find pleasure in our own company – but always the chance we could get lost there. I could never have predicted, even after all the years, all the tournaments, that I'd feel our particular magic once again.

You could say the something began at any number of times and places, maybe as early as the day, long before Mel Brooks' story of the five thousand year old man, when one of that gang of apes who'd lost the waterhole realized that if bones could become weapons, so could rocks. There'd been a lot of grunting and chest pounding, but among all the theatrics there was that magical moment when an ape, weapon in hand, saw a rock flying towards him and instead of waiting for his chance to avenge himself, swung at the rock, hit it squarely and watched with a sense of wonder he'd never felt before as it sailed far into the distance. And for each of us a moment, a catch, a pitch, a well struck ball, when the field was suddenly alive with a sense we were capable of remarkable things.

This time round I was aware that in earlier times, there'd been close, well played games that challenged us beyond the point of comfort and took us to the edge of our abilities. I'm not sure why on this day, with just the two teams and the accumulated rust of a more or less gameless season that the games were no less satisfying. Gilles eventually tired, but was pretty much unhittable for five innings in Game One. Warren got hit hard, but gave no quarter and hung around to get the win. He continued for three innings into Game Two. I'd decided the Moonlight Graham thing was too much a cerebral exercise and decided on taking a turn at bat. All I could manage was a weak ground ball. Back on the bench Marc H said,

"Did he give you a pitch to hit?"

"No bleeping way. The first one broke a foot outside. The second one was a change up. The third one jammed me.'

It was better that way. We both understand the game requires your best. Fred told me later that Warren had been in tears after turning the mound over to Luke, knowing he might never pitch again.

There were plays that might have been made on another day, but some gems as well. Stephen darting to his left to field a hot grounder a few feet from second, throwing to first for to double up the runner at first. Some good infield play from Chatz, Fred and Hugh. Stephen also had a big day at the plate. It seemed he hit the ball harder with each at bat. The last one sailed ten feet over the centre fielder's head. Megan came over to the dugout as if to say, 'That's my guy.' Mike M was a sparkplug behind the plate and hit a rope that would have gone for the distance had it not been for Luke playing rover. Lorne DH'd in Game Two. He struck out the first two times and someone on the bench wondered aloud if he was seeing the ball. One pitch later, he hit a sharp liner past first. It was only right. We've had players who hit the ball farther, but Lorne has done it for forty-three years.

After the last out and Iden taking the photo with everyone in it, we headed over to Frank's and Susan's. Canada Geese fly south, we go to 84 Wilson Park Road. As we eat, I'm sitting beside Hugh and his son and we getting talking about Hugh's swing. It's effortless. It comes from the feet and the core and a quiet upper body. He says he doesn't think about that. Sue Breitner asks me how my writing is going. The question reminds me of her love for music. It's not just polite interest, it's that sense of another person and what brings them joy. I talk to Iden who was so pumped about playing in the Tournament he couldn't relax. He settled down after a few innings and got himself in front of balls that came his way. He was more himself behind the camera and left us with a wonderful slide show. We talked about cars, mostly his BMW X3 and agreed that when you find a car you can make friends with, you don't rush to get rid of it. I'm a sucker for car talk, but thinking back, what he said about learning the art of photography struck a deeper note. 'Looking at you, I don't think of it the way most people do, I think about the how the light reflects from your face.'

When I got home, I had the strange sense of having been away much longer than six hours. We like to think of time as something that defines itself by the hands of a clock. You don't have to be Albert Einstein to know it's not like that. It's what we put into it, what we make of it.

Fri Oct 26/18: One of our larger offseason gatherings - Steve, Frank, Mike M, Fred, Lorne, Ben, Chatz, George, Sandy, John St J, Nelles - due mainly to the presence of Steve Shapiro whose contribution in the early years provided the foundation from which we were able to move forward. It was deeply satisfying to be able to say thank you with forty-three years of FNB around the table. Frank talked about the moment each Friday afternoon when he'd dig the equipment out from under the front porch and gather it together and the feeling of sheer joy he felt knowing it was the first step in creating a game, praying all the while it wouldn't rain. I ventured the opinion that it was remarkable he felt that way given the ordinariness of the task, and was quickly interrupted by Steve who said he felt the same way when he was taking care of the equipment in the eighties. FNB was the best day of the week and the tournament was the best day of the year. Except for the Friday he said to himself, 'I'm not going to the pub with the guys, I'm going home and I'm going to propose to Pat.' She was resting on the couch when he came through the door. He got down on his knees and popped the question. She didn't say anything. She started making lists about who to invite to the wedding.

20

Eric Hellman, Frank's Play, The NRA, Hugh, Daniel Hudson

Fri May 24/19: The word came from Fred that Eric was visiting from Vancouver and would join us at Amicos. He's found himself an apartment with a view of Stanley Park and the mountains. Real estate is pricey, but the rents are still doable. During the course of the talk, we found out he chaired a project which led to the creation of the blue box program. He's discovered that working with people in smaller groups gets better results than working with organizations who often end up squabbling with one another. He said he often mentions tells friends and associates about our balance of camaraderie and competition. He's worked with a lot of people in many different situations and he's never seen anything to match it.

Fri July 19/19: A lively, informative evening at the pub. Franks' play had finished its run at the The Fringe. *Failed* is about a drug addict who dug himself out of the habit. Frank was the producer, writer, director and probably some other took on some not so visible tasks as well. A huge achievement. There were 100 people in the audience closing night and a standing ovation. The cast didn't know what to do and Frank had to shout from the back to let them know they should take another curtain call.

A chilling moment in the news, the crowd at Trump's North Carolina rally shouting 'Send her back.' The need as Lorne pointed out for an educational system that encourages critical thinking. I thought it might be a useful educational experiment to have a course on the constitution which had been put together by great men. George reminded us while the men were exceptional we had to remember that Washington and Jefferson were slave owners. It seemed to me that all this could be part of the course. My worry. Teacher who belongs to the NRA spends the whole semester on the second amendment.

The rest of the season was plagued by low numbers and rain begging the question of whether or not there were enough players interested in getting together for The Tournament. It required a lot of persistence, but we ended up with enough for two teams.

Tournament 2019

Sun Sept 22/19: There were eighteen of us sitting around the big table upstairs at Amicos. I was sitting across from Luis who never stopped smiling the whole time. We met him Friday. When I crossed Lake Shore Blvd, the gang was playing work ups and Luis was in left field. I went over to say hello and ask him if he was one of the guy's friends. 'No English. Just Spanish.' We learned he's from Venezuela. His being there reminded us of the recurring theme where we'd meet someone at the park who'd end up playing. It was written in the grass that we'd invite him to join us for the big day.

I'd made up my mind beforehand that I wanted to pitch to the first batter. Not just the ceremonial thing. I tried that last year and no one noticed. No way the same thing was going to happen this year. I wanted to pitch a real, actual one third of an inning and have the result verified in the box score. I didn't think it would be fair to the team's starting pitcher if I walked the leadoff hitter which was all too likely, but figured he'd understand. I found my release point just in time and got Chatz to pop up for the first out. Warren observed that since I started when I was ten, I'd pitched in eight different decades.

When Gilles tired in Game Two, I went in to relieve him. My arm stiffened up and I couldn't throw strikes, but still managed to get a couple of outs. Lorne came to the plate for his one at bat of the day and I threw four straight balls, none of them close. I got the ump to wave the walk and hit Lorne with the next pitch. He says I beaned him. Sounds more dramatic that way. Okay with me. Any drama he could find in the ignominious event required significant creative thought.

It was good to see Mark Riddle again. He told me his knees hurt along with a lot of other stuff. He played some good shortstop and hit a monster shot over George in deep, deep left field. Chatz moved back to take George's throw as Mark was rounding third. His knees were saying enough is enough, but four bases are twice as good as three. In the meantime, Luis was looking more like eighteen than seventy-eight. There was a lot of chatter about his sweep tag at second. What you see from the major leaguers. If the MVP award went to the player who had the most fun, Luis would be the guy.

Sandy told me he was playing in two other games that day and still managed to join us for an hour at Amicos. He got us some Steam Whistle which we drank at Frank's and Susan's before crossing the street to Amicos. Eric (as in Chadwick) beat out a routine ground ball to his dad at short. If you were just following the ball, you'd have assumed the out, but the kid was ten feet past the bag when the dad's throw got to first. What to say about Hugh? Good field, sweet swing, pure love of the game, comes all the way from London to be with us. He invited his son, Ryan, to join us. The kid (forty years old) had a great time.

Good to see Wayne again. He's looking for something to carry him through his later years. I don't push Tai Chi, but it's the best set of exercises devised by the mind of man. And more than exercise. It's an art. You never stop learning. Peter Roach will turn 80 next spring. Still dragon boating. Still can hit. Warren looked tight in the first game more relaxed in the second. Most fun guy to talk bb with ever. Fred still plays a mean third base. Printed out the rosters in bold colours as he's always done. Didn't want the occasion to feel like a couple of pickup games. Wonderful to see Jim Betts after not sure how many years. He met Frank at Julia Pagels' wedding and Frank invited him to the tournament. He's still doing a lot of writing, getting shows produced with a couple of exciting projects in the works.

On Fri Oct 4: At Amicos Frank talked of his memories of watching his dad catch. He was the best catcher in a Senior A softball league. Sunday Oct 22, 2019, Frank caught ten innings on his seventy-six year old legs. His dad would have been proud. When my dad was in his twenties, he was the best pitcher in Norfolk county. When he moved to Madsen Red Lake Gold mines, my mother took me to watch him on the large patch of mill tailings which served as a ball field. I was too young to understand much about what was going on, but noticed that he never got a hit. I asked him why it was that Mr Dick always struck him out. He must have been thinking, 'What kind of kid is this who only remembers when I screw up?' I visited him when he was retired in Simcoe, going down the slope of the big front yard and pitching to my brother while he watched. 'Here's my rise ball.' 'Here's the drop.' 'Here's the curve.' What he showed me all those years ago.

Lorne had the just one ignominious at bat, but is still a force over beer and pizza. He was disappointed no one commented on what he'd written to accompany Sandy's photo.

> You captured a historic moment in the history of baseball. From humble beginnings in the coal mines of Cape Breton to a sun drenched ball field in Toronto an illustrious career comes to an end; beaned by a stray pitch thrown by his arch rival and good friend from the gold mines of Red Lake Ontario, N. Van Loon. All good things come to an end. It's not like the poem: "Casey at The Bat" but FNB has its own poetry.

Once again, what Hugh has brought our game. Or maybe it's just that I know he likes me. But what the heck, he likes all of us. At Amicos he said words to the effect that anyone who had turned eighty on Sept 16, in the year of Our Lord 2019, should be feted by those present.

Some of you probably saw the amazing post season play. Astros vs Tampa. Batter hits the ball into the gap in left centre, Kiermaier races over to play it off the wall, turns, makes a perfect throw throw to Adames. Alteuve is rounding the bases, gets the go ahead from third base coach, Adames makes a perfect throw to D'Arnaud who's perfectly positioned to make the tag. Beautiful. But sad to see Atlanta go out so brutally. The kid pitcher will remember that merciless first inning far too long, same with Joe Kelly who gave up the slam to Howie Kendrick. The game can be cruel. No. That's wrong. What happened to Bill Bucker was cruel, but that wasn't the game. It was some mistaken idea of what sport is all about. Go for Kiermaeir to Adames to D'Arnaud.

Some of us will remember Daniel Hudson's first 2019 appearance. A two (three?) run homer with the Blue Jays. As he watched the ball sail high and far, he'd never in his wildest dreams have imagined he'd get the last out in the seventh game of the World Series. He had his ups and downs, but was a key to the repair of the incendiary Washington bullpen that cost the Nats a record number of late inning leads early in the season. Amusing article about him in *The Star* a few weeks ago. He hates closing. Never heard a pitcher be that honest. What I used to feel in the tournament. Very happy for him.

Have to admit I was asleep while it happened. Made it till the top of the sixth. Loved the way Greinke was getting outs with an eighty-nine mph fastball and four other pitches. One of those games where I was cheering for everyone. Hats off to the Nats. But it wasn't the Nats. It was the Expos. Remember the year of the strike, the year there was no world series. Who was in first place?

Once again, hooray for Daniel Hudson. My kind of guy.

21

All Good Things

As noted earlier, this book started out as a collection of reports I'd written from 2004 to 2019, each a description of a particular game. I thought of them as similar to a captain's log. Like Ferdinand Magellan's daily observations on his journey round the world. Good weather, bad weather, crew working together, crew restless and rebellious, sometimes going ashore somewhere the food was good. You'd keep reading because it was the stuff of daily life, with the question of whether they arrive safely back home hovering above the details. But my entries were never just reports. There was always something about each game, a certain way of looking at it, a theme, a plot, characters, all based on fact of course. But what about an idea that would hold them together? What they ask when you read in writer's workshops. 'What's it about?' If you can't say, you're in trouble. Somewhere along the way, I thought it might be that we never lost that kids in the schoolyard feeling. Yes, but we also wanted to play well and while there were games that felt patched together, there were others which attained palpable beauty. Good pitching, good - occasionally spectacular - fielding, long home runs. The outcome uncertain until the last out.

So yes, you have to know what it's about, and it helps you get somewhere satisfying, but really, you never know. There's always something between the lines, all the more powerful for being unstated. Perhaps what's between these lines, sometimes there to see, but usually implicit, (along with other things, but this more than the rest) the love of the game. You don't start out loving, you have to fall. It's a letting go, an opening of the mind and heart, imagination, longing, desire.

Steve Chadwick, aka Chatz, has been sending a daily email, each with a story about one of the greatest one hundred players of all time. It's been fun, but it begs the question, 'What is greatness?' Was Babe Ruth greater than Willie Mays? Was Warren Spahn greater than Bob Feller? Was Ty Cobb greater than Ricky Henderson? Maybe it's the need to believe in some higher order of things. Why the Greeks invented the gods. Ares the god of war, Aphrodite the goddess of love, each looking down on the Trojan war unable to resist the impulse to turn the outcome in their favour. And the heroes, Hector the venerable old warrior versus Achilles the arrogant young phenom. Which brings us back to The Hand. The ball intent on landing safely, Austin's sixty-five year old body out of position to make the catch, his bare hand appearing as if out of nowhere. The gods of baseball were smiling down on us that magical evening. Perhaps it was always the case, and they chose that occasion to make their presence known. To say, yes, we exist, but only for those who love the game and believe in its wonders.

Eddie Matthews is on the list of the one hundred greatest. For me, he was a good third baseman, a force to be reckoned with. For Warren he led the way to The Grail.

My older brother's all-time favourite player. My first baseball memories are from the 1957 World Series between the Braves and Yankees. As a 5 year old, I was mighty impressed that this game unfolding on TV could bring my 10 year old brother such joy and grief. I was hooked.

For Chatz, it was Ernie Banks.

One of my favourite players, being a shortstop and the joy baseball brings me. I was in Chicago at Wrigley Field in 2015 the year he died;

they gave out little pins with the number 14; Ernie's number. I was flooded with memories of my childhood and playing baseball with friends in the school yard close by, remembering Ernie Banks.

Chatz was Ernie Banks, I was Robin Roberts, Warren's bro was Eddie Matthews. But heroes live in another world. Even the big kids, the ones you watch every time you get the chance, inhabit the unattainable. And then one day you're there with your big brother and they're short a player. It's spring, of course, and that in itself is a miracle. One winter, I pitched to my dad in the basement after almost dying of complications from a ruptured appendix. That spring, while trying out for our midget team, I was pitching to Lloyd Stansell the captain of the senior team. The ball was going smack into his glove. He took the ball in his hand, looked at it, and said as if the whole world was listening, 'There's your pitcher.'

But it was catching fly balls I loved most. The impossibility when seen through the eyes of a seven year old. So high, so far. How could a person manage such a thing? I'm not sure I remember the first one, but I seem to recall being in right field (where they put the weakest fielder) seeing the ball rise above the first baseman, taking the necessary steps to get under it, thinking that it was not for the likes of me to actually catch it. And then, as if by magic, the ball falling into my glove. The wonder of knowing I could do it. The higher and farther the better. And that it came along with spring, followed by long summer days when all you needed was a bat and a ball (and a glove if you were lucky) and just one other person, and you could spend all day at it. And the games themselves. Almost too good to be true knowing you were really there. In the field expecting on every pitch the ball would be hit to you. Waiting your turn to hit. Seeing the field spread out in front of you. Hit the ball into one of the empty spaces and you could run the bases. If you touched them all you could try for home. If you got there before the throw, you'd scored a run and they'd mark it down in the score book beside your name.

That's where it starts. You see a ball field and it's not just a dirt and grass. It's a magical place. Close your eyes and the players emerge from the cornfield. It's what must have happened to Luis in September 2019 when he was walking along Lake Shore Blvd and saw a group of us playing workups. That so splendid a thing as Coronation Park should appear across from a busy urban throughway would surely have surprised him. And then to see us playing catch and chasing fly balls, would have surprised him further. He must have thought he was dreaming. When we told him about The Tournament he wasn't quite sure, with his limited English, what it was all about. Two games. Sunday morning. Beer and pizza afterwards. He showed up with a big smile, maybe not the biggest, but no smile could have been bigger. I can still see the sweeping tag that said, 'I'm a ballplayer.' No one at Amicos, not even those of us who'd been together for forty-five years looked happier.

It was just before Christmas that Fred got the email:

> Fred friend, l thank you for your sport support with your senior team, which l could play on September 18 and 20 the double game, l live in Venezuela and l leave on January 7, 2020, the next time l come to Toronto, l will try to be in the month of April to play more games with you, merry Christmas for all and a successful 2020. my phone +58-0414-4098866
>
> Luis

I wondered how Fred would explain, except for the scaled down tournament, that we were no longer playing on Friday nights. I see Luis looking across Lake Shore Boulevard towards Coronation Park and I can't think of a way to break the news that wouldn't feeling like explaining to a six year old there's no Santa Claus. I forgo the explanation and close my eyes, but see nothing. Nothing will come from nothing. Maybe my faith, my love, my capacity for wonder are not strong enough. Maybe they never were. Maybe they were part of some vain desire to be special in a way I had no real claim to. I'm about to return to the reality of a world without Friday Night Baseball when I realize I'm trying too hard. The mind's flow cannot be forced, it must be allowed to find its way. A moment passes and my mind's eye is no longer clouded by disbelief. Soon I have managed to call up a view of the field in all its summer splendor. I know without having to think further that Frank and Lorne will appear and unload the equipment and Fred and Mike will start putting down the bases. In fact, they were here all the time. Joe is here. Sluggo and Ron and Bill D are here, along with everyone who has taken the field with us. Bill Barnes who got a spring training hit off Dizzy Dean is here. Randy whose dad used to yell at him from the hill behind first base at Ramsden Park is here. The old guys who sat behind the bench at Viewmount are here. Lorne's nephew who hit three home runs into the trees at Upper Keelesdale is here. George Gamester who wrote about us in the *Toronto Star* is here. Art who played one game in July 1998 is here. Billy Parrott who took calls on his cellphone in right field is here. Jim Wilson, who postponed his trip to the cottage till Saturday morning because he loved calling balls and strikes for us is here. Too many to name, but they all are here. The world is green, summer is stretched out ahead of us as far as the mind can see, and winter is a word from some other place and time. Luis will cross Lakeshore Boulevard and it will be like the first time. The day you caught the towering fly ball or got a big hit or struck out the other team's best hitter.

We are such stuff as dreams are made on.

FNB - Final Season Tournament - 2018

Addendum

About a dozen of us were there from the beginning, but our longevity was largely due to the players who joined us along the way, some for just a game or two, some for a good many years. There was something democratic about it which requires acknowledgement. Here, partly for the fun of it and partly for reasons of historical truth, is as complete a list as I can manage of everyone who took the field with us. In some cases we never got round to last names. For example, Randy who we met at Ramsden who was with us for three or four years at Ramsden Park, whose dad used to sit on the side of the hill and yell at him. And a good many players I don't remember included on the assumption that the name itself gives substance to their presence. All placed in no particular order. Most of the names from memory, but many from old scores books and players lists. An occasional name so badly handwritten I can't make it out. Digging through it all made me feel like a genuine historian. Finding the early score books and player's lists was akin to discovering the Dead Sea Scrolls.

Nelles Van Loon, Craig Donovan, Luke Donovan, Curtis Smith (Craig's tenant), Gilles Morin, Fred Breitner, Stephen Breitner, Cam (friend of Stephen), David Breitner, Frank Trotz, Anna Trotz, Marcus Farrugla, Lorne Mitchell, Lorne's nephew (Paul), Jim Conlin, Will Kennedy, Howard Gerhard, Perry Gerhard, Jason Gerhard, Remo Brassolotto, Bob McKenzie, Dave Bolland, Mark Bolland, Chris

Bolland, Don Crawford, Nelson Smith, Jamie Crammond, Doug Jones, John Jarvis, Steve Shapiro, Eric Hellman, Mike Marino, Austin Repath, Wayne Oake, Joe Leonard, Steve Chadwick, Eric Chadwick (Steve's son), Bill Davidovitz, John LeSarge, John's sons Mike and Greg, Ron LeSarge (John's younger brother), Milton McCrystal, Walter Weary, Billy Parrott (real estate agent, friend of Walter), Paul Pernette, Dave Fisher, Fred Cohen, Mike Walshaw, Tom Christopher, Dan Christopher, Peter Handley, Dave LeChaz and his pal Jay, Monty and John and Jeff from the Rockets in the TASL, George Wheeler, John St James, Jim St James, Ken Pagel, Jim Betts, John Larocque, Jack Alvo, John Dorsey, Bill Barnes, Tom O'Sullivan, Peter Dales, Sandy Douglas, Gavin Douglas (Sandy's son), Peter Roach, Ben Woolfitt, Ted Bradanovich, Phil Klumak, Russ Ford, Damian Ford (Russ's son), Danian DeSouza, Paul Casey, Mark Riddle, Rolando from the Philippines, Rocko (guessing he was Rolando's son), Warren Quinn, Gavin Quinn, Brandon Quinn (Warren's sons) Rick Czepita, Ben Czepita (Rick's son), Richard Cox, Nicole Dimson, Doug Densmore, Lee Johanson (came to the game in his work boots), Stan Bachinski, Wayne Nicholas, Rick Traugott, Randy, Randy's dad, David Greisman, Rob Johnson, Tim Bryson, Jake Zabusky, Richard and Dorothy Quinlan, David Wells, Ray Kerr, Ross via Ray Kerr, Pete McCarthy from Red Lake, Adam from France, Mike Pearson (no relation to Lester), Iden Ford, Peter Hajdasz, Taylor and Brock (met them at the park, played just one game), Alex Bierk, Ian (friend of Alex), Nick Bierk, Mark Hershoran (Chatz's nephew), Richard Veldhoen, Dan DosSantos, Wilmer Gonzalez, Kevin (Richard's pals), Jon Brooks, Mike D (friend of Sandy, played in The Tournament in 2012), Justin (just a few games summer 2012), Hugh Moran, Hugh's son Ryan, Jim Biggar (early days at Jesse Ketchum), Kristy (pal of Anna), Rob Baral and his pal Zak (met them at the park summer 2014), Jean Marc (definitive ringer, pal of Sandy), Roberto, Harvey Bradley, Marty Thomas, Elan Thomas (Marty's son), Andrew Faria, (loved to steal a base, we called him Rocket Man), Neil (knuckle baller from Nfld), Tom Cain, Philp Moyer, Steve Smith, Bob Canuel, Craig Doyle, Mike Broadribb, Nick Power, Bob Lewis (student of mine from Ryerson), Stuart Grant, Ted Grant (no relation to Stuart), Peter Markle, Phil Marchand, Larry Sone, Norval Wiener, Lorne Seagal, Philip Ames, Frank Schmidt, David Wood, Sam Longo, Kevin Adams, Barry Wilson, M. Wise, John Vatafu, Sean Carney, Hersh Chadwick, John Thompson from the Amigos in the TASL, Hersh Chadwick, Lawrence Pengelly, Brian and Monty from the Rockets in the TASL, Ted McGee, John Spzic, John Tucheroni, Jesse Craney, John Pitt, Larry Forsner, Jerry Johnson, John Sestito, Jon Mok, Ben from Yellowknife, Dale Whittacre from Cincinnati, Jim Cottrell and the other umps who played with us when the numbers were down, Gagan, Grubir (friend of Gagan), Will (friend of Wayne), Will's brother, Warren (Alex's brother in law), Nathalie (from the TASL) via Sandy, Jordain and Jaclyn (met them at the park), Ari Elkouby, (1996-97), Larry (June -July 1996), Roberto (May 1997), Luis (not Luis from Venezuela, 1997-99), Sheldon Gocool July 2001, Mike Z c. 1990 (name appears just once, four at bats, but no hits) Lionel (name appears just once July, 2006), Patrick just once, Mark McCauley, Brad only twice 1999, David Thornely, George Gamester, Jeff Kwok, Jason Prole, Dez Oku (Frank's neighbour, good field, hit for power), John Silva, John Polito (name appears on 2004 list, but no record of him ever playing), same with Donna Green, Fred Hunt, R Payne, Mike Hollinger, Robert Greenberg, Don Turner, Mike Balkwill, Rick Wilks, Don Richardson, Richard Bryant, David Fahl, John Brewin, Ted Weber, someone named Art who played one game in July 1998. Maybe, like Doc Graham in *Shoeless Joe,* he was faced with the choice of saving a life or achieving immortality and did the honorable thing.

Thanks to David Bolland for clearing my mind about
what this piece is. Not a diary, something more.
And to Iden Ford for his wonderful photos.

About the Author

Nelles Van Loon grew up in Red Lake, Ontario, where he acquired a lifelong passion for baseball. His play, Babe Ruth Comes to Pickle River, has had productions in a number of theatres across the country. We Never Came to Lose, written with catcher and long-time friend Frank Trotz, was part of the 2007 Toronto Fringe Festival. Several musicals for children have been produced in theatres in Nova Scotia and Ontario.

CPSIA information can be obtained
at www.ICGtesting.com
Printed in the USA
LVHW070730250422
717137LV00007B/66

9 780228 872207